The Development of Antisocial Behavior and Crime

Marc Le Blanc

The Development
of Antisocial Behavior
and Crime

Replication with the Montréal Cross
Sectional and Longitudinal Studies

 Springer

Marc Le Blanc
University of Montréal École de Criminologie and Psychoéducation
Montreal, QC, Canada

ISBN 978-3-030-68431-0   ISBN 978-3-030-68429-7   (eBook)
https://doi.org/10.1007/978-3-030-68429-7

This Springer imprint is published by the registered company Springer Nature Switzerland AG
The registered company address is: Gewerbestrasse 11, 6330 Cham, Switzerland

Dedication
Thanks *to 15,000 adolescents who voluntarily gave us their time to complete our interviews and questionnaires and for many of them up to six times during their life. Without their generosity, the Montréal Two Samples Four Generations Cross-sectional and Longitudinal Studies could not have emerged as an original source of criminological knowledge.*

Foreword

The Montréal Two Samples Four Generations Cross-sectional and Longitudinal Studies (MTSFGCLS) was an unplanned research program. It paralleled the evolution of empirical criminology, queries of the researchers involved, funding opportunities, governmental revisions of laws and policies, and questions from clinicians. Marcel Fréchette, a psychologist, was the office neighbor of Marc Le Blanc, a sociologist and criminologist. In the early 1970s, each was designing a biennial gathering of data. Their sampling targets were, in the first case, the total population of the 1973–1974 juvenile court convicted males with a focus on perpetration of crime and personality and, in the second case, it was a replication of Hirschi's (1969) landmark study with a random sample of the Montréal adolescent population and additional self-reported delinquency and social control measures. For the second gathering of data during adolescence, the two studies were merged in a common research program and some measures were shared: self-reported delinquency, personality questionnaires, and social-control variables.

Later data gatherings were responses to the question "Why not?"; first, about repeating data gathering when the court subjects were in their 20s, 30s, 40s, and 50s and, second, for the addition of a court sample in the early 1990s. On the way, population samples were added to the program in the 1980s, 1990s, and 2000s, when a diagnostic instrument was created and validated to be used in social services and the juvenile justice system. These samples are the foundations of this book as illustrated by the subtitle "Replications by generations, genders, delinquency status, ages, and types of behavior."

This book contains terms that need to be defined immediately for reasons of simplicity in the writing of the text and the clarity in understanding between the author and the readers.

The term *crime* reflects offenses that are defined in the Canadian Criminal Code. In this book, the offenses, or the official crimes, are the result of a conviction by a juvenile or an adult court. A crime may also be self-reported during an interview. The term *antisocial* points to conduct that is "contrary or injurious to the interest of society in general" (Collins, 2005). In social science, it is a behavior that is contrary to the laws and customs of society; it is antagonistic to conventional social practices. The scientific or operational definitions of antisocial behavior vary enormously as is discussed in Chapter I. The MTSFGCLS contains all the types of crimes and a spectrum of deviant behaviors that are considered, in criminology, as equivalent to crime. They are recognized as problem behaviors in some laws, some institutions (schools, work places, etc.), and persons (parents, peers, and adults). They manifest as conflict and violence or risk-taking behaviors (drug use, sex, etc.).

In this book, nine distinctive **periods** define the life cycle. Psychologists (Magnusson and Cairns, 1996), sociologists (Elder, 1998), and developmental criminologists (Loeber and Le Blanc, 1990) have subscribed strongly to an axiom. Life course refers to a sequence of age-graded biological, psychological, social, and behavioral phases. In this book, the life cycle is divided into nine periods: (1) childhood from age 8 to 11; (2) early adolescence from age 12 to 14 (12 is the age at entrance into secondary school in Québec); (3) late adolescence from age 15 to 17; (4) early youth from age 18 to 21 (18 is the legal age in Canada to be recognized as an adult); (5) middle youth from age 22 to 25; (6) late youth from age 26 to 29; (7) early maturity from age 30 to 39; (8) middle maturity from age 40 to 49; (9) late maturity from age 50 to 60 (the last age included in the longitudinal data sets).

Preface

Quételet compiled a table with the first age–crime data in 1835. The spinal of the criminal career was identified for criminology. He later deduced the first criminological law.

> *The propensity for crime, toward adulthood, increases very rapidly; it attains a maximum and decreases thereafter slowly until the limit of life.* (1869, p. 366).

In 1986, the "Criminal Career Paradigm" was proposed in the two volumes *"Criminal Careers and Career Criminals"* by Blumstein, Cohen, Roth, & Visher. These volumes were the synthesis of the criminological knowledge on the measurement of official and self-reported criminal activity. First, it standardized its descriptive (participation, variety, frequency, and seriousness) and boundary parameters (age at onset, duration, and age at termination). Second, it identified the dominant developmental mechanism of crime, aggravation. Third, the criminal career was mathematically formalized. Fourth, a complete paradigm was proposed because methodological directions were laid down for the study of the criminal career. Later, researchers within this paradigm explored the unlimited list of risk and protective factors, from biological, psychological, social, and environmental factors within many domains: peers, family, school, work, marriage, routine activities, and communities (see reviews in Farrington, Kazemian, and Piquero 2019). Fifth, a list of policies and practical implications was formulated for general and specific crime prevention, crime control, the functioning of justice, and correctional programs.

A few years later a second paradigm was formulated, developmental criminology. The adjective "developmental" was chosen because the nominator's training was in psychology (Fréchette & Le Blanc, 1987; Le Blanc & Fréchette, 1989; Loeber & Le Blanc, 1990; Le Blanc & Loeber, 1998). They were reflecting on *"the study of within individual changes"*. This perspective focuses, first, on individual changes in antisocial behavior and crime, with particular attention given to self-reported behaviors. Second, explanatory factors that occur in continuous processes throughout life and individual development that is observable in the behavioral, biological, psychological, interpersonal, social, societal, and historical spheres (see reviews in Morizot and Kazemian, 2015). Third, their development is intimately and continuously interconnected and embedded along the life span. Fourth, the preferred method for the study of developmental changes is the longitudinal research design. Fifth, these researchers showed that there are three developmental mechanisms, activation, aggravation, and deactivation. These mechanisms collaborate in a system to construct numerous trajectories within the age–crime curve trajectory. Sixth, the developmental empirical knowledge on antisocial behavior and crime and self (biological and psychological), social controls (interpersonal and social), and their contexts (societal and historical) must serve to conceive preventive and treatment interventions by the State. The applications that they proposed were more focused on individual prevention and treatment of antisocial behavior of all sorts. As argued by Le Blanc (2015), the criminal career and the individual growth paradigms are part of the developmental criminology perspective.

A related paradigm was formulated in sociology, the life-course perspective. It is stated that human development is influenced by historical and macro societal conditions, not only characteristics of the individual and particular conditions of its immediate environment (Elder, 1974). This "Life-course Paradigm " was adapted to criminology by the Sampson and Laub team (Sampson and Laub, 1993; Laub and Sampson, 2003). Criminologists should look at the impact on antisocial behavior and crime of the major role transitions during late adolescence and youth: leaving school, entering into the work market, going into the army, getting married or divorced, becoming a parent, adopting a religion, being treated for an addiction or a mental health problem, and going to prison (see Benson, 2002, 2013; Siennick and Osgood, 2008).

The maturation of the criminal career, individual growth, and life-course paradigms is reflected by the fact that developmental criminology was formally recognized as a division of the American Society of Criminology in 2012, nearly 60 years after its creation and 200 years after Quételet's observations on the age–crime curve.

In this book, a 50-year journey into the antisocial behavior and crime country is revived with the Montréal Two Samples Four Generations Cross-sectional and Longitudinal Studies through replications by generations, genders, delinquency status, and type of behaviors.

Montréal, QC, Canada   Marc Le Blanc

List of Abbreviations by Categories and Synonyms

ABC   Antisocial behavior and crime

     SRABC   Self-reported antisocial behavior and crime
     CFA   Confirmatory factor analysis

Court Sample—convicted

     CS70 Court Sample of the 1970s
     CS90 Court Sample of the 1990s
     CSF90 Court Sample of Females of the 1990s
     CSM70 Court Sample of Males of the 1970s
     CSM90 Court Sample of Males of the 1990s

Crime—official

     OC   Official criminal career
     OCS   Official offending system
     OO   Official offending
     SRO   Self-reported official offenses

Generation

     G60 1960 generation, five birth cohorts born around 1960
     G80 1980 generation, five births cohorts born around 1980

ISRDS   International Self-reported Delinquency Study

Laws

     JDA   Juvenile Delinquents Act of Canada
     YCJA   Youth Criminal Justice Act of Canada
     YOA   Young Offender Act of Canada
     YPA   Youth Protection Act of Quebec

MTSFGCLS   Montréal Two Samples Four Generations Cross-sectional and Longitudinal Studies

Problem behavior

OPB Official problem behavior
PBS Problem behavior scales
SRPB Self-reported problem behavior

Representative sample of the population

RSP70 1970s
RSP80 1980ss
RSP90 1990s
RSP00 2000s

SSI Semi-structured Interview
Types of crimes

PO Covert property offenses
VO Overt violent offenses
LSO Lifestyle offenses

Acknowledgements

A 50-year scientific journey needs an extensive and regular research infrastructure. An army of research professionals, undergraduate and graduate student research assistants, data managers, and statistical analysts. The list of persons enrolled in this army would cover numerous pages of dedicated persons.

This journey was prepared with Professor Denis Szabo, my mentor, in a multi-disciplinary research program on social structure, personality, and delinquency in the late 1960s. In early 1970, Marcel Fréchette, an office neighbor, opened my eyes to the developmental perspective and the importance of psychological factors. From the early 1980s on, David Farrington encouraged and sustained the MTSFGCLS. The next stage, in the middle of the 1980s, was meeting Rolf Loeber, who unfortunately died in the fall of 2019. It was decisive for the author's theoretical and empirical contribution to developmental criminology. Rolf Loeber was innovative and vision-ary in his enormous empirical works, his theoretical trajectory formulation, and his list of proposed interventions. He was a true gentleman and an eminent and land-mark psychologist and criminologist, and a cofounder of the Individual Growth paradigm.

During the first decades of the MTSFGCLS, Aaron Caplan, Louise Biron, and Hélène Beaumont played a central role in data collection, management, and analy-ses. In the 1990s, they were replaced by a second generation of dedicated and com-mitted assistants at data gathering: Suzanne Langelier and Viviane Lorie. The data management task became increasingly complex over time; it was in the competent hands of Pierre McDuff. In the 2000s, Céline Dufresne, Nadine Lanctôt, Julien Morizot, and Martine Lacroix managed the data gathering and organization for the court and representative samples. Lila Kazemian organized the longitudinal official crime data. Finally, Annie Lemieux executed the multivariate statistical analyses for Chapters 4 and 5.

The Université de Montréal was our home and a generous and understanding parent. Many federal and provincial funding agencies abundantly and continuously supported us: Social Sciences and Humanities Research Council of Canada, Québec Social Research Council, FCAR Québec, the Ministries of Solicitor General, Justice and Health and Welfare of Canada, the Ministry of Health and Welfare Services of

Québec, and the Health Institutes of Canada. Many organisms of the governments of Canada and Québec facilitated interviewing and locating the subjects such as youth centers, school boards, juvenile and adult courts, correctional services, shelters, mental health centers, federal, provincial, and municipal police agencies, Equifax, etc.

The making of this book received funding from l'École de psychoéducation of the Université de Montréal and la Chaire de recherche du Canada sur le placement et la réadaptation des adolescentes et des jeunes femmes en difficulté de l'Université de Sherbrooke.

For the contribution of all adolescents, teachers, educators, managers, and institutions of all kinds, research professional and assistants, we express our sincere thanks and our greatest gratitude.

Introduction

What Kind of Journey Will We Have?

I began my criminological career in 1966 during my graduate studies, with the following empirical research assignment: the study of the variations of juvenile crime over time in Montréal with police arrest files and the comparison of self-reported delinquency (Nye and Short, 1957, questionnaire) between a working class and an upper class neighborhood in Montréal. This task was the launch factor of my career on the study of antisocial behavior and crime. This book synthetizes my journey. That is, the theoretical and empirical studies over the 50 years of the MTSFGCLS. This journey is distinguished by the application of five views on the antisocial behavior and crime scene: the measurement, epidemiological, process, system, and course views.

First, in this book it is assumed that crime always has to be studied in close interaction with the whole spectrum of forms of antisocial behavior. As a consequence, the criminal career paradigm is incomplete because it is centered on crime. Second, it is hypothesized that the developmental of crime grows in the same manner for all forms of antisocial behavior. Third, similar static and dynamic indicators, developmental mechanisms, system functioning, and trajectories apply to all forms of antisocial behavior, not only crime. Fourth, it is taken for granted that replications are necessary in criminology. In this book, the development of antisocial behavior and crime is studied as a whole and as a close system that has its own autodynamic and that is partly independent of the contribution of all explanatory, risk, and protective factors for each age period of the life cycle.

Beyond Crime, Toward Antisocial Behavior

From Sellin (1938) to Hirschi (1969), many criminologists, from each generation, have debated the object of criminology. Le Blanc and Fréchette (1989) showed that some criminologists advocated a legal definition of crime, the violation of criminal law, or official crimes, whereas others preferred a sociological definition, deviant behavior that is in conflict with current social norms. The historical distinction between crime and deviance was not reintroduced in this millennium because the criminal career and the individual growth paradigms were conceived as members of the same developmental family. In addition, now, criminologists tend to agree with the theoretical proposition of Gottfredson and Hirschi (1990) that all deviant behaviors are in essence "*analogous*" or "*equivalent*" to crimes (p. 42).

Along this line of thinking, Le Blanc (2015) proposed that all behavioral sciences use, as their common object, the generic construct of ***antisocial behavior***, that is, all forms of behaviors that "*are contrary or injurious to the interests of society in general*" (Collins, 2005). This choice reduces potential confusion between scientists and professionals of different disciplines, such as criminology, sociology, psychology, psychoeducation, social work, and psychiatry. A common construct limits misunderstandings between theoreticians and empirical researchers of these disciplines and with practitioners and clinicians in different domains of practice inside and outside of the justice system. In sum, the generic construct of antisocial behavior refers to a wide range of behaviors and it is not limited to Criminal Code offenses.

In the first chapter, it is argued theoretically that antisocial behavior is an inclusive and generalizable construct that is recognized by all behavioral sciences and that it takes the form of a heterotypic structure. Then it is verified empirically if this latent construct is subdivided into two main categories, crime and problem behavior, each respectively composed of forms of behavior, overt, covert, and lifestyle for delinquency and reckless behavior, and authority conflict for problem behavior. Each of these forms is operationalized into specific official and self-reported measures in Appendix B.

The second chapter exposes the epidemiological view of the journey scenery with data on static and dynamic parameters. These data by genders, types of samples (population and court samples), age ranges, and generations (adolescents in the 1970s, 1980s, 1990s, and 2000s) are analyzed to find generalizations.

At the end of the first two chapters, the reader should be convinced that some generalizations stand out from the measurement and epidemiology of antisocial behavior and crime. Particularly, that these two phenomena are in essence part of the same family. In addition, they must be conceived as generalizable across gender, generations, age ranges, and types of sample.

From an Epidemiological Perspective, Toward a Developmental View

Sylvester (1984) stated that Quételet wrote "... *the first scientific treatise ever published on crime* (page V)". The criminal career, the life course, and the individual growth paradigms were then intuitively conceived to constitute what we now call developmental criminology. Quételet displayed the first global age–crime curve and specific curves by types of crime and compared them by gender and Europeans state. He deduced the first criminological law, the age–crime curve:

The propensity for crime, toward adulthood, increases very rapidly; it attains a maximum and decreases thereafter slowly until the limit of life. (Quételet, 1869, p. 366)

Quételet concluded that "*Age is without contradiction the cause, which acts with the most energy to develop or moderate the propensity for crime.*" (Sylvester, 1984, p. 64).

After Quételet, age became an imperative variable in the analysis of the propensity for crime and numerous criminological textbooks of the last 20 years have commented on its importance. Along the way, it reappeared as an empirical controversy on the invariance of the age–crime curve in 1980 with Hirschi's and Gottfredson' challenge (1983). Today, criminologists would not use the word "*cause*" as Quételet did. However, the accumulated knowledge on the age–crime curve indicates that all the descriptors of the criminal career are patterned by the age-graded life course: participation, onset, frequency, versatility, duration, offset, co-offending, types of offender, and criminal trajectories, according to its recent comprehensive description by Piquero, Farrington, and Blumstein (2007) and recent synthesis (Delisi, 2015; Britt, 2019; Eggleston Doherty, and Bacon 2019). What criminology should now study is the cycle of antisocial behavior in general and for each of its forms alone and, particularly, in parallel and interaction between these forms and crime.

From a methods point of view, Quételet showed us the way by using prevalence data over time that would become the preferred method of developmental criminology. He also noticed the significance of distinguishing hidden and observed crime and accusations and convictions. The first age-related official and self-reported crime curves for population and adjudicated samples were published in Le Blanc and Fréchette (1989). It reflected, as in many subsequent studies, the impact of the justice system because self-reported crime peaks earlier than official crime on curves that have the same shape in comparable cycles. These particular phenomena are important distinctions in the analysis of the development of antisocial behavior and its forms.

Quételet describes the progression into crime, what we now call "*the aggravation process*" (Blumstein et al. 1986; Fréchette et Le Blanc 1987) and the changes in the crime mix that have been recognized by today's developmental criminologists.

Although it is around the age of 25 that the maximum number of different types appears, this maximum is found advanced or retarded by some years. However, for certain crimes according to more or less tardy development of some qualities which are in relationship with these crimes. Thus, man pushed by violence and his passions at first yields to rape and indecent assaults. He enters almost at the same time into a career of theft, which seems to follow as by instinct until his last breath. The development of his strength carries him to all acts of violence, to homicide, rebellion, and thefts on the public ways. Later, reflection turns manslaughter into murder and poisoning. Finally, man, advancing in his career of crime, substitutes more cunning for strength and becomes a forger more than at any other period of his life. p. 65 (Translation by Sylvester, 1984).

In sum, Quételet proposed the developmental law of the cycle of offending or the age–crime curve, and he suggested a developmental mechanism of the criminal career, the aggravation process. The test of these laws came back into the criminological agenda with the landmark study by Wolfgang, Figlio, and Sellin (1972) and was reformulated by Blumstein et al. (1986), Le Blanc and Fréchette (1989), Loeber and Le Blanc (1990), and Le Blanc and Loeber (1998). Today, the vast body of knowledge on the development of crime is reviewed in several books and papers: Piquero, Farrington, and Blumstein (2003, 2007), Liberman (2010), Benson (2002, 2013), Morizot and Kazemian (2015), and Farrington, Kazemian, and Piquero (2019).

The next three chapters jump into a developmental criminology that integrates the criminal career and individual growth paradigms. Three views of the journey scenery, that were progressively included in the MTSFGCLS, are contemplated.

The third chapter is devoted to the developmental processes of antisocial behavior and crime. The developmental mechanisms of quantitative changes, activation and deactivation, and qualitative changes, aggravation and deaggravation will be explored. It is expected that for males these mechanisms will be replicated for antisocial behavior and crime in general and their specific forms, and by generations.

The fourth chapter offers a system view of the antisocial behavior and crime scene. Alfred Blumstein, in 1967, imported the system morphology and methodology into criminology and produced the first system analysis flowchart of criminal justice. Drawing from the system, developmental psychology, and the chaos–order perspectives, Le Blanc (2009) integrated their methodological principles for the analyses of the coevolution of antisocial behavior and crime.

The fifth chapter focuses on trajectories that grow out of the above analyses of the developmental processes. A fashionable subject, as numerous studies were conducted around the turn of the millennium according to reviews (Piquero, 2010; Jennings and Reingle, 2012; Piquero, Reingle Gonzales, and Jennings, 2015; Morizot, 2019). Three meso-trajectories are expected to be found in a sample of the population: abstinent, transitory, and persistent antisocial behavior and crime trajectories and three to five trajectories in a sample of court males. As in the previous four chapters it is anticipated that the shapes of the trajectories will be similar for the generations and the forms of antisocial behavior and crime.

From Replication to Reproducibility, Toward Generalizability and Universality

I began my career in 1970 designing a research project that was intended to be a replication of Hirschi's (1969) most important book on empirical criminology of the twentieth century *"Causes of Delinquency."* It was a planned as a two-wave, 2 years apart, panel study. As in his study, the school sample was stratified randomly for the school district of the Island of Montréal. However, private high schools were added because they recruit an significant group of students, mainly from parents with average and higher socioeconomic status. The sample differed from Hirschi's one because all subjects were French speaking, Catholic, and white. All his measures were used with an improvement of his self-reported delinquency (SRD) questionnaire, social control measures, and self-control scales were integrated. Hirschi's bivariate relationships between social control measures and self-reported delinquency were all confirmed except for one (Caplan and Le Blanc, 1985).

When the MTSFGCLS began we were not aware of the necessity for reproducibility and the conditions of scientific replication. We did not know that in the seventeenth century, the chemist Robert Boyle had insisted on the importance of reproducibility in science and that this principle was immediately challenged by Descartes and Hobbes. More recently, that Popper reinforced Boyle's point of view *"… non-reproducible single occurrences are of no significance to science."* (1959, p. 66). Today, replications are still neglected in social sciences (Schmidt, 2009) and psychology (Makel, Plucker, and Hegarty, 2012). It is also the case in criminology. McNeeley and Warner (2015) report data for the period 2006 to 2010; out of 691 publications, only 6 (0.9%) were direct replications, 10 (1.4%) were empirical generalizations or conceptual replications. Pridemore, Makel & Plucker (2018), in a systematic review up to 2014 on the Web of Science, found only 178 replications (0.45%) out of 39,275 papers and 98% consisted of original research. In criminology, the proportion of original research is 98–99%; this level is in the same range for social sciences (97%), natural sciences (99%), and psychology (99%) according to Makel et al. (2012). These authors calculate that 79% of the replications are successful in psychology (73% for direct replications and 83% for conceptual ones). In criminology, McNeeley and Warner report that 50% of the direct replications are not consistent with prior results, whereas only 10% of the empirical generalizations are in the same situation; however, the number of papers is insufficient to draw reliable conclusions (6 and 10 publications respectively). Pridemore et al. (2018) conclude that 75% of the replications are successful and the percentage is lower for independent studies, 69% without the participation of an author of the first paper.

The essence of science, its unchanging and unchangeable feature, is to discover descriptive, developmental, and explanatory laws of the antisocial behavior phenomenon, laws that transcend samples, communities, time, societies, and cultures. For example, a descriptive fact would be: 80% of male adolescents commit at least one crime (usual SRD measures) between age 12 and 17. A developmental fact could be: the earlier the age at onset of SRD, the longer its duration, or the

developmental stages toward drug abuse are the use of alcohol followed successively by soft drugs, chemical drugs, and hard drugs. An antisocial behavior explanatory close system could be: drug use is the launch factor of an antisocial behavior
career; it is followed by minor self-reported delinquency; their continuation needs
the contemporaneous interaction of drug use and crime along the ages; toward the
termination of the career, when drug use diminishes crime will diminish.

These few examples of facts that characterize the phenomenon of antisocial
behavior will become laws if they are reproduced after replication. A fact will attain
the status of a proven law, the quality of the study notwithstanding, when two goals
are attained: generality and universality. Generality can be concluded when four
confirmations are obtained: (1) a number of independent samples produced the
same conclusion; (2) the fact is reported in diverse types of communities (counties,
cities of various sizes, rural areas, countries, etc.); (3) the fact is observed in a number of time periods; and (4) there are observations of the same fact in a variety of
cultures. In summary, the universality of a fact is virtually impossible to demonstrate because it is extremely difficult to accumulate such a variety of studies.

The MTSFGCLS will give us an opportunity to evaluate the generality of some
descriptive and developmental facts about the antisocial behavior and crime career,
because it was built on many samples from succeeding decades controlling for the
type of community, a metropolitan area, a society, Québec, and a culture, a French
Canadian white Catholic population. This cultural specificity will not refrain us
from concluding with a certain level of universality, as there are studies in the USA
and Western Europe that produce comparable descriptive and developmental facts.
However, it will be difficult to untangle historical and maturational changes in a
particular social and cultural context. When data are presented on these questions,
we will be in the heart of the life course paradigm of developmental criminology.

In the new division of developmental criminology of the American Society of
Criminology three paradigms are recognized: criminal career (see Piquero et al.
2003–2007), individual growth (see Le Blanc and Loeber, 1998; Le Blanc, 2015),
and life course (see Benson, 2002, 2013). This book adopts premises from each of
the three perspectives. The criminal career view insists on the importance of official
crime and SRD measures, descriptive and boundary markers, and implications for
the criminal justice system. The individual growth demands more attention to the
interconnection between crimes and other antisocial behaviors, developmental
mechanisms and trajectories, and prevention and treatment. The principal focus, the
life course, is the influence of societal and historical conditions on individual
growth. To be in tune with this paradigm, the evolution of the state of Québec from
1960 to 2000, the historical and sociological context of the MTSFGCLS is synthetized in Appendix C, from Langlois, 1999; Langlois, Baillargeon, Caldwell, Fréchet,
Gauthier, and Simard, 1991, and Langlois, 2005).

Contents

List of Figures

List of Tables

About the Author

Marc Le Blanc is Emeritus Professor in Criminology and Psychoeducation at The University of Montréal. He was trained in sociology and criminology. He received a Doctorate Honorius Causa in Belgium, several fellowships and prizes from international scientific societies, the American Society of Criminology, and the Québec social sciences prize for an outstanding contribution to criminology. There was a Festschrift in honor of his career. He has been involved in theoretical and empirical research and the conception, implementation, and evaluation of treatments for delinquents. He participated in numerous governmental consultations in Québec, Canada, and in other countries concerning juvenile delinquency and antisocial behavior, juvenile justice, and the treatment of delinquents. He has published in French, English, Spanish, Portuguese, and Arabic. He is the author of numerous reports and edited books, monographs, refereed empirical papers, computer-assisted clinical evaluation instruments, and a cognitive–emotional–behavioral treatment program for antisocial adolescents and delinquents.

Chapter 1
The Constructs of Antisocial Behavior and Crime: A Measurement View

1 Introduction

At the beginning of the MTSFGCLS in 1970, I was convinced that the epidemiology and etiology of criminal activity should not be studied independently, but in continuous interconnectedness with all forms of antisocial behavior. Two decades later, reviews of the literature on the development of antisocial behavior comforted us with this position (Le Blanc and Fréchette 1989; Loeber and Le Blanc 1990; Le Blanc and Loeber 1998). Then, the goal of the Montréal Two Samples Four Generations Cross-sectional and Longitudinal Studies (MTSFGCLS) became to empirically test if the proposed descriptive and dynamic parameters of criminal activity, the mechanisms of its development, and the nature of its courses also apply to all other forms of antisocial behavior. In Le Blanc (2015), it was positioned as a priority to extend the object of developmental criminology to the study of the life-course within individual variations of all forms of antisocial behavior interrelated with crimes.

In this chapter, it is assumed that five underlying and long- standing controversies have now been resolved to the satisfaction of the vast majority of behavioral scientists. First, there is a very solid consensus on the behavioral acts that should be composed of the whole spectrum of official and self-reported antisocial behavior (SRAB) that is needed to measure the antisocial behavior construct.

Second, the developmental view implies the heteromorphic character of many of these behaviors during the life cycle from childhood through to late adulthood and this statement will be tested with SRAB. Third, criminologists now concur to say that they can measure antisocial behavior reliably and validly. The doubts have been put aside, for official data, with the study by Wolfgang et al. (1972) and, for self-reported data, with the experimental study by Hindelang et al. (1981) and later reviews (Elliott and Huizinga 1989; Le Blanc 1989; Thornberry and Krohn 2000).

Fourth, criminology went through a design quarrel: is the longitudinal research design necessary for theory testing and making policy propositions? Gottfredson

© Springer Nature Switzerland AG 2021
M. Le Blanc, *The Development of Antisocial Behavior and Crime*,
https://doi.org/10.1007/978-3-030-68429-7_1

and Hirschi (1987) rejected its utility on several grounds (methodological, theoretical, factual, policy, and cost). Their point of view was challenged by Blumstein et al. (1988a, b). These authors argued that longitudinal data are superior to cross-sectional information in testing statistical causal hypotheses. They are the only ones that permit the description of the time ordering and the control of extraneous variables. It should be added that the longitudinal design stands as an equivalent to the natural life cycle, the advance of humans over years.

Fifth, the first interpretation of the age–crime curve discovered by Quételet was that age was the principal cause of crime. Modern criminologists recognize the universality of the age–crime curve and its importance for practical criminology (Loeber 2012; DeLisi 2015; Rocque et al. 2015; Britt 2019). However, Blumstein et al. (1988a, b) argued that participation in offending and not frequency, as suggested by Gottfredson and Hirschi (1986), is the key dimension that varies with age.

With this background, let us start with the content of the antisocial behavior construct, then move to the demonstration of the fractal structure of these heteromorphic behaviors and its metric properties. Subsequent chapters will investigate the developmental mechanisms and the course of antisocial behavior. To investigate these questions the representative population and juvenile court longitudinal and cross-sectional samples recruited in the 1970s, 1980s, 1990s, and 2000s will be used (Appendix A).

2   The Constructs of Antisocial Behavior

Two sources must be looked upon to guide the selection of antisocial behaviors to include in a scientific measure: normative legal and social meanings, and the research operationalization.

2.1   The Legal or Societal Construct of Antisocial Behavior

Literally, the Collins English Dictionary (2005) defines antisocial as "*contrary or injurious to the interests of society in general.*" With this general notion in mind, let us outline the evolution of the legal definition of delinquency from an elastic set of behaviors to today's specific legal constructs of criminal and statutory delinquency and problem behavior. The content of these subconstructs became increasingly specific as time passed in modern occidental societies, particularly in Québec, Canada (Fréchette and Le Blanc 1987).

With the creation of the Juvenile Court in North America at the end of the nineteenth century (Platt 1969), the notion of delinquency was an all-inclusive idea. In Canada, the 1908 Juvenile Delinquent Act defined a "delinquent" as:

… a child (under eighteen years of age in Quebec or sixteen or seventeen in other provinces) who commits an infraction of any of the provisions of the Criminal Code, or a federal or provincial statute, or a regulation or ordinance of a municipality or who is guilty of sexual immorality or any similar form of vice, or who commits any other infraction….

This legal definition of delinquency had the disadvantage of being rather expansive. It covered minor antisocial behavior as well as serious criminal acts. The conduct described goes from activities that adults consider improper for a minor (sexual promiscuity, use of alcohol, etc.) to the most serious crimes specifically defined by the Criminal Code, from behavior prohibited by various laws and regulations (such as the municipal regulations on curfews) to those especially provided for juveniles (school attendance, etc.) or those passed in provincial legislation in which the child is a victim (against neglect, abandonment, situations of moral or physical danger, etc.). This Canadian definition of delinquency, by the way, was not very dissimilar to those adopted by most of the American states, Canadian provinces, and European countries until the 1980s (Corrado et al. 1983).

When the MTSFGCLS was implemented, it was feasible to select the infractions that represented the spectrum of crimes defined by the Criminal Code and the list of statutory offenses from federal, provincial, or municipal laws. It was possible to make sure that the selection of offenses for the self-reported measure represented the participation in crimes, minor, major, and statutory infractions according to the yearly Juvenile Court Statistics of Statistic Canada. As a consequence, the construct of delinquency was composed of two subconstructs: criminal activities and statutory infractions. In addition, it is customary, in criminal statistics and in criminology, to distinguish between crime against property, persons, and without victims. Consequently, all these types of offenses were represented in the MTSFGCLS self-reported questionnaires.

In Canada, as in many other countries or states in the USA, new delinquency acts were voted in the last quarter of the twentieth century. In Canada, it was the 1982 Young Offenders Act, and all its revisions since then. They all maintained the separation between delinquency and problem behavior (for an analysis of this process, in Québec: Fréchette and Le Blanc 1987, and in Canada: Corrado et al. 1992). As a result of this evolution, problem behavior was defined in the Article 38.f of the Youth Protection Act of Quebec in 1979 and was revised a few times later on. Problem behaviors are:

… serious behavioral disturbance refers to a situation in which a child behaves in such a way as to repeatedly or seriously undermine the child's or others' physical or psychological integrity… (revised Québec Youth Protection Act, 1979, 2016).

This legal definition is extremely vague; it does not specify particular behaviors. The professionals (social workers, psychologists, psychoeducators, criminologists, and others) that apply this law have come to a consensual set of standards reasons to refer such a case to juvenile court according to Messier's (1989) analysis of a large sample of files. These problem behaviors are concerned either by behaviors that are permitted for adults but not recommended for adolescents (frequent sexual promiscuity, abuse of alcohol and drugs, addiction to gambling, gaming, etc.) or behaviors that are prohibited specifically for adolescents (driving a car before a certain age, not going to school until a particular age, being in a place where alcohol is sold, etc.) or behaviors that violated educational norms (rebellious behaviors in school, dropping out of school, running away from home, insubordination to parents, etc.). Court professionals adjust the list of such behaviors over time; they are the standard reasons they used to refer an adolescent to juvenile court under the Youth Protection Act.

In summary, it is clear that in Canada and throughout most contemporary Western societies, legislative developments were considerable toward the conceptual specification and operational specification of the idea of delinquency and problem behavior. Three types of infractions to laws were finally identified under the legal construct of antisocial behavior. First, the crimes that are violations to the Criminal Code and they seem to give rise to socially significant fear, concern, and anxiety. Second, there are statutory offenses that defined the violations to regulations governing particular aspects of social life, such as driving, alcohol consumption, drug and alcohol distribution and use, and public order. Last, there are problem behaviors that are the violations of social norms in the family, at school, and in society. This set of subconstructs represent a structure of antisocial behavior from the point of view of laws in occidental societies.

This chapter begins with the understanding that antisocial behavior is composed of two general categories: crimes and problem behavior. Crimes can be criminal, they are against property and persons, or statutory, violations of other state regulations. All of them apply to all citizens, whereas problem behavior refers to specific rules for children and adolescents, families, and school life. All the statutory and criminal behavior can be observed in police and court statistics published by Statistic Canada and the reports on youth protection in Quebec and all of them can also be measured with self-reported instruments.

In the MTSFGCLS, official juvenile and adult data are court convictions because these files, contrary to police files, were available for the whole territory of Québec and for many decades. In addition, agents of the justice system recognize that they have been of virtually the same quality in Québec during the last six decades.

2.2 The Scientific Construct of Antisocial Behavior

Immediately after the Second World War, epidemiological studies with self-reported questionnaires were published (Murphy 1946; Porterfield 1946; Wallerstein and Wyle 1947). Criminology had to wait for the second half of the 1950s for the first scale. Nye and Short (1957) put together a questionnaire composed of 23 behavior descriptions that started with the introductory instruction "*Check those (rules and regulations) that you have broken since the beginning of grade school.*" The proposed responses were: "*very often, several times, once or twice,* and *no.*" Le Blanc (1969), for the first time in Canada, used this questionnaire and the scale for a comparison of self-report delinquency (SRD) by social class in Montréal.

Of these behaviors, seven were summed to compose the first so-called Nye and Short SRD scale: Driven a car without a driver's license or permit? Skip school without a legitimate excuse? Defied your parents' authority? Taken little things (worth less than $2) that did not belong to you? Bought or drank beer, wine, liquor? Purposely damaged or destroyed a public or private property that did not belong to you? Had sex relations with a person of the opposite sex?

Of these seven behaviors only two operationalized the constructs of crime as specified by criminal law (take little things and purposely damage), whereas the other five were deviant or behavioral problems according to the sociological norms of that time and today. The selection of the term *"delinquency"* to name this scale was misleading because only two out of the seven behaviors referred to legal offenses. It would have been better to have named that scale *"problem behavior,"* as is most often the case in psychology, or *"deviant behavior,"* as id often done in sociology. In the MTSFGCLS, it became self-reported *"antisocial behavior"* (SRAB).

Immediately, this SRAB scale became the most frequently used dependent variable in epidemiological and etiological studies of juvenile delinquency. The scientific norms for the construction of SRAB questionnaires and scales were formally adopted by the research community 8 years later (Hardt and Bodine 1965). However, some criminologists were still skeptical about self-reported measures, particularly of delinquency, a rather sensible topic of reporting on its own undetected criminal and problem behavior. Some of their methodological questions became unchallenged after the landmark experimental study of Hindelang et al. (1981). However, some questions resurface once in a while. What should be the behavioral content of a SRAB measure? Is the phenomenon of SRAB a one-category or multicategory phenomenon? Is SRAB a hierarchical structure of subconstructs? What is the likelihood of the truth of personal responses to such questionnaires? What should be the window and the responses categories? Should we use a self-administered questionnaire or a personal interview? What is the level of reliability of scales? What is the degree of their validity?

3   The Measurement of Self-Reported Antisocial Behavior

Each of these questions could be the object of a long review of the literature (see the last extensive review by Thornberry and Krohn 2000). This section concentrates on the spectrum of antisocial behaviors and the metric properties on the scales in the MTSFGCLS.

3.1   The Spectrum of Antisocial Behaviors

Rapidly, researchers wanted to improve the Nye and Short list of questions and their omnibus scale by covering a broader range of antisocial behaviors. In the MTSFGCLS, during the 1970s, the objective was to improve its content. Questions were added because they were often used in existing questionnaires, particularly Hirschi's list of behaviors, which was to be replicated in Montréal. In addition, more serious criminal offenses were added because they were often recorded in the Juvenile Delinquent Statistics of Canada but rarely included in SRAB questionnaires. In the selection of behaviors, questions that were clearly formulated, simple, and referring to more serious behaviors were preferred. Thirty years later, these choices were still in line with Thornberry and Krohn's (2000) recommendations for the development of a SRAB questionnaire.

As the Nye and Short questionnaire and scale were loaded with minor problem behaviors and delinquent acts, some more serious conduct problems were added. They came from motives that court professionals stated in their reports when they referred an adolescent to Juvenile Court under the Youth Protection Act of Québec (Messier 1989).

Later, in late 1980s and early 1990s, new behaviors were included in the adult questionnaire to cover all the categories of antisocial behavior. As a consequence, for example, the initial drug question was subdivided into four: soft, chemical, hard, and selling drugs. The end product of the step-by-step gathering of a more comprehensive set of antisocial behaviors was 63 acts that were classified into two classes, problem behavior and delinquency, four categories, overt or violent and covert or property delinquencies, and conflict and reckless problem behaviors for 16 types of behaviors (Appendix B and Table 1.1).

In criminology, a third generation of longitudinal studies was launched during the 1980s and they had to revise the existing antisocial behavior questionnaire (Le Blanc 2015). At the same time, the MTSFGCLS was producing a more comprehensive questionnaire for a clinical instrument and preparing a longitudinal study of a new court sample. The subjects had to be measured at various windows of the life cycle from childhood to late adulthood. As a consequence, researchers were confronted with a serious difficulty, construct continuity (Le Blanc 1989; Thornberry and Krohn 2000). The antisocial behavior list had to be adapted in terms of context, content, and seriousness, and to childhood, adolescence, or adulthood.

Researchers responded to this challenge with five strategies:

1. They composed a special list of antisocial behaviors, for example, for children, which was checked by parents or teachers (for example, the Achenbach Child Behavior Checklist, Achenbach 1992).
2. They incorporated some minor crimes, for example, petty larcenies and less serious violent behavior; they identified age-related behaviors such as temper tantrums, lying.
3. Some others researchers created an adapted questionnaire from existing ones for adolescents, for example, for pre-teens (Loeber et al. 1989; Le Blanc and McDuff 1991, administered using a Walkman, because pre-tests showed that pre-teens understand the delinquent and problem behavior questions, the reliability of the scales was comparable with what was obtained with adolescents, and the validity was sufficient as the scales was predictive of later antisocial behavior.

Table 1.1 List of self-reported antisocial behavior scales and behaviors in the MTSFGCLS samples: court samples CS70 and CS90 and population samples (POS) of 1970, 1980, 1990, and 2000

		CS70[a] and POS70-80-90[b]		CS90[c] and POS20[d]	
		Scales	Behaviors[e]	Adolescent behaviors	Youth behaviors
Delinquency		Theft	4, 14, 36, 45, 51, 58[c]	4, 14, 25, 36, 45, 46, 51, 56	4, 14, 25, 36, 45, 46, 51, 56
	Covert	Motor vehicle theft		T1–T2: 50, 58, 60	T3–T4: aut06, 50, 58, 60
		Fraud		T1–T2: 33, 40,	T3–T4: 33, 69, 71
		Vandalism[a]	7, 12, 41, 54	7, 12, 37, 41, 54	7, 12, 37, 41, 54
	Overt	Physical violence	5, 10, 21, 38, 43, 44	5, 10, 21, 38, 43, 44	5, 10, 21, 38, 43, 44
		Psychological violence		16, 27, 49, 61, 62	16, 27, 49, 61, 62
		Sexual aggression		63, 64, 65	63, 64, 65
	Serious		14, 21, 36, 58	14, 21, 36, 58	14, 21, 36, 58
Problem behavior	Conflict	School or work[a]	1, 12, 17, 32, 35, 42	School T1–T2: 1, 17, 32, 35, 41	Work T3–T4: 1, 7, 17, 29, 32, 35, 41
		Home Intimate Child	3, 8, 24	3, 8, 13, 22, 24 54, 57, 58a, 87	3, 8, 13, 22, 24 54, 57, 58a, 87 Children: enf38 … 45
Reckless		Drug use	11, 48, 52, 55, 59	11, 48, 52, 55, 59	11, 48, 52, 55, 59
	Arouser	Sexual promiscuity	18, 28, 39, 47	T1–T2: 18, 28, 39, 47	T3–T4: act19, 18, 28, 39, 47
		Gambling		T1–T2: 30	T3–T4: act25
		Risky driving		T1–T2: 23	T3–T4: aut5, aut8, aut9, aut10
	Risky	Disorderly conduct		T1–T2: 15, 34	T3–T4: 70

[a]The scales and behaviors for the MCS of the CS70
[b]The scales and behaviors for the POS of the RSP70. RSP80, RSP90
[c]The scales and behaviors for the CS of the CS90. There were repeated measures, T1 and T2
[d]The scales and behaviors for the CS of the 1990s. There were repeated measures, T1 and T2 during adolescence. For adult ages, T3 and T4, the behaviors were adapted to the youth period of the life course
[e]Appendix B lists all antisocial behavior acts of the SRAB questionnaires

4. Concerning adults, because the questionnaire was initially worded with their definition in the Criminal Code in mind, as for the MTSFGCLS, there was the need to incorporate a greater diversity among violent offenses, for example, homicide, sex offenses, domestic violence; among frauds, for example, false representation, income tax evasion, credit card-related offenses; and among driving offenses, for example, driving under the effect of alcohol and drugs, excessive speeding. Regarding problem behaviors, there was no consensus in the research community on the need to adapt the adolescent questionnaire. In the

MTSFGCLS, authority conflict questions at school and in the family were replaced by similar questions about work, marital relations, and the treatment of aging parents. In addition, drug questions had to be included because of new substances on the illegal market, and sexual activity questions had to be diversified with deviant sexual activities.

5. Today, there are new activities that researchers must investigate, those relative to electronic devices and, particularly, the Internet. Exploratory studies, such as Brewers et al. (2018), show that half of adolescents are involved in cyber deviance. There are often journalistic reports of such behaviors by adults.

The MTSFGCLS advanced in these five directions, but much work was still to be done to take into account the life span heteromorphy of antisocial behavior.

Among these additions of behaviors, a last improvement was the introduction of specific acts that are appropriate only for adults, such as some sophisticated forms of motor vehicle theft, fraud, sexual violence, lack of discipline at work, conflict with parents, spouse, and with their children, risky driving, gambling, and disorderly conduct. Appendix B lists 75 antisocial behaviors. Table 1.1 classifies these acts, first, in two sets of scales, those available for 1960 and 1970 versus those for 1980 and 1990 generations, and second, as an internal structure of antisocial behavior, which we will justify subsequently (Fig. 1.1). Before answering that question, let us analyze the metric properties of the scales and the heteromorphy between the adolescent and adult scales.

A final note, in the MTSFGCLS, the form of the questions took into account the landmark experimental study by Hindelang et al. (1981). As with other researchers, the length of the recall period was tested and the decision was to retain an ever response window and a last year response window and an ordinal measure of frequency (Caplan and Le Blanc 1985). New descriptors of the behaviors were introduced, such as participation, frequency, seriousness, onset, and offset, which were recommended by Elliott and Huizinga (1989) and Le Blanc (1989) and which would become requisite in the criminal career paradigm (Blumstein et al. 1986). As for the procedure of data gathering, in our longitudinal waves, a common self-administered questionnaire and an interview on 14 types of crime were used. All the available antisocial behavior measures, official and self-reported, in the MTSFGCLS, are listed in Appendix B.

3.2   The Metric Properties of the SRAB Scales

About 20 years after the first few studies of SRD, Hardt and Bodine (1965) outlined the content of the work to be done on its measurement properties. However, in the middle of the 1970s, Reiss (1975) concluded that sociologists' measuring of SRD, contrary to that of psychologists, lacked attention to the metric properties of their scales. Notwithstanding, many criminologists were much more concerned with the likelihood and honesty of responses of the subjects.

Theoretical and EmpiricallyTested (light grey) models

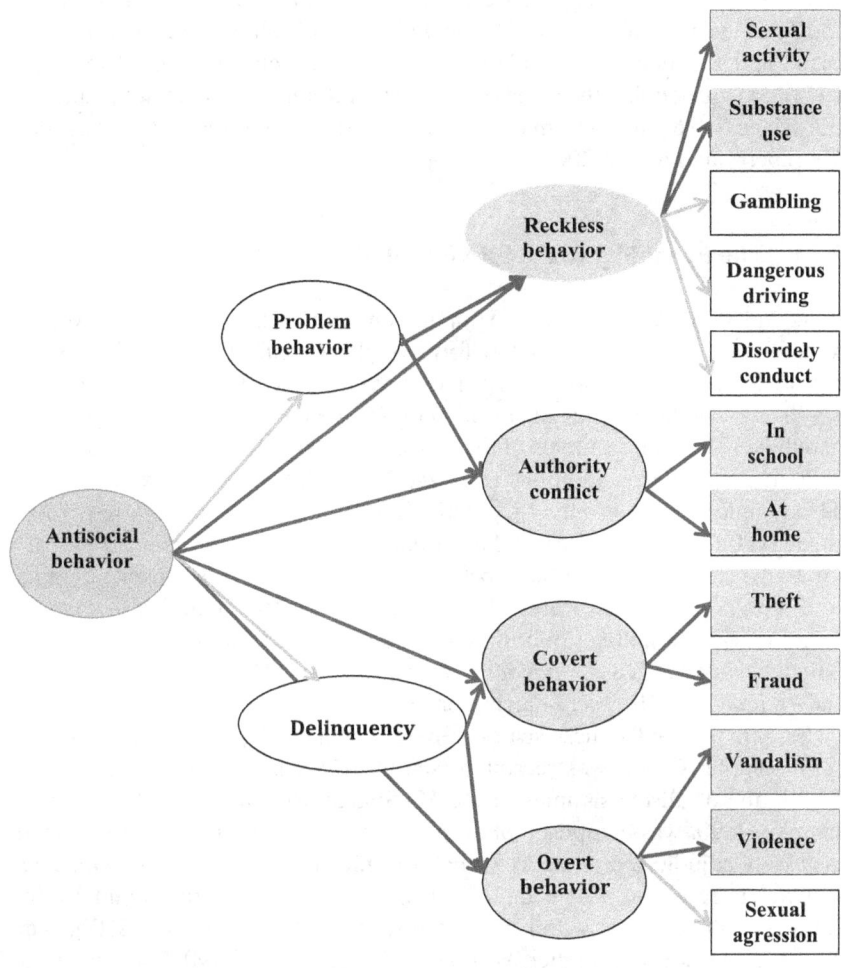

Legend:
        In light grey: the tested model.
        White ovals: not tested.
Adapted from Le Blanc and Bouthillier (2003) and Le Blanc (2009)

Fig. 1.1 The hierarchical structure of antisocial behavior: theoretical and empirically tested (light gray) models. Legend: In light gray: the tested model. White ovals: not tested. (Adapted from Le Blanc and Bouthillier 2003 and Le Blanc 2009)

Before and after these high points, there were numerous studies that tested potential bias. Farrington's (1973) investigation was about the test-retest reliability and the comparison of SRD with official crime. Later on, reviewing the literature and conducting such tests in their landmark experimental study, Hindelang et al. (1981) concluded that, particularly for variety scales, that SRD measures were "*impressively reliable*". However, many procedures were used to verify if respondents systematically tried to appear more or less delinquent or under- or over-reported their SRD. The most important tests were realized with (1) the lie detector (Clark and Tiff 1966), (2) a lie scale (Nye and Short 1957; Whitehead and Smart 1974; Le Blanc and Fréchette 1989), (3) an experiment on cheating (Erickson and Smith 1974), (4) introducing the same questions at different locations in the questionnaire (Le Blanc 1996), and (5) making a test-retest (Farrington 1973; Weis 1986, and Thornberry and Krohn 2000).

3.2.1 The Reliability of the SRAB Scales

In the MTSFGCLS (all court and population samples are described in Appendix A), reliability was calculated in the form of the Cronbach alpha (Cronbach 1951) adjusted for a comparable number of behaviors: 12 (Nunnaly 1967). Le Blanc (1996) reports the coefficients of the initial content of the scales constructed for the population and court samples of the 1970s and 1980s. In the representative samples, 7470 adolescent girls and boys from age 10 to 19, the adjusted alphas by independent samples, status groups (population and court), genders, and age groups were above 0.80 for all the scales of the delinquency category in Table 1.2 and over 0.75 for all the scales of the problem behavior category. Such coefficients compare very well with psychometric standards of the American Psychological Association and they have been qualified, in criminology, at different time periods, as "*impressive*" (Hindelang et al. 1981), "*particularly impressive*" (Thornberry and Krohn 2000), and "*reliable*" (Jolliffe and Farrington 2014).

Early in the 1990s, these scales were revised and adapted because a new juvenile court sample (CS90) was recruited (see the 75 behaviors in Appendix B and the description of all the samples of the MTSFGCLS in Appendix A). The new court sample, CS90, was composed of all boys (506) and girls (150), born around 1980; they were adjudicated at the Montreal juvenile court in 1992 and 1993. The objective was to replicate the results obtained with the boys born around 1960: CS70. Corrected alphas were within the same range as those for the CS70 group. They were even a few points higher, as shown in Table 1.2 for CS90. Later, in 2006–2007, the MTSFGCLS recruited a random sample of high school pupils, RSP00, composed of 4023 girls and boys born around 1990. The alphas were again within a similar range to the previous population samples (Le Blanc 2017).

Because to our knowledge nobody ever reported the reliability coefficients for adult females and males convicted by a juvenile court, these data are presented in Table 1.2. It may be noted that for the delinquency scales, the coefficients are over 0.80 for adolescent and adult males, except for fraud with 0.74. However, for females, the alphas are somewhat lower and some are below 0.70. It is interesting to note that these coefficients were calculated on a small sample (150) and are associated with a scale for which female participation in antisocial behavior is extremely low, as we will see later (vandalism and physical violence), particularly during adulthood.

Table 1.2 Scale reliabilities for females and males of the CS90 during adolescence and youth

	Scales[1]	Middle and late adolescence	Early and late youth
Delinquency	Theft	4, 14, 25, 36, 45, 46, 51, 56 F: .91 M: .93	4, 14, 25, 36, 45, 51, 56 F: .89 M: .92
Covert	Motor vehicle theft	50, 58, 60 F: .82 M: .85	50, 58, 60 F: .75 M: .85
	Fraud	33, 40[1] F: .74 M: .84	33, 68, 69, 71 F: .69 M: .74
	Vandalism	7, 12, 37, 41, 54 F: .73 M: .72	7, 12, 37, 41, 54 F: .64 M: .79
Overt	Physical violence	10, 21, 26, 31, 38, 43, 44, 57 F: .85 M: .83	10, 21, 26, 31, 38, 43, 44, 57 F: .69 M: .82
	Psychological violence	5, 16, 27, 49, 61, 62 F: .85 M: .90	5, 16, 27, 49, 61, 62 F: .84 M: .88
Problem behavior	School-work[2]	School 1, 7, 9, 17, 29, 32, 35 41 F: .75 M: 79	Work 1, 7, 9, 17, 29, 32, 35, 41 F: .75 M: .82
Conflict	Parents	3. 8. 13.22. 24 F: .70 M: .74	3. 8. 13.22. 24 F: .79 M: .74
	Intimate		Ami 54, 57, 58a, 87 F: .79 M: .72
	Child		enf38 ... 45 F: .71 M: .75
Reckless	Drug use	11, 48, 52, 55, 59 F: .87 M: .87	11, 48, 52, 55, 59 F: .78 M: .82
Arouser	Sexual promiscuity[3]	18, 28, 39, 47 F: .70 M: .76	act19, 18, 28, 39, 47 F: .50 M: .59
Risky	Risky driving[3]		23, aut5, aut8, aut9, aut10 F: .87 M: .85
	Disorderly conduct	15, 34[1] F: .84 M: .84	15, 70[1] F: .74 M: .79

1.   In each cell, the first lines listed the behaviors composing a scals; the second lines present the reliability Alphas for females (F) and males (M). Reliability coefficients for scales with less then three items are reported because we have no idea of what they could be in existing.
2.   These questions are independently formulated for school and work and respondents answer the questions that are appropriate to their actual situation.
3.   When the list of questions composing a scale changes in adulthood, it operationalizes according to the heteromorphous nature of the behavior.

Concerning problem behavior scales, alphas were generally lower than 0.80, except for drug use. However, they were, in most cases, over 0.70, except for adult sexual promiscuity. In the case of adults, some improvements were included in the terms of formulation of the content of acts and new scales were conceived, such as risky driving, disorderly conduct, and conflict with intimates, parents, and spouse.

In summary, the alpha reliabilities for adolescent girls and boys born around 1960, 1970, 1980, and 1990 are not only impressive but the internal consistency of the scales is excellent. This conclusion is generalizable from the conceptual replications by generations, genders, age groups, and types of sample. The generalizability of MTSFGCLS scales has also been established in other cultures: Algeria (Bergheul and Le Blanc 2006), Brazil (Bazon and Estevâo 2010), France (Brandibas and Favard 2003), and Spain (Le Blanc et al. 2004). In spite of that clear and irrefutable scientific conclusion for adolescents, there is still a need for continued conceptual and empirical work because of the heteromorphous nature of antisocial behavior for adults and lower reliabilities in comparison with scales for children and adolescents.

3.2.2   The Validity of the SRAB Scales

If internal consistency is essential, it is insufficient. Tests of content, construct, concurrent, criterion, predictive, and differential validity are unavoidable. In the MTSFGCLS, content validity was attained, as reported previously, through three procedures with the objective of creating the most comprehensive SRAB measure in a context of parsimony of its length. First, the initial questionnaire was compared with existing ones to identify behaviors that could be integrated. Second, the diversity of acts was guaranteed by a comparison with frequent acts that were reported in official statistics for delinquency and problem behavior and in previous studies. Third, the wording of the behaviors was pretested with numerous adolescents in various decades.

Construct validity refers to the extent to which the scales are related in theoretically expected ways to self and social controls (Le Blanc 1997, 2006, 2019). The construct of self-control was measured using the standard personality scales of Jesness and Eysenck. Social controls were assessed as family, school, peer, routine activity, and normative controls operationalized along the lines of Hirschi's (1969) constructs of attachment, commitment, involvement, and beliefs, and Nye (1957) constructs of formal and informal social sanctions. In the population samples of each decade, the correlations between the delinquency and problem behavior scales were stronger within the domain of antisocial behavior than within the scales of the social and self-control domains (Le Blanc 1995, 2019).

Concurrent validity refers to the extent to which scales agree with other ways to assess the nature and level of antisocial behavior. A first test was the comparison of the respondent answers on the same behaviors with the perception of other intimate persons. Examples of these tests involved parents (Loeber et al. 1989), mothers (Le Blanc and McDuff 1991), siblings (Hindelang et al. 1981), peers (Gold 1970), a best friend (Hindelang et al. 1981), and teacher reports (Patterson et al. 1992; Achenbach et al. 1987; Charlebois et al. 1995; Farrington et al. 1996).

A second test consisted in the assessment of the concordance between self-reported and official delinquency. In the 1981 landmark experimental study by Hindelang et al. (1981), they calculated, for females and males in their stratified random school sample, correlations between self-report and official contact with police and court and formal contact with this agency. They concluded that the concurrent validity coefficients were "*in the moderate to strong range.*" Since then, other reviews have not challenged that evaluation, in late 1980 (Elliott and Huizinga 1989; Le Blanc 1989), at the turn of the century (Thornberry and Krohn 2000), and more recently (Piquero et al. 2012; Forrest and Vassallo 2014; Gillman et al. 2014; Farrington et al. 2014). Without challenging this type of validity, now authors have identified the "scaling-up factor" by calculating the number of self-reported crimes by convictions for the same crime (Theobald et al. 2014; Gomes, Maia, and Farrington, 2018).

The criterion or know group validity refers to the ability of a scale to distinguish subjects on an external criterion that is conceptually an alternative measure of antisocial behavior. The operationalization of this form of validity test can be cross-sectional and longitudinal. There are many cross-sectional criteria, for example, a nondelinquent group is contrasted with delinquent groups, either official or self-reported, or with a delinquent status group (police, court, institution, and so on). These results were discussed by Hindelang et al. (1981) and by Thornberry and Krohn (2000). They conclude that these minimal tests of criterion validity present moderate to strong agreement between the self-reported and official contemporary measures. Thornberry and Krohn state that:

> The majority of individuals who have been arrested self-report their delinquent behavior and the majority of the offenses they commit are also reported. p. 54.

It can be assumed that it is also the case for all forms of problem behavior as it is the case for drug use according to these authors. All the MTSFGCLS (Tables 1.1 and 1.2.), in the population and juvenile court samples, distinguished statistically, at least at $p \leq 0.0001$, between adolescent reporting and not a contact with police or court (Le Blanc 1996, 2010a, b).

The longitudinal or predictive validity was rarely tested until the launch of major longitudinal projects in the middle of the 1980s (see an historical analysis in Le Blanc 2015). In the MTSFGCLS, two tests were performed (Le Blanc 1996). The first test involved the prediction of the second half of adolescence antisocial behavior with first half data. All the results for all the scales were statistically significant at $p = 0.0001$. The second test included scale at time 1 (an average age 15) or time 2 (17) and adult court convictions between ages 18 and 28. All the results were statistically significant at least at $p = 0.001$. More recently, Jolliffe and Farrington (2014) reviewed the validity studies on the concordance of self-reports and registers of official delinquency. They conclude that:

> In most cases, officially arrested or convicted offenders admit their arrests or convictions and admit the types of offences that led to these official records. More impressively, self-reports of offending by currently unrecorded persons predict their future arrests or convictions for the same offences. According to commonly accepted psychometric criteria, self-reports of offending are reliable and valid, at least for young males. p. 225.

In addition, the predictive validity has been investigated with developmental criminology parameters. Le Blanc and Fréchette (1989) compared self-reported and official participation, frequency, seriousness, onset, offset, and duration. They showed that the official parameters were only the tip of the iceberg compared with the self-reported ones. In summary, the participation in official adolescent and adult delinquency was lower, had a later onset, lower frequency, shorter duration, and a later offset. In a recent analysis of the Cambridge criminal career data, Farrington et al. (2014) arrived at the same conclusions.

There is a last form of validity, which is called differential. Thornberry and Krohn (2000), reviewing the literature on this unresolved issue, concluded that "*the responses of African-American males appear to have lower levels of validity.*" p. 58. In the MTSFGCLS, it is not an important point to consider because until the 1990 the Black population in Montréal accounted for less than 10% of the adolescents in the population and court samples. A recent publication of the International Self-report Delinquency Study (Enzman et al. 2018) brought forward the question of the cultural variability in reporting SRD. They showed that their response integrity measure varied enormously between samples recruited in 34 countries and in opposite direction of the prevalence rate in each country. In consequence, they recommend refraining from comparing participation rates. It is not a problem in the MTSFGCLS data set as Montréal was characterized by cultural homogeneity (Appendix C).

In summary, the validity of the self-report method that measures antisocial behavior appears to behave very well when judged by standard metric criteria available to criminologists and in other behavioral sciences. The biases with SRAB measures are well known in experimental studies (Gomes and Farrington 2019), but they appear to be surmountable. These measures will always be a rather sensitive subject. However, they do not appear to be flawed from the numerous and repeated results on content, construct, concurrent, criterion, predictive, and differential validities. Their content validity is acceptable; the construct validity is high; the criterion validity is strong; the predictive validity is increasingly often confirmed; the differential validity does not exist for genders (in the MTSFGCLS), but it may be questionable in samples with a high proportion of African Americans and Asians. However, criminologists should still be lucid, there is most likely a degree of either concealing or forgetting past antisocial behavior, and there is still most probably some under-reporting or over-reporting. In conclusion, SRAB scale metric measures were exact replications for genders, status groups, ages, and decades, and there are numerous conceptual replications. Their generalizability is "*authoritative.*" An opportunity exists to exactly replicate the above conclusions on reliability and validity, that is, the data sets of the International Self-reported Delinquency study 1 through 4. These data sets contain similar measures to SRAB in many countries and cities around the world. However, the researchers never published any reliability and validity data (Junger-Tas et al. 1994, 2003, 2010, 2012; Enzman et al. 2018).

4   A Test of the Heteromorphy of Antisocial Behavior Measures

The term heteromorphy was initially used for insects. It referred, according to the Collins English Dictionary (2005), to *"having different forms at different stages of the life cycle"*.= In the MTSFGCLS, it was theoretically postulated as a formal rule that was the case for all kinds of antisocial behavior (Le Blanc 2015). Researchers in developmental behavioral science have been intuitively aware of this phenomenon and they used distinctive formulations in their questionnaires for behaviors of theft, aggression, rebelliousness, and so on, for children and adolescents. However, heteromorphy is not a question that is neither discussed nor investigated, in the last two impressive handbooks on developmental criminology (Morizot and Kazemian 2015; Farrington et al. 2019). In the MTSFGCLS this measurement strategy was adopted, particularly between adolescence and youth, as illustrated in Tables 1.1 and 1.2 and Appendix B, particularly for fraud, undisciplined behaviors in school and at work, risky driving, disorderly conduct, conflict with parents, teachers, boss, and intimates such as girlfriend and spouse.

Let us agree, first, that the reliability and the validity of the scales of all forms of antisocial behavior are well documented in Table 1.2; second, that the content validity of the new youth scales is excellent, even if the choice of youth behaviors could be challenged and improved. The relationship between past and future criminal activity was often reviewed in criminology (Le Blanc and Loeber 1998; Piquero et al. 2003; Jennings et al. 2016), particularly its continuity between adolescence and youth. As a consequence, published correlations between adolescence and youth scales could not indubitably confirm the heteromorphy of antisocial behavior during the life cycle. The theoretical position is that a form of antisocial behavior, for example, fraud, has to be measured by distinct behaviors with adolescents and adults, in summary adapted to their age. Nevertheless, different scale composition is an integral part of the common concept of fraud. To our knowledge there is no recognized analytical procedure to assess such a construct and the life cycle validity of heteromorphous measures.

In this book, the Goldberg (2006) procedure is adopted; it is a top-down factorial analysis strategy to identify a hierarchical structure with psychological measures. This procedure is composed of the following steps. (1) An unrotated principal components solution is extracted using, for example, the adolescence fraud scores, middle and late, and the youth fraud scores, early and late (let us remember the CS90 adolescents were around 16 at time1, the first interview, and 18 at time2, and youths were around 24 at time3 and 30 at time4). (2) If the results are statistically sound, a two-principal axis solution is extracted with a Varimax rotation solution. It is then expected that the adolescence fraud scales will saturate one factor and that the youth scales will be part of a second factor. (3) If a three-factors solution complies with the Goldberg criteria, that none of the measures of fraud has its highest loading on a third factor, then the two-factors solution is retained. If the conclusions on these steps are positives, it can state that adolescence- and youth-specific fraud scales are constituents of the life cycle concept of fraud.

Table 1.3 Test of the life cycle concept for forms of antisocial behavior with the Goldberg factorial analysis procedure[a]

	Fraud		Undiscipline school - work		Disordely conduct		Risky driving[2]		Conflict parents-intimate		Fraud	
Principal component % variance	41.31		36.17		34.71		45.96		41.93		41.3	
Saturations												
Adol16	.62		.52		.24				.56		.62	
Adol18	.56		.47		.10		.43		.57		.56	
Youth24	.67		.72		.81		.80		.70		.67	
Youth30	.71		.67		.81		.75		.74		.71	
Two factors % variance	66.71		62.11		63.54		77.82		65.73		66.7%	
Saturations	Youth[3]	Adol[4]	Youth[3]	Adol[4]	Youth[3]	Adol[4]	Youth[3]	Adol[4]	Adol[3]	Youth[4]	Adu[3]	Ado[4]
Adol16	.15	.58	.15	.26	.06	.40			.62	.18	.15	.58
Adol18	.13	.41	.03	.60	.02	.40	.07	.33	.57	.20	.13	.41
Youth24	.56	.14	.44	.20	.58	.03	.54	.32	.13	.47	.56	.14
Youth30	.60	.21	.67	.03	.64	.03	.56	.07	.18	.46	.60	.21
Path coefficients between factors scores[5]	Youth Pc .95[5]	Adol .67	Youth Pc .83[5]	Adol .63	Youth Pc .79	Adol .98	Youth Pc .93	Adol .70	Adol Pc .94	Youth .64	Adol Pc .78	Youth .79

1. The detail listings are available from Marc Le Blanc.
2. The risky driving behviors were not included in the first interview because most of them were not old enough to obtain a driving permit.
3. During youth, the average age at the first interview was 24 and 30 at the second interview.
4. During adolescence, the average age at the first interview was 16 and 18 at the second interview.
5. All path coefficients are statistically significant at at least 0.000.

Table 1.3 shows that for the scales of fraud, undisciplined in school and at work, disorderly conduct, risky driving, and conflict with parents and intimates are hetero-morphous phenomena. All these constructs are characterized by substantial satura-tions on a common principal component factor, a first indication that the four scales assessing these phenomena are measuring a life cycle construct. In addition, the two-principal axis factor solutions with a Varimax rotation increase the explained proportions of variance from at least 62% to at most 78%. The highest saturations for adolescence scales are attached to the same factor and they are much lower on the youth factor. the reverse is observable for the youth scales. Finally, in most cases, very high path coefficients, highly statistically significant, between the prin-cipal component factor scores and the adolescent and youth factor scores are reported in Table 1.3. In addition, they are significantly higher for the correlations of the youth factor scores as expected from existing empirical knowledge on the continuity of offending, which is the progressive diminution of the correlation between earlier and more distant criminal activities (Le Blanc and Loeber 1998; Piquero et al. 2007).

The same results were obtained for adjudicated girls, but they are not reported because the sample was small, 150 at the first interview, and 64 at time4. In addi-tion, it is well documented in criminology that their participation in antisocial behavior (SRAB and observed antisocial behavior [OAB]) has been very low for many decades (Lanctôt and Le Blanc 2002) (detailed results can be obtained from the author).

These results on the validity of the life cycle concepts of SRAB are confirmed for the first time in developmental criminology. In consequence, criminologists should direct more attention at the measurement and test of life cycle concepts within and between early and late childhood, adolescence, and youth, and other adulthood peri-ods. In this context, replications of these results are still necessary because they were only obtained with a court sample of adolescents born around 1980 and inter-viewed until age 30.

5   The Empirical Structure of the Antisocial Behavior Construct

About a quarter of century after the first studies of SRD, scientists in behavioral sciences had explored the level of participation of adolescents in a large spectrum of antisocial behavior and it became evident that there was a need for particular-ized measures. Dentler and Monroe (1961) were the first to identify some, while maintaining what was called "*a general delinquency scale.*" In the 1970s, with access to convivial statistical computer packages proposing a variety of factor and cluster analysis, it became easy to investigate the structure of a pool of antisocial behaviors.

5.1   The Theoretical Model, What Do We Know?

Later, Hindelang et al. (1981) reviewed ten studies and reported the following most common four categories of antisocial behavior: physical aggression, drug use, property crimes, and parental defiance. In their own study, five categories emerged: serious offending, general delinquency, drug use, and school and family conflict.

A series of exploratory factor analysis with the RSP70 sample were calculated (a stratified random sample of the adolescent population in and out of school on Montréal Island, see Appendix A). The existence of the following subscales was established for delinquency: physical aggression, vandalism, minor theft, major theft, and serious delinquency (serious thefts and physical aggression) and problem behavior: sexual promiscuity, use of alcohol and drugs, authority conflict in home and at school (Le Blanc et al. 1977). These scales were replicated with the CS70 sample (all adolescents adjudicated in Montréal Juvenile Court during a period of 2 years, see Appendix A). Later, these factor analyses were confirmed with a aggregation of samples, 8237 adolescents from the 1970s and 1980s school populations of Montréal and the Juvenile Court: girls and boys from age 12 to 18 (Le Blanc 1995). At that time, these categories of antisocial behavior were conceived as independent dimensions because of the use of the Varimax rotation. Anyhow, all these scales were strong on all criminometric criteria for reliability and validity, as reported in Sect. 1.3.2.

During the same period, between 1985 and 2000, a total of 19 studies of the antisocial behavior structure were published according to Le Blanc and Bouthillier (2003). Since then, this topic has been investigated six times (Bartlett et al. 2005; Bongers et al. 2004; Childs and Sullivan 2012; Farmer et al. 2009; Hemphill et al. 2007; Zamboanga et al. 2004).

These studies of the millennium, like previous ones, were not direct replications except for the Hemphill paper comparing samples in Australia and USA. A direct replication demands similar composition of samples, a common set of AB, and an identical statistical analysis. The Hemphill study used a limited number of behaviors (attack, gang involvement, vehicle theft, alcohol, marijuana, and cigarette use) and they confirmed a two-factor model, as in many studies with a larger set of antisocial behaviors: delinquency was composed of the first three behaviors and drug use with the last three. What was most interesting was that the structure held in Australia and in the USA for two particular states, Maine and Oregon.

Except for this study, all other studies were conceptual replication. They used, as a roof, the construct of antisocial behavior, but they operationalized it with a diversified set of behaviors and with various types of samples and statistical analysis. All these replications report the existence of a latent construct and they had in common the use of one form or another of grouping analysis. Ordinary factor analysis, confirmatory factor analysis, and structural equation modeling were the most frequently employed statistical techniques. The grouping procedure was applied on a certain number of behaviors from various forms; each of them was represented by a set of a higher or lower number of behaviors. Some of the following 12 forms were identified in these studies: theft, vandalism, physical and nonphysical interpersonal violence, sexual violence, school problems, parental defiance, sexual intercourse, forms of acting out, use and trafficking of drugs, and use of alcohol and tobacco. A few studies considered behaviors from nine of these 12 forms and most of them analyzed five types of behaviors or less. The vast majority of the studies involved some measures of theft, violence, drug use, vandalism, and alcohol use. Sexual violence, dangerous driving, and use of tobacco were very rarely introduced. Some studies included measures that were not intrinsically antisocial behavior such as academic results, going to church, grade point average, social conformity, psychiatric diagnosis, or health measures.

The vast majority of studies analyzed self-reports and mixed gender samples. Some studies used national samples of US residents, whereas most of the samples were local (regions, counties, cities, or schools) and only two studies used samples of juvenile court adolescents. A few conceptual replications had taken place outside the USA: Australia, Canada, and New Zealand. Very few studies were conducted with specific ethnic or racial groups. Some studies confirmed the latent construct with age groups: children, adolescents of various ages, and adults. The samples were recruited in the 1970s, 1980s, 1990s, and 2000s and only one study compared equivalent samples from two decades (Le Blanc and Girard 1997). A latent construct was confirmed with official delinquency (Parker and McDowall 1986).

In summary, more than 30 conceptual replications support the following conclusions: (1) There is no doubt that the empirical construct of antisocial behavior is empirically observable. (2) It is composed of two major categories, delinquent and problem behaviors. (3) These categories are subdivided into a variety of types. These solid conclusions are independent of the informant, the set of behaviors, the statistical grouping method, the source and composition of the sample, the historical period, and the site of the study. Three questions still need more investigations. Will these generalizations stand for the last four historical periods covered by the MTSFGCLS? Can a five-level complex fractal structure model be confirmed? Can the construct of antisocial behavior be confirmed with developmental career indicators of OAB and SRAB, such as onset, duration, and offset?

5.2 A Test of the Antisocial Behavior Theoretical Model

During the 1990s, the position of the MTSFGCLS became that all forms of antisocial behavior are under the synthetic latent construct of AB. This theoretical position was stated and first tested in psychology by Jessor and Jesor (1977). In criminology, Gottfredson and Hirschi (1990) argued convincingly that the classical tradition "… *ignored many forms of behavior analogous to crime in terms of social reaction and identical in terms of causation.*" (p. 3) That position has not been challenged. The construct of AB adopts various dominations; it is the "*general deviance syndrome*" in criminology, "*problem behavior*" in psychology, "*antisocial behavior*" in psychiatry, "*deviant behavior*" in sociology, "*externalizing behavior*" in psychoeducation, and any of these names in social work. In Sect. 1.2.1, it was argued that today, in western society, this construct is subdivided into distinctive laws, criminal law and problem behaviors or protection laws, and independent justice and youth social and protection systems.

During the last 40 years, researchers did not try to group the diversified types of SRAB into meaningful categories. In laws, in the mind of journalists and the population, and in the publications of researchers, it is customary to distinguish criminal behaviors into two subconstructs, property and violent crimes as documented in Sect. 1.2.1. Loeber and Hay (1997) were the first to empirically extract three subconstructs composed of specific SRAB scales. They proposed *"covert"* antisocial behavior, such as property crimes, *"overt"* antisocial behavior, analogous to violent behaviors, and *"authority conflict"* at school and in the home. In 1990, Gottfredson and Hirschi (p. 10) introduced the notion of *"reckless or imprudent behavior,"* which points to *"natural harm or physical sanction.".* Le Blanc and Bouthillier (2003) proposed that these reckless behaviors take the forms of sexual activities, alcohol and drug use, risky driving, disorderly conduct, and gambling. In summary, SRAB can be measured with a wider taxonomy than in previous empirical studies.

Figure 1.1 proposes that a four-level hierarchical fractal structure portrays the latent construct of antisocial behavior, either SRAB or OAB. This figure summarizes existing knowledge on this legal and scientific construct. The first column on the right in Fig. 1.1, the lower level of the fractal structure, level one, enumerates specific forms of antisocial behavior, 12 scales. This number may increase as laws, morals, theory, and empirical research evolve. There is an underground to that level, the specific acts that compose each of the 12 scales (see the list of acts in Table 1.1, their reliability in Table 1.2, and the formulation of the questions in Appendix B). The second column from the right, level two, proposes the four basic types of antisocial behavior: overt, covert, conflict, and reckless behaviors. The third column from the right, level three, consists of the two general categories of antisocial behavior, delinquent and problem behavior, which reflect the legal construct of antisocial behavior. Finally, in the last column from the right, level four, is the overall latent construct. This hierarchical theoretical structure was tested with two the parameters of the career, age at onset, a developmental descriptor, and frequency during the last year, a descriptive parameter (Le Blanc and Bouthillier 2003).

With the juvenile court sample of the 1990s, the test of the SRAB model was carried out using confirmatory factor analysis and some statistical barriers were encountered. The relatively large sample, 655 adolescents, offered high participation rates for most antisocial acts, whatever their seriousness. First, the test of the theoretical model was conducted with only three of its four levels (in light color in Fig. 1.1) because, to our knowledge, no statistical software package was available that could handle this complexity, a four-level model. Only Mplus offered the possibility of a hierarchical confirmatory factor analysis with three levels. We had to drop the third level, the distinction between delinquent activities and problem behavior. Second, for various conceptual, measurement, and statistical reasons, some scales in Fig. 1.1 (in white) had to be dropped for the final test. In a first case, gambling, disorderly conduct, and dangerous driving had too few behaviors representing their scale and some acts were not that well adapted for the middle age of adolescence. In a second case, sexual aggression was dropped because it had an extremely low prevalence rate. In addition, the number of scales greatly exceeded existing tests of such models and some scales had to be dropped because some of the correlations between them were very small in comparison with others that were much higher, without being excessively high. At term, the light gray fractal structure of SRAB in Fig. 1.1 was submitted for Mplus Hierarchical confirmatory factor analysis.

This model fitted well with the frequency data (NFI 0.90, CFI 0.91) and the age at onset data (NFI 0.92, CFI 0.95). These results were replicated independently for females and males and with a gender group comparison. The results were satisfactory for the frequency data (males: NFI 0.90, CFI 0.92; females: NFI 0.92, CFI 0.95) and the group comparison (equal loadings: NFI 0.88, CFI 0.90). The results were comparable for the onset data (males: NFI 0.92, CFI 0.95; females: NFI 0.77, CFI 0.91) and for the group comparison (equal loadings: NFI 0.88, CFI 0.95).

In conclusion, the model tested with CFA confirms that SRAB is a fractal phenomenon composed of forms and categories of behaviors under the general umbrella of the construct of antisocial behavior. However, it was an imperfect test from a strictly statistical perspective. Some statistical conditions were not optimal; they incorporate a limited range of scales and of antisocial acts (45 instead of 61), and it was not replicated with other samples of the MTSFGCLS because the list of acts changed across decades. In addition, an important level of the theoretical model, between the global construct of antisocial behavior and its four categories, was not tested, i.e., the legal differentiation between criminal activities and problem behavior.

At the beginning of this section, three questions were formulated. A partial response was proposed by the above test. First, the model is confirmed with two parameters of antisocial behavior, the actual frequency and the onset (see the list of parameters of a career in Table 2.1). However, there is still a need to reproduce the test with other parameters, for example, participation, variety, and offset. Second, only three levels were confirmed because the CFA software cannot handle four levels. Third, in this book there are four criteria for attaining generalization, that is, the reproduction of the results for genders, the phases of the life cycle, the status group, and historical periods. Only one of these criteria has been confirmed up to now, the reproduction of the model for genders. Let us see if better results can be obtained with the Goldberg procedure.

5.3 The Generalization of the Antisocial Behavior Hierarchical Model

In the introduction to the book, it was stated that its central theme was the generalizability of empirical results on the phenomenon of antisocial behavior. Criminological knowledge is extremely rarely reproduced with exact replications and once in a while with conceptual replications (McNeeley and Warner 2015). It is also the case with the empirical results in behavioral sciences (Schmidt 2009; Makel et al. 2012) and criminology (Pridemore et al. 2018). The MTSFGCLS spans through five historical periods and 40 years of the life cycle of some subjects. In consequence, the SRAB questionnaire was adapted to individual development in these socio-historical contexts taking into account the growth of criminological thinking, the explosion of developmental empirical knowledge, the advent of the numeric world, and the maturation of researchers.

Looking back at all the data sets of the MTSFGCLS, it became evident that a direct replication with exact common measures of SRAB for all the samples and all the time periods could not be made. To conform with the basic criteria of generalizability, seven scales enumerated in Table 1.1 and Appendix B were analyzed: sexual promiscuity, alcohol and drug use, conflict at home and in school, vandalism, physical violence, and theft. All the population and court samples are described in Appendix A. The population samples of each decade do not show the exact same composition of sociodemographic characteristics. For their part, the court samples were recruited using the same criteria, being convicted in the same juvenile court during a 2-year period, but they differed because of the legal, criminal justice, and demographic changes in Montréal during the 20-year interval (see Appendix C). In summary, the generalizations will be strong because of the use of the same scales of SRAB and a common statistical procedure. However, it will be decreased by the diversity in the composition of each of the categories of samples.

The analytical strategy is the following. The Goldberg hierarchical factor analysis procedure from the top down (Goldberg 2006) is used with the scales and the last-year variety parameter. Since Hindelang et al.'s (1981) landmark study, most researchers have considered this descriptor to be the pivot and the most efficient measure of SRAB for descriptive and explanatory purposes. The Goldberg procedure is applied with the total MTSFGCLS data set, genders (Table 1.4), age groups of males (Table 1.5), populations of males of sociohistorical periods (Table 1.6), and status groups (population and court samples) (Table 1.7).

As the Goldberg procedure has six steps, the tables are reporting the three most essential ones. First, the principal component results are reported to test the hypothesis that the seven scales are saturating a common factor, level four of the theoretical model (Fig. 1.1). Second, the principal axis solution with a Varimax rotation is displayed to test the hypothesis that the scales are saturating two factors that can be interpreted as delinquency and problem behavior, the two main dimensions of SRAB, that is, level three of the theoretical model in Fig. 1.1. Third, the principal axis four factors solution with a Varimax rotation is presented to test the hypothesis that the scales are saturating four factors that can be interpreted as the four categories of SRAB: overt and covert delinquency and reckless and conflict problem behavior (level two of the theoretical model; Fig. 1.1). Two steps of the procedure are not reported. The three factors solution between the second and third steps is not of interest in clarifying the above questions. The analysis with five factors is also not displayed because all the SRAB scales show saturations below 0.30 on a solution with five factors (a closure criterion recommended by Goldberg). All results not presented are available upon request to the author.

The response to the first question is clearly yes. It is displayed in the four Tables 1.4, 1.5, 1.6, and 1.7, which show that one principal component factor can be extracted in analysis of all 13 principal component factors. This factor explains

Table 1.4 The gender reproduction of the SRAB structure for all MTSFGCLS samples: last year variety with the Goldberg procedure

Results	MTSFGLS 13,037[1]	Females 4,200[1]	Males 8,831[1]
Principal component %[2]	46,26	43,87	46,56
Saturations[3] **Sex**	.64[3]	.63	.62
Drug use	.75	.72	.75
Conflict in home	.66	.70	.67
Conflict at school	.67	.68	.68
Vandalism	.59	.52	.59
Physical violence	.75	.72	.75
Serious theft	.70	.64	.72

Two factors[4] %[2]	MTSFGLS 60,39		Females 59,32		Males 61.07	
Saturations	Factor 1	Factor 2	Factor 1	Factor 2	Factor 1	Factor 2
Sexual relation	.14	**.75**[5]	.13	**.72**	.13	**.70**
Drug use	.30	**.73**	.25	**.74**	.32	**.72**
Conflict in home	.47	.34	.52	.36	.52	.30
Conflict at school	.43	.40	.38	.45	.50	.34
Physical violence	**.66**[5]	.08	**.56**	.06	**.66**	.07
Serious theft	**.68**	.31	**.73**	.24	**.67**	.31
Serious theft	.46	.41	.47	.30	.48	.43

Four Factors[5,6] %[2]	MTSFGLS 80,49				Females 80,07				Males 80.46			
Saturations	Factor1	Factor2	Factor3	Factor4	Factor1	Factor2	Factor3	Factor4	Factor1	Factor2	Factor3	Factor4
Sexual relation	**.71**	.09	.17	.09	**.72**	.01	.14	.33	**.68**	.05	.19	.09
Drug use	**.75**	.21	.32	.16	**.71**	.23	.34	.03	**.68**	.20	.24	.19
Conflict in home	.20	.27	**.48**	**.44**	.21	.36	**.48**	.21	.23	.29	**.51**	.26
Conflict at school	.28	.25	**.62**	.10	.31	.24	**.54**	.09	.27	.30	**.61**	.20
Vandalism	.06	**.66**	.24	.17	.03	**.53**	.22	.09	.07	**.66**	.22	.13
Physical violence	.29	**.60**	.21	.24	.19	**.66**	.18	.35	.31	**.53**	.21	.31
Serious theft	.44	.45	.05	**.35**	.21	.31	.14	**.57**	.36	.43	-.09	**.30**

1. The number of subjects in analysis with all the MTSFGLS samples.
2. The percentage of variance explained by a factor.
3. The factor analysis saturations of each scale and each factor.
4. The factors extracted on request with the Principal axis method and a Varimax rotation.
5. The saturations in bold indicate which are highly significant for the interpretation of the meaning of a factor.
6. The three factors solution is not reported because because it does not help to understand the SRAB structure and the five factors solution is not displayed because no saturation are above 0,30 following Goldberg criteria to stop extracting more factors ikn this case. All these results are available on demand to the author.

Table 1.5 The age reproduction of the SRAB structure for males: last year variety with the Goldberg procedure

Males age groups	10 to 13 3,602[1]	14-15-16 3,483[1]	17 to 20 1,173[1]
Principal component %[2]	43,89	48,78	45,89
Saturations[3] Sex relation	.61[3]	.63	.53
Drug use	.70	.77	.69
Conflict in home	.62	.68	.66
Conflict at school	.70	.67	.59
Vandalism	.61	.62	.64
Physical violence	.77	.77	.82
Serious theft	.58	.73	.77

Two factors[4] %	56,76		61,06		60,03	
Saturations	Factor 1	Factor 2	Factor 1	Factor 2	Factor 1	Factor 2
Sex relation	.28	.46[5]	.18	**.66**	.11	**.77**
Drug use	.30	**.65**	.38	**.68**	.43	**.59**
Conflict in home	.52	.22	.50	.36	.57	.18
Conflict at school	**.54**	.33	.49	.35	.50	.15
Vandalism	**.56**	.22	**.64**	.13	**.64**	.06
Physical violence	**.65**	.37	**.61**	.41	**.72**	.35
Serious theft	.21	**.52**	.47	.47	.59	.42

[5]Four Factors[5][6] %	77,36				80,65				80,12			
Saturations[6]	Factor1	Factor2	Factor3	Factor4	Factor1	Factor2	Factor3	Factor4	Factor1	Factor2	Fector3	Factor4
Sexual relation	.09	.47	.33	.15	**.65**	.21	.08	.16	.15	**.65**	.09	.07
Drug use	.18	.34	**.48**	.27	**.58**	.32	.22	.29	.19	**.53**	.43	-.05
Conflict in home	.36	.24	.16	.30	.20	.33	.19	**.56**	.29	.15	**.55**	.23
Conflict at school	.36	**.61**	.12	.17	.36	-.01	.43	**.52**	.23	.15	**.54**	.04
Vandalism	**.65**	.16	.20	.13	.09	.26	**.62**	.19	**.59**	.04	.32	.01
Physical violence	**.54**	.33	.26	**.40**	.32	.44	.39	.29	**.65**	.37	.33	.03
Serious theft	.19	.13	**.64**	.085	.34	**.65**	.24	.15	**.58**	.45	-.8	**.33**

1. The number of subjects in analysis with all the MTSFGLS samples.
2. The percentage of variance explained by a factor.
3. The factor analysis saturations of each scale and each factor.
4. The factors extracted with the Principal axix method and a Varimax rotation.
5. The saturations in bold indicate which are highly significant for the interpretation of the meaning of a factor.
6. The three factors solution is not reported because because it does not help to understand the SRAB structure and the five factors solution is not displayed because no saturation are above 0,30 following Goldberg criteria to stop extracting more factors ikn this case. All these results are available on demand to the author.

Table 1.6 The historic reproduction of the SRAB structure for male population samples: last year variety with the Goldberg procedure

Males populations	Population 1970s 1672[1]	Population 1980s 365[1]	Population 1990s 244[1]	Population 2000s 1,964[1]
Principal %[2,3]	40,13	43,60	57,26	57,92
Sexual relation	.55[3]	.60	.68	.66
Drug use	.67	.73	.85	.75
Conflict home	.55	.58	.69	.73
Conflict school	.67	.73	.61	.76
Vandalism	.66	.70	.80	.65
Physical viole.	.65	.71	.81	.75
Serious theft	.66	.53	.77	.79

Two factors[4]	Population 1970s		Population 1980s		Population 1990s		Population 2000s	
% Saturations	53.17		56.56		67.88		71.75	
	Factor 1	Factor 2	Factor 1	Factor 2	Factor 1	Factor 2	Factor 1	Factor 2
Sexual relation	.23[5]	**.70**	.48	.46	**.68**	.48	.11	**.87**
Drug use	.21	.45	**.60**	.16	.42	.45	.29	**.77**
Conflict home	.36	.28	.32	.37	.40	.49	.53	.38
Conflict school	.38	.45	**.65**	.32	.21	**.73**	.43	.56
Vandalism	**.64**	.20	.30	**.61**	.57	.50	**.71**	.09
Physical viol.	**.56**	.23	.45	.45	**.67**	.41	**.73**	.23
Serious theft	.48	.33	.13	**.52**	**.81**	.21	**.76**	.39

Four Factors[5,6]	Population 1970s				Population 1980s				Population 1990s				Population 2000s			
Saturations[6]	74.93				77.93				83.37				86.16			
	Fac 1	2	3	4	Fac 1	2	3	4	Fac 1	2	3	4	Fac 1	2	3	4
Sexual relation	**.63**	.05	.39	.15	.46	.09	**.40**	.35	**.60**	.49	.44	.07	.40	**.81**	.11	.05
Drug use	.46	.16	.07	.15	**.64**	.25	.13	.15	.32	.16	**.58**	.16	.15	**.81**	.24	.01
Conflict home	.20	.15	.15	**.47**	.10	.15	.22	.12	.23	**.70**	.20	.20	**.57**	.23	**.40**	.08
Conflict school	**.50**	.32	.06	.25	.48	.17	.12	.18	.11	.33	**.49**	.36	.43	.45	**.40**	.05
Vandalism	.19	**.66**	.22	.18	.19	**.50**	.33	.24	.45	.25	.30	**.61**	**.74**	.18	.12	.02
Physical viol.	.20	.37	.20	.36	.29	.43	.24	**.52**	**.55**	.34	.31	.29	**.73**	.31	.17	.09
Serious theft	.18	.29	**.60**	.22	.10	**.53**	.09	.12	**.78**	.17	.20	.23	**.75**	.32	.15	**.30**

1. The number of subjects in analysis with all the MTSFGLS samples.
2. The percentage of variance explained by a factor.
3. The factor analysis saturations of each scale and each factor.
4. The factors extracted on request with the Principal axix method and a Varimax rotation.
5. The saturations in bold indicate which are highly significant for the interpretation of the meaning of a factor.
6. The three factors solution is not reported because because it does not help to understand the SRAB structure and the five factors solution is not displayed because no saturation are above 0,30 following Goldberg criteria to stop extracting more factors in this case. All these results are available on demand from the author.

Table 1.7 The historic reproduction of the SRAB structure for males by court samples of the 1970s and 1990s: last year variety with Goldberg procedure

Court samples	Court males 1970s 470[1]	Court males 1990s 506[1]	Court females 150[1]
Principal %[2,3]	43.70	43.05	48.37
Sexual relation	.52	.30	.37
Drug use	.74	.61	.67
Conflict in home	.60	.69	.76
Conflict at school	.68	.73	.66
Vandalism	.67	.61	.76
Physical violence	.71	.75	.73
Serious theft	.70	.79	.83

Two factors %	Court males 1970s 470[1] 59.75		Court males 1990s 506[1] 57.49		Court females 150[1] 63.56	
Saturations	Factor 1	Factor 2	Factor 1	Factor 2	Factor 1	Factor 2
Sexual relation	-.14[3]	.46[4]	.21	.31	.06	.38
Drug use	.25	**.85**	.02	**.55**	.33	**.48**
Conflict in home	.32	.32	.35	**.50**	.58	.38
Conflict at school	.38	.42	.42	**.51**	.57	.18
Vandalism	**.76**	.11	**.74**	.06	**.74**	.15
Physical violence	**.57**	.27	.49	.47	**.67**	.15
Serious theft	.48	.36	.56	.49	**.80**	**.51**

[5]Four Factors %	Court males 1970s 470[1] 83.37				Court males 1990s 506[1] 79.44				Court females 150[1] 81.46			
Saturations[6]	Factor1	Factor2	Factor3	Factor4	Factor1	Factor2	Factor3	Factir4	Factor1	Factor2	Factor3	Factor4
Sexual relation	.13	**.56**	.09	.03	.03	.33	.09	.30	.03	.48	.09	.03
Drug use	.19	**.66**	.33	.22	.17	.20	**.59**	.30	.25	**.65**	.33	.22
Conflict in home	.22	.20	**.46**	.12	.26	.51	.14	.23	.35	.30	.25	**.50**
Conflict at school	.20	.18	**.49**	.18	.26	**.71**	**.65**	.12	.40	.13	.22	.42
Vandalism	**.67**	.08	.24	.12	**.59**	.25	.06	.09	**.61**	.09	.42	.21
Physical violence	**.61**	.28	.13	.12	**.78**	.40	.06	**.35**	**.78**	.17	.11	.20
Serious theft	.37	.20	.33	**.41**	**.69**	.19	.44	.20	.30	.38	**.74**	.31

1. The number of subjects use in analysis.
2. The percentage of variance explained by a factor.
3. The factor analysis saturations of each scale on each factor.
4. The saturations in bold indicate which are highly significant for the interpretation of the meaning of a factor.
5. The number of factors extracted on request with the Principal axix method and a Varimax rotation.
6. The three factors solution is not reported because because it does not help to understand the SRAB structure and the five factors solution is not displayed because no saturation are above 0,30 following Goldberg criteria to stop extracting more factors in this case. All these results are available on demand to the author.

between 30% and 58% of the variance; the lowest saturation for the scales is always above 0.53 and the majority of them are between 0.60 and 0.70. In most of the cases, the physical aggression and theft scales present the highest saturations and they are followed by sexual relations and drug use. In summary, the results of these direct replications confirm that the seven SRAB scales are constituents of the same construct and this conclusion is valid for the whole data set and for females and males (Table 1.4), age groups of the life cycle (Table 1.5), population and court samples (Table 1.6), and historical periods (Table 1.7) of the MTSFGCLS data set. Overall, the prevailing theoretical position that problem behaviors are analogous to crimes and that they are constituents of the antisocial behavioral construct becomes an unbreakable generalization, at least for the last half-century in Quebec. Such diversity of controls was never attained, in spite of the numerous studies of the structure of SRAB.

The second question on the agenda was about the postulate, illustrated in Fig. 1.1, that SRAB consists of two subconstructs, a delinquency factor (vandalism, physical violence, and theft) and a problem behavior factor (sexual relations, drug use, and conflict in home and at school). Each table has three results; the second row responds to the existence of these two main dimensions of SRAB. All the analyses explained between 53% and 72% of the variance and in 9 out of 13 analyses around 60%. In all these analyses, one of the two factors is highly saturated, at least higher than 0.60, by the three delinquency scales, vandalism, physical aggression, and theft. These saturations are very much higher on the delinquency factor than on the problem behavior factor. The opposite results are observed for two of the four problem behavior scales, sexual relations and drug use. However, the two conflict scales, in home and at school, display lower saturations than those of the five other scales on the delinquency or problem behavior factors, generally from 0.30 to 0.50. For these scales, some higher saturations are on the delinquency factor, 6 out of 13 analyses, on the problem behavior factor, 2 out of 13, and similar on the two factors, 5 out of 14. The home conflict scale has its highest saturation on the delinquency factor in 12 out of 13 analyses, whereas the school conflict scale has its highest saturation on the delinquency factor in 9 out of 13 analyses, 3 on the problem behavior factor and in 3 cases the saturations are almost equal on the two factors. In summary, there are, first, two subconstructs that are clearly dominant and independent of each other in all 13 analyses, delinquency (vandalism, physical violence, and theft) and problem behavior (sexual relations and drug use), and, second, a secondary subconstruct, conflict behaviors, which contributes marginally to them; these behaviors sustain these two categories of SRAB. Our hypothesis of the existence of two clear types of SRAB is not generalizable. The distinction between criminal behavior and problem behavior proposed by laws and most justice systems is not sustainable with SRAB. As a consequence, the third level of the theoretical model of Fig. 1.1, which has never been empirically tested, should be erased. It then becomes essential to push forward and extract the expected four factors solution that is postulated by the theoretical model. The extractions of a solution with three factors did not lighten the understanding of the composition of the SRAB construct. Except for the delinquency factor, the other two factors present all sort of mixes of the five problem behavior scales and they were difficult to interpret.

Let us look at the four factors solutions and start with the gender reproducibility. Table 1.4 reports the results of the factor analysis with four factors for all MTSFGCLS subjects (13,037). They explain 80% of the variance for all subjects (13,037) and for females (4200) and males (8831). With all subjects, the first factor measures reckless behavior, such as sexual relations and drug use. The second factor contains overt behavior, vandalism, and physical aggression. The third factor is composed of conflict behaviors in home and at school. The fourth factor is a mix of conflict at home and theft, with significant lower saturation than their highest ones on the conflict and delinquency factors respectively. These results vary by gender. Four factors are totally clear for females: reckless (sexual relations and drugs), conflict (in home and at school), overt (vandalism and physical violence), and covert (serious theft). For males, there is some shadow ambiguity because the four factors solution is the best; however, serious theft saturates three factors at 0.30 or more: reckless, overt, and the fourth factor. These results tell us that male thieves put into practice all other forms of delinquencies, as well as the use of drugs and sex.

Table 1.5 presents the results by male age groups; the age reproducibility. The principal component and the two factor solutions are reproducing the theoretical model for the middle adolescence group (age 14 to 16). That is clearly four categories of SRAB: reckless, conflict, covert, and overt behavior. For the younger group (age 10 to 13), no clear structure exists except for overt behavior (vandalism and physical violence); sexual relations is associated with conflict at school, drug use with theft, conflict in the home and physical violence, conflict in the home with vandalism, and physical violence, etc. As is shown in Chap. 3, at that period of life some behaviors are just starting and the participation rate is low for many SRABs. It can be concluded that SRAB has not really taken shape before adolescence. It may also be a measurement misinterpretation, the formulation of the behaviors may have been better adapted for middle adolescence and some equivalent child behaviors may have been forgotten. Finally, for the oldest age group (17 to 20), the four factors solution is the best, with solid reckless, conflict, and delinquency (vandalism, physical violence), and serious theft factors. In this case, we could probably reverse the arguments that were stated for the younger group.

The results of the historic replication for the four male population samples are presented in Table 1.6. As in previous tables, a strong principal component factor is displayed with all the SRAB scales. Then, a two principal axis factors solution, with Varimax rotation, was obtained as usual, that is, clear delinquency and reckless factors in the four time periods, whereas the conflict scales are secondary components, alternatively with a stronger saturation on one of these two factors. As for the gender and age comparisons, the conflict scales show lower saturations on one or the other category (delinquency and problem behavior) or about equally on both factors.

Before drawing conclusions on all of these reproducibility results, let us look at Table 1.7. The comparison of the two male court samples, at a 20-year interval, confirms the previous results. First, a strong principal axis SRAB factor was extracted; second, a very independent delinquency factor was obtained with a diluted problem behavior factor owing to the conflict scales; finally, the usual four factors solution is observable for the 1970 sample, overt, reckless, conflict, and covert, whereas the picture is troubled for the 1990 males as the reckless and conflict factors are identified with delinquency and physical violence factors. For the female court sample of the 1990s, the results are similar to previous results for females of the population samples.

The objective of this section was to empirically generalize the hierarchical theoretical model of SRAB in Fig. 1.1. (1) It was established that the seven scales measuring SRAB could be regrouped under one construct, antisocial behavior, as was theoretically expected. (2) It was impossible to sustain a clear and independent distinction between delinquency and problem behavior; there was a strong and independent delinquency category of SRAB, but the expected problem behavior category was unclear because the conflict behaviors did not match strongly with the reckless behaviors, as was expected from the theoretical model. (3) In most factorial analyses, the seven SRAB scales could be distributed on four forms of SRAB of the theoretical model. Overall, the theoretical model empirically tested is generalizable to genders, age groups of the life cycle, male population samples of four decades, and court samples 20 years apart.

This conclusion is powerful because statisticians and criminologists are well aware of the volatility of factor analysis. Its results could be easily influenced by variations in the composition of samples and their context. However, this conclusion could still be a challenge from the following perspectives: the seven scales are not sufficiently representative of all the diversity of antisocial behavior, even if they are exact measurement replications. The samples can only permit conceptual replications and the above replications were only conducted in one culture and society; as a consequence, social change can explain part of the variations of the results. An opportunity exists to replicate or discard the above conclusions and the theoretical model; it is the last few decade data sets of the International Self-reported Delinquency Study that contain similar measures of SRAB in many countries and cities around the world (Junger-Tas et al. 1994, 2003, 2010, 2012).

5.4   A Network View of the Patterns of Antisocial Behavior

The above successful replication tests were conducted with seven SRAB scales. Over time, the questionnaire was enlarged to include behaviors from other forms of SRAB and adult-specific scales. These improvements had the impact to increase to 15 the total number of SRAB scales. Three were rapidly discarded: intimate violence, gambling, and conflict at work. This decision was taken for at least two of the following reasons: their correlations with other scales were low (less than 0.20), the communalities were also around that level, the prevalence of these scales was low (under 30%), and the measurement of gambling did not seem an appropriate representation of that phenomenon. A factor analysis, with the Goldberg procedure, was conducted with the 12 scales listed in Table 1.8.

Table 1.8 Exploratory factor analysis of the onset of SRAB scales, court sample of males of the 1990s

Onset of SRAB[1]	Exciting[2,3]	Covert[2]	Strolling[2]	Conflict[2]	Overt[2]	Arousing[2]
Sexual relations	0.086	0.050	0.153	0.060	0.128	0.897
Drug use	0.185	0.456	- 0 .043	0.238	0.102	0.559
Disordely conduct	0.054	0.282	0.844	0.025	0.009	0.092
Vandalism	0.135	0.059	0.757	0.223	0.319	0.067
Theft	0.207	0.785	0.253	0.210	- 0.038	.066
Fraud	0.181	0.618	0.223	- 0.002	0.410	0.152
Motor vehicule theft	0.922	0.132	0.135	0.084	0.119	0.111
Risky driving	0.934	0.136	0.041	0.066	0.084	0.082
Physical violence	- 0.025	0.606	0.102	0.312	0.487	0.116
Psychological violence	0.172	0.154	0.176	0.106	0.875	0.149
Conflict at school	0.001	0.034	0.238	0.806	0.112	0.163
Conflict at home	0.152	0.295	- 0.022	0.743	0.051	0.016

1. In previous replications there were seven scales; we began the exploration with fifteen sclales and we had to discord three of them: gambling and conflict at work and with intimate.
2. The name given to each patterns of AB.
3. The ordre of the factors reproduce the order of their extraction.

As in previous analysis, all the scales saturated one factor with coefficients between 0.48 and 0.68; this factor can be called antisocial behavior, and these variables explain 36% of the variance for 1990-adjudicated boys and 41% for girls. Following the Goldberg procedure, the best solution was six factors that explain 78% of the variance for boys and 80% for girls. Table 1.8 presents the saturations for Varimax rotated solution with six factors (all the results of all the steps of the procedure are available from the author). These six factors are made up of a dominant pair of SRAB scales with saturations well above other saturations of other scales. Factor 1 is composed of motor vehicle theft and risky driving and it is called "exciting behavior." Factor 2 regroups "covert behavior" and the most important scales are theft and fraud. Factor 3 presents "strolling behavior"; this is wandering around with disorderly conduct and vandalism. Factor 4 reflects what is manned "conflict behavior" or authority conflict and manifests by authority conflict in home

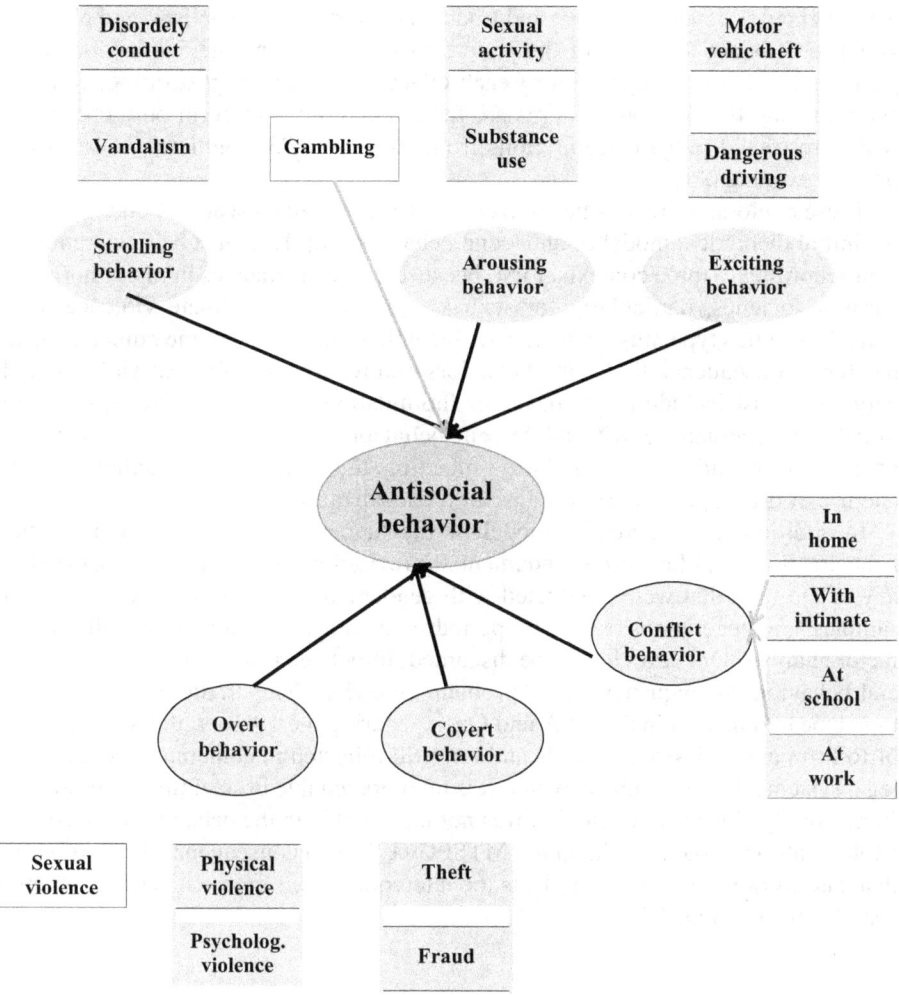

Fig. 1.2 A broader theoretical model of the network of behavioral patterns of self-reported antisocial behavior

and at school. Factor 5 is about physical and psychological violence; this is called "overt behavior." The factor 6 is about "arousing behavior" and the principal scales are drug use and sexual relations; they evoke a reaction in the form of a sensation, an immediate response. Figure 1.2 illustrates this broader theoretical model of the construct of antisocial behavior.

What is also interesting is that two of these six patterns are composed of secondary forms of antisocial behavior. First, the covert pattern, theft and fraud, can be associated with physical violence and drug use. Second, the overt pattern may be accompanied by complementary behaviors, vandalism and fraud. It is interesting to note that these four forms of SRAB are behaviors that are habitually defined as delinquency, as covert with theft and fraud, and overt, with vandalism, and physical violence. It is not the case for the pattern that are called problem behavior; these patterns are clearly independent of each other, that is, exciting, strolling, conflict, and arousing. If these four patterns are factor analyzed, they form only one factor with a restricted range of saturations from strolling 0.73, conflict 0.72, arousing 0.66, to exciting 0.62.

These exploratory results become challenges for future research. Some scales of the initial theoretical model of antisocial behavior (Fig. 1.1) must be reoperationalized according to three contexts. First, because of recent changes in moral norms in western societies, particularly for sexual aggression and intimate violence, new behaviors of this type must be included. Second, the explosion of the numeric world has for a consequence that some behaviors relative to psychological violence and gambling must include these means of intimidation. Third, as many scales were initially conceptualized with adolescent behaviors in mind, they must be better adapted to the adult contexts and ways of acting; this is the case for conflict at work and use of drugs, particularly because of the legalization of marihuana.

In addition, the theoretical model of the hierarchical structure of antisocial behavior (Fig. 1.1) has to be fundamentally revised because it is not supported in any of the tests that were conducted with genders, ages of the life cycle, types of samples, and generations or historic periods and with exploratory and confirmatory factor analysis. One level had to be discarded, in-between two categories of antisocial behavior, "delinquency" and "problem behavior." This traditional differentiation appeared in laws in the USA and Québec during the 1860s with the distinction of Reform and Industrial Schools and it is still reflected in contemporary laws and legal systems. From the above result, it is no more tenable in scientific criminology. Behaviorally, this legal distinction was not measurable in the behavioral patterns of adolescents and young adults in the MTSFGCLS. As a consequence, it is proposed that a network representation reflects the interconnections between patterns of antisocial behavior (Fig. 1.2).

6   Conclusion

In this chapter, existing empirical knowledge on the measurement of self-reported antisocial behavior was reviewed and a set of scales was empirically tested with population and court samples from the last four decades. The generalized conclusion is that a large spectrum of scales are criminometrically solid in terms of reliability and validity. In addition, the results were replicated by genders, ages of the life cycle, population and court samples, and historic periods in the social and cultural context of Montréal, Québec. Two sets of data could go beyond this limitation: the 1985 cohort of North American longitudinal studies in some cities (Le Blanc 2015) and the data sets of the International Self-reported Delinquency Study that contain similar measures of SRAB for many countries and cities around the world (Junger-Tas et al. 1994, 2003, 2010, 2012).

This chapter reports an accomplishment with the test of the heteromorphy of some patterns of SRAB between adolescence and youth, particularly for fraud, undisciplined in school and at work, disorderly conduct, risky driving, and conflict with parents and intimates. Criminologists now face the challenge of replicating the heteromorphy of these patterns and including other patterns and not only for those two periods of the life span but also between childhood and adolescence, between youth and maturity.

A good part of the chapter was devoted to the analysis of the hierarchical structure of antisocial behavior and its replication. A revision of the theoretical model was proposed and it was confirmed for genders, ages of the life course, population and court samples, and generations. These results pointed to a network model to be tested with new statistical technics. The main challenge for the criminologist is the operationalization of antisocial behavior that integrates behaviors that grow out of the numeric world.

Chapter 2
Antisocial Behavior and Crime: An Epidemiological View

1 Introduction

In criminology an enormous quantity of conceptual thinking and empirical studies have been devoted to the measurement of official crime and SRAB, particularly to the identification of the criteria for creating credible and reliable such data sets for the description of the epidemiology of these vital dependent variables. Today, there are still imperfections in the criminal statistics, but a large common set of data emerged over time in western societies and their credibility is sufficiently high. In addition, it was demonstrated in Chap. 1 that in criminology there is also access to believable data sets of SRAB because of the existence of solid and generalizable criminometric measures that have been constructed and validated by numerous other empirical studies and in the MTSFGCLS.

The landmark synthesis on criminal careers (Blumstein et al. 1986; Piquero et al. 2003, 2007), developmental criminology (Le Blanc and Fréchette 1989; Loeber and Le Blanc 1990; Le Blanc and Loeber 1998), and the latest textbooks (Morizot and Kazemian 2015; Farrington et al. 2019) confirmed that criminologists had agreed on a set of descriptive and boundary parameters for many decades. Criminologists now distinguish static and dynamic measures.

Snow (1855) invented the epidemiological method in his study of cholera. Eisner (1969) adapted it to criminology and applied it to official offending data. It was defined as the comparison of the risk, prevalence or incidence, of a condition for segments of a population. Now, in criminology, static descriptive parameters are distinguished from their dynamic counterparts.

The static epidemiological parameters are participation or prevalence, frequency (Lambda), and other measures of incidence such as seriousness, variety, and crime mix, whereas the dynamic or boundary measures of an career of antisocial behavior are age at onset, age at termination or offset, duration, and crime switching. Some descriptive parameters, prevalence and frequency, have always been in use in criminology since Quételet, to obtain an account of the state of the official career (OC).

© Springer Nature Switzerland AG 2021
M. Le Blanc, *The Development of Antisocial Behavior and Crime*,
https://doi.org/10.1007/978-3-030-68429-7_2

Others are more recent additions to the criminological tools. Variety was introduced into the first SRAB studies, particularly with the Nye and Short scale, whereas seriousness was redefined by Sellin and Wolfgang (1964) as a population estimation of the dangerousness of each crime. Finally, Blumstein et al. (1986) pointed out the importance of the ages at onset and offset and the duration, and they introduced the crime mix and switching measures. All these parameters have been applied to describe the course of the whole OD and forms of OC and SRAB. The definitions of all these parameters are given in Table 2.1

Psychologists (Magnusson and Cairns 1996), sociologists (Elder 1998), and individual growth criminologists (Loeber and Le Blanc 1990) have subscribed strongly to two axioms for a long period of time. The first of these universal laws is that the life cycle refers to a sequence of age-graded biological, psychological, social, and behavioral phases. The second law is that these developments are influenced by social and historical conditions and changes. The basic framework of this book is the comparison of the development of SRAB and crime across generations, genders, and particular groups during the second half of the twentieth century and the beginning of the twenty-first century.

It is expected that the well-known and universal gap between genders on antisocial behavior will be observed (Lanctôt 2015). As sociology describes the historical growth of societies and that the life course developmental criminology point to the

Table 2.1 The analytical tools for the study of the epidemiology of official and self-reported antisocial behavior

Descriptive parameters
Participation: an individual takes part in at least one behavior: currently, during the last year, or cumulatively for a specific time window
Frequency: number of times a behavior is enacted within a given time period: annually (Lambda) or cumulatively for a specific time window
Variety: the number of types of behaviors of a particular category at a particular point in time, for example, the number of sorts of drugs experienced
Seriousness: a score based on a legal classification, the harmfulness of an act, or by ratings of severity by experts or the population for antisocial behaviors
Mix: a combination of forms of behaviors at a particular point in time, for example, committing a mix of property crimes and person crimes
Boundary parameters
Onset: the age of an individual at his first behavior
Offset: the age of an individual when he carried out his last behavior
Duration:
(a) The career span: the time interval between the first and the last behavior
(b) Duration: the percentage of active years over the career span
Measures of change
Direction: percentage of subjects who progress or regress on antisocial behavior
Degree: percentage of subjects who are stable or change their antisocial behavior
Velocity: percentage of change over time or age on antisocial behavior

This table is adapted from Loeber and Le Blanc (1990), Le Blanc and Loeber (1998) and Le Blanc (2015)

impact of social change, it is anticipated that a gap will exist between the generations of the 1970s, 1980s, 1990s, and 2000s on antisocial behavior and crime in the MTSFGCLS. Numerous criminologists and our previous studies (Fréchette and Le Blanc 1987) have pointed out the normative gap; it manifests by the fact that particular groups, for example, adjudicated males, display antisocial behavior and self and social characteristics that distinguish them from the general population. There is a fourth gap that has been recurrently studied in criminal career research; it is the overlap between OC and SRO particularly in the Cambridge (Farrington et al. 2013b) and the Pittsburg (Jennings et al. 2016) longitudinal studies.

After the developmental epidemiology antisocial behavior has been described, it will be possible to contrast their evolution with the changes in the criminal justice system in Québec and the macro sociological evolutions that occurred over time in Montréal society. These data will facilitate the interpretation of the empirical results on these four possible gaps, that is, identification of the major changes in the justice and sociological contexts that were experienced by the four generations of subjects from the MTSFGCLS. This is from the birth of the first samples of subjects, around 1960, to the last interviews and data gathering on official offending in the 2000s.

2 The Epidemiology of Official Antisocial Behavior and Crime Careers

Official offending and problem behavior are measured by court convictions in the MTSFGCLS. They represent the output of the juvenile (delinquency and protection laws) and adult justice systems and convictions are far away from police arrest data. In Canada they are the most reliable source of data on the criminal career because they have existed for the longest period of time and they are carefully gathered and kept owing to the consequences of a court decision on the life individuals and their importance in the functioning of the criminal justice system. In addition, juvenile and adult data have a common base with the court paper files. Consequently, data sources such as the police register of arrests, accusations, convictions, and sentences were available directly to the MTSFGCLS.

Appendix B contains the list of delinquent offenses and problem behaviors. The offenses are grouped into 25 categories, six forms of crimes against property without violence, ten forms of crimes against persons, nine other forms of crimes, and all the Canadian criminal code numbers are also listed. In total, 76 criminal offenses were committed for which there was a court conviction. At the end of Appendix B, the official definition of the problem behaviors is given. In addition, two appendixes can be consulted. First, Appendix A describes the characteristics of all the samples. Second, Appendix C presents a short description of the evolution of the legal statuses and the criminal justice system as well as sociological indicators of historical changes in Québec from the 1960s to the 2000s.

The main question of this section is: do specific generations produce a similar or dissimilar criminal career? Five sub-questions are addressed. (1) How does the criminal career in a representative sample of adolescent differ from that in a court sample? (2) Is there a difference between a criminal career that began in the 1970s and one in the 1990s? (3) How does the criminal career of males and females of the 1980 generation differ? (4) How does the offenses mix that constituted a criminal career vary by decade, gender, age, and sample? (5) How does the OC differ from the problem behavior career during childhood and adolescence, in general and between genders?

The samples of the first generation, called the 1960 generation (G60), are composed of the 1970 court population (all the cases referred to the Montréal juvenile court during a 2-year period) and it is made up of five birth cohorts that were born between 1956 and 1960 with a median of 1958 (470 males) and, second by a representative sample of school adolescents (RSP70) was also composed of five birth cohorts with a median of 1959 (458 males). All the subjects included these samples were males. The members of this first generation went through adolescence during the 1970s, and their criminal career span from the early 1970s until 2017, from age 8, the legal age of responsibility, to age 61.

For its part, the court population of the generation of 1980 (recruited in the same way as for the first generation) also constituted five birth cohorts. The males (506) were born between 1974 and 1978 with 1976 as the median, whereas the years of birth of the female cohorts (150) were 1975 to 1979 with 1977 as the median. The members of this second generation went through their adolescence during the 1990s and their criminal careers covered the period from the early 1990s until 2017, from age 12, the new legal age of responsibility, to 45. The descriptive measures of offending available were defined in Table 1.1.

2.1 The Official Offending Career

2.1.1 A Descriptive Statistic View

Tables 2.2 and 2.3 respond to the previous four questions. In these tables, the left column lists the descriptors of the criminal carrier, whereas the middle column presents the results for the two samples of the generation of 1960, that is, the representative sample and the court males. The reader will note that only 13% of the males of the population sample were convicted for an offense between age 8 and 61 compared with 92% for the court sample and 8% of them were adjudicated under the youth protection authority. Le Blanc and Fréchette (1989) reported, in a contemporary historical period and an age span from age 8 to 30, that the level of convictions was very similar to those of Wadsworth (1979) in England and Jason (1982) in Sweden. Farrington et al. (2013b) report a prevalence of 40% in a working class

Table 2.2 The official criminal career for the 1960 and 1980 generations of the MTSFGCLS: an epidemiological view

Parameters	1960[a] males 8 to 61[b]		1960[a]–1980[a] 12 to 45[b] males females		
	Population[c]	Court[d]	1970 Males[d]	1980 Males[d]	1980 Females[d]
Participation (%)	12.9	91.7	89.4	89.3	32.7
Years active					
Minimum	1	1	1	1	1
Maximum	11	22	20	20	3
Mean	2.1	6.5	6	5	1.4
SD	2	4.4	4.2	3.7	1
Median	1	6	5	4	1
75th percentile	2	10	9	7	2
Frequency					
Minimum	1	1	1	1	1
Maximum	31	207	207	150	11
Mean	3.6	20.1	19.7	15.9	2.2
SD	5.8	21.8	21.5	17.3	2
Median	1	13	12	11	1
75th percentile	3	30	28	22	3
Variety					
Minimum	1	1	1	1	1
Maximum	8	15	15	15	6
Mean	1.9	5.8	5.7	5.9	1.7
SD	1.6	3.4	3.4	3.3	1.1
Median	1	6	5	6	1
75th percentile	2	8	8	8	2
Onset					
Minimum	15	8	12	12	13
Maximum	61	55	43	40	21
Mean	28.7	17.9	17.3	15.8	16.6
SD	11.9	12.5	5.1	2.3	1.9
Median	33	16	16	15	16
75th percentile	23	19	19	17	18
Offset					
Minimum	15	13	13	13	14
Maximum	61	60	45	44	23
Mean	32.9	35.6	32.1	25.5	17.6
SD	12.7	11.9	9.2	8.6	2.4
Median	30	37	34	22	17
75th percentile	44	43	39.8	33	19
Duration[e]					
Minimum	1 8.5%	1 14.5%	1 14.5%	1 20%	1 24.6%
Maximum	38	47	33	28	6
Mean	4.8	20.5	15	9.9	1.6
SD	7.3	11.1	9.6	7.6	1.4
Median	1	21	17	5	1
75th percentile	5	27	24	17	1.5

[a]Birth cohorts born around 1960 or 1980
[b]The range of ages for the career span
[c]A representative sample of French-speaking adolescents living on the Island of Montréal
[d]All adolescents referred to Montréal juvenile court by a prosecutor during a 2-year period and adjudicated under a delinquency or a youth protection law
[e]Duration is calculated in the following way: age of offset minus age of onset; the percentage refers to the number of subjects that have only 1 year of participation in offending

community of South London for a follow-up until age 55. Jennings et al. (2016) records 50% for Pittsburg inner city youngest and oldest cohorts from onset to their 30s. It is hazardous to compare other contemporary descriptive measures of the criminal career because not only does the composition of the samples vary but also the laws, the criminal justice systems, and the socioeconomic characteristics of the communities.

Question (1): how does the OC differ between a representative sample of a population of adolescents and a contemporary juvenile court population? Le Blanc and Fréchette (1989) showed that the gap between these groups was enormous, at least before they attained the middle of youth, for all the descriptive parameters: participation (annual and cumulative), variety, frequency (annual and cumulative), variety (presence and degree), gravity (Sellin and Wolfgang 1964 measure), onset, and duration. Table 2.2, with data from age 8 to 61, displays statistics that are to the order of six times or more for the court males whatever the measures. It is interesting to note that similar gaps had also been found with numerous measures of social and self-controls during adolescence (Fréchette and Le Blanc 1987). It is untrustworthy, even with contemporary data for the Pittsburg Study, to compare the OC results in Table 2.2 with the published results of these studies because of variations in the characteristics of their samples, the length of their follow-up, and their criminal laws.

Question (2): is there a distance between an OC of delinquents of the generations of 1960 (G60) and 1980 (G80)? The response is yes. According to the descriptive statistics in Table 2.2, when the generations of males are compared using a similar age span, that is, from age 12 to 45, most of the results for the males of G80 are lower than the figures for the males of G60. The only variable for which the statistics are equal is variety. We will come back to the interpretation of these results after the analyses of the age–crime curves.

Question (3): how does the OC vary by the nature of crimes? The criminal career literature is unambiguous on this question. It is expected that property crimes will dominate the career crime mix whatever the age and that violent crimes play a secondary role among all the types of offending. The figures from Glueck's 1940s arrest data (Laub and Samson 2003) and the later Cambridge Study in Delinquent Development conviction data (Farrington et al. 2013a) clearly show that, whatever the age group, the property offenses dominated the violent ones. Table 2.3 confirms this expected result for the G60 court males with the descriptive career descriptors.

In Table 2.3 two new categories of crime are displayed. First, as in Laub and Samson (2003) one column presents the figures for alcohol and drug offenses. They have a later onset and the lowest incidence results (frequency, participation, duration) compared with property and violent offenses. In addition, the fourth column replaces what is often named victimless crimes by the category "*delinquent lifestyle.*" Naylor (2003) has argued in favor of introducing a new distinction among

Table 2.3 The epidemiology of the criminal career by types of offending for the court sample of males of ages 8–61 and born around 1960

Types of offending Parameters	Property	Violence	Drugs/alcohol	Delinquent lifestyle
Participation	84.3	69.4	60.6	73.8
Years active				
Minimum	1	1	1	1
Maximum	19	11	10	14
Mean	4.8	3.1	2.3	3.1
SD	3.7	2.112	1.5	2.2
Median	4	2	2	3
75th percentile[a]	7	4.25	3	4
Frequency				
Minimum	0.17	0.08	0.25	0.14
Maximum	33.7	4.7	4.3	3.4
Mean	2.3	0.59	0.84	0.66
SD	2.9	0.71	0.20	0.56
Median	1.3	0.33	0.25	0.43
75th percentile	3.2	0.75	0.50	0.86
Variety				
Minimum	0.17	0.08	0.25	0.14
Maximum	1	0.67	1	0.86
Mean	0.51	0.23	0.42	0.33
SD	0.25	0.14	0.20	0.18
Median	0.50	0.17	0.25	0.29
75th percentile	0.67	0.33	0.50	0.43
Onset				
Minimum	8	10	10	10
Maximum	54	57	59	59
Mean	17.8	22.3	24.8	22.8
SD	6.7	9.3	10.1	9.4
Median	16	19	21	19
75th percentile	19	25	30	24
Offset				
Minimum	12	13	14	14
Maximum	60	59	60	60
Mean	30.3	33.3	32.8	33.3
SD	12	10.9	11.4	11.3
Median	29	34	33	33
75th percentile	38.8	40	40	40
Duration				
Minimum	1 22.3[b]	1 23	1 27	1 25.1
Maximum	47	44	39	44
Mean	12.7	11.3	8.4	10.9
SD	11.7	10.3	9.6	10.1
Median	10	10	4	7
75th percentile	21	19	13	19

[a]All adolescents referred to the Montréal juvenile court by a prosecutor during a 2-year period and adjudicated under a Delinquency act or the Youth protection law
[b]Percentage of cases with 1 year or less duration: age of offset–age of onset

official crimes that he calls illegal market crimes. In the MTSFGCLS official data, there are a significant number of convictions for such crimes: the importation and trafficking of drugs, cigarettes, and alcohol, sexual services (not as a client), and other underground activities such as gambling, shylocking, selling stolen goods, etc. Cusson (2005) has developed the construct of delinquent lifestyle around a behavioral and a routine activities dimension that includes the above-mentioned market crimes. Other illegal activities, such as driving dangerously and under the effect of alcohol or drugs, buying stolen goods and services on illegal markets, fighting, etc., are included in the lifestyle and market offenses (LSOs). These types of criminal activities were regularly mentioned during adult interviews with G60 and G80 males. Very often, newspaper articles describe such illegal activities by known criminals.

Table 2.3 shows that for G60 property offenses (POs) dominate violent crimes (VOs) and LSOs for four of the seven career descriptors: participation, frequency, variety, and duration. However, the onset and offset of POs are earlier than counterparts VOs and LSOs, whereas POs show a longer duration. In Table 2.3, the LSOs occupy the second position, in-between POs and VOs, for participation, number of active years, frequency, variety, and the third position for onset, offset, and duration. In sum, property offenses dominate VOs and LSOs whereas, for prevalence and incidence, LSOs overtake VOs in the crime mix and LSOs tend to appear later in the career crime mix.

Then, the question is: what types of offending occupies the second and the third positions to POs? Table 2.3 lists the response to this question. For G60, VOs and LSOs are about equal on four parameters: active years, variety, onset, and offset. This position of LSOs may be an indication of the possibility that these crimes are less frequently reported and sanctioned because the victims are voluntary clients. It is probable that LSOs come to the attention of the criminal justice system following a police-initiated investigation. Only self-reported data may clarify that situation. However, the participation is higher for LSOs, whereas the frequency is much higher for VOs spine. In summary, the spine of the OC mix consists of POs. This observation is confirmed in Table 2.4, which compares the same data for G60 and G80 based on a common career span from age 12 to 45. In Table 2.4, the dominance of POs is also evident and, for the three types of offenses, the general tendency is that the entire statistics are lower for the G80 males. The generation gap hypothesis is sustained for the total OC and types of offenses. The respective role of VOs and LSOs may be clarified by the analysis of age–crime curves.

To conclude the analysis of the offending career with descriptive statistics, some questions have to be investigated to conclude on the similarity or the dissimilarity of the criminal career from one generation to the next 20 years later. Why is the level of participation much lower for G80? Why are the careers of the females so short? Does the role of VOs and LSOs in the offending mix change over time?

Table 2.4 The epidemiology of the official criminal career from ages 12 to 45[a] by types of offending for the 1960 and the 1980 generations of the MTSFGCLS

Parameters	Property		Persons violence		Lifestyle	
Generation[b]	1960	1980	1960	1980	1960	1980
Participation %	83	63.4	66.6	65.2	70.4	56.7
Years active						
Minimum	1	1	1	1	1	1
Maximum	17	17	11	14	12	13
Mean	4.6	3.6	3.1	3	3	2.8
SD	3.5	3	2.2	2.4	2.1	2.3
Median	4	3	2	2	2	2
75th percentile	7	4	4	4	4	4
Frequency						
Minimum	1	1	1	1	1	1
Maximum	198	129	57	61	24	57
Mean	13.6	8.8	7	6.4	4.6	5
SD	17.3	11.6	8.6	6.9	3.8	5.6
Median	8	5	4	4	3	3
75th percentile	18	11	8.5	8	6	6
Variety						
Minimum	1	1	1	1	1	1
Maximum	6	6	8	6	6	6
Mean	3	3	2.7	2.6	2.3	2.2
SD	1.5	1.5	1.6	1.4	1.2	1.2
Median	3	3	2	2	2	2
75th percentile	4	4	4	4	3	3
Onset						
Minimum	12	12	12	12	13	12
Maximum	45	27	45	36	45	40
Mean	17.5	16.6	21.2	16.8	21.4	18
SD	5.4	2.5	7.5	3.1	7.4	4.2
Median	16	16	18	16	19	17
75th percentile	19	18	24	17	23	19
Offset						
Minimum	12	12	13	13	14	12
Maximum	45	44	45	43	45	44
Mean	27.9	24	30.8	23.8	30.2	24.2
SD	9.3	7.9	9	8.3	8.5	8.1
Median	27	21	33	20.5	31	21
75th percentile	36	29	38	30	37	30
Duration						
Minimum	1 23.4	1 24.5[c]	1 22.8	1 30	1 25.1	1 22.6
Maximum	33	28	31	28	30	26
Mean	10.6	8.1	9.9	7.7	9	6.8
SD	9.1	7.8	8.8	7.9	8.4	7.5
Median	9	5	14	4	6	5
75th percentile	19	13	20	14	16	11

[a]The range of ages for the career span
[b]Five birth cohorts born around 1960 or 1980
[c]Percentage of cases with 1 year or less duration: age of offset–age of onset

Table 2.5 The distribution of crimes in France from 1826 to 1829: number of persons by age, type, and gender, the original Quételet data[a]

Ages	Crimes against		Accused	
	Persons	Property	Males	Females
Less than 16	80	440	438	82
16 to 21	904	3723	3901	726
21 to 25	1278	3329	3762	845
25 to 30	1575	3702	4260	1017
30 to 35	1153	2883	3254	782
35 to 40	650	2076	2105	621
40 to 45	575	1734	1831	488
45 to 50	445	1275	1357	363
50 to 55	288	811	896	213
55 to 60	168	500	555	113
60 to 65	157	385	445	97
65 to 70	91	184	230	45
70 to 80	64	137	163	38
80+	5	14	18	1

[a]Adapted from Quételet (1833), pp. 65–66

2.1.2 An Age–Crime Curve View

Age has been one of the central long-term themes in criminology. Quételet (1831) was the first criminologist to describe the distribution of crimes by age 185 years ago. Table 2.5 displays his original aggregate data for France from 1826 through 1829. It is adapted from his tables on pages 65 and 66. Quételet interpreted these data in terms of four laws. Are they still valid in criminology? (1) The crime propensity attains a peak and then declines; in his data the maximum is between age 25 and 30. (2) The criminal career of females starts later and stops earlier than the careers of males. (3) Crimes against property are much more numerous than crimes against persons. (4) As age increases, the proportion of crimes against persons increases.

Over time, these Quételet statistics became age–crime curves. It was most often compiled with aggregate statistical reports on criminality in a country, a state, or a city and with court convictions. Later, it was calculated with other measures from various agencies of the system of justice. With the advent of longitudinal research a 100 years later, with Glueck's studies (1930, 1934, 1937, 1943), it became a meaningful variable in the analysis of the individual development of the criminal career. Half a century later, the age–crime curve became topical with papers by Hirschi and Gottfredson (1983) and Farrington et al. (1986). Counter-attacks and arguments followed (Gottfredson and Hirschi 1986, 1987; Blumstein et al. 1988a, b). Later, a prospective paper outlined future research to undertake (Loeber 2012). More recently, reviews of DeLisi (2015) and Britt (2019) are the last summaries on this subject. DeLisi (2015) lists a dozen papers that support the invariance, the equivocal or the critical positions about the shape of the age–crime curve using various sources of aggregate and individual data. His conclusion was that aggregate data lean more toward the equivocal and the critical points of view, whereas the invariance conclusion was more often supported by individual longitudinal data.

Interesting enough, the paradigmatic papers on developmental criminology by Loeber and Le Blanc (1990) and Le Blanc and Loeber (1998) did not review the literature on the age–crime curve. They focused on the importance of an early onset for the development of antisocial behavior and crime. They positioned that variable as the central moving force of the mechanisms of the developmental process of antisocial behavior and crime such as activation, aggravation, and desistance following Le Blanc and Fréchette's (1989) empirical investigation. In summary, age became the spine of modern developmental criminology when the trajectory perspective soared in the 1990s and it replaced the descriptive statistics above in the epidemiological description of the criminal career.

The landmark paper by Hirschi and Gottfredson (1983) demonstrated that the age distribution of crime is *"invariant"* in time and place. Twenty-five years later, Loeber (2012) stated that the age–crime curve is *"universal"* across nations, historical periods, data sources, birth cohorts, sample composition (gender, race, socioeconomic status), and forms of offending. Le Blanc (2015) proposed that criminology should test if the shape of the age–crime curve applies to all forms of antisocial behavior. This hypothesis will be tested in this chapter and in Chap. 5 on trajectories. The question is: can the general shape of the age–crime curve be replicated, even if it has significant specificities or irregularities, short-terms significant ups and downs, particular peak, velocities, and so on? Can the curve be replicated by generation, genders, types of samples, and types of offenses, even if many social, cultural, legal, and criminal justice conditions changed between 1960 and 2000?

Measurement Issues with Official Offending Data Sets

There are measurement issues with published curves that will be avoided. First, most age–crime curves are drawn with aggregate data sets and the MTSFGCLS proposes individual longitudinal curves in accordance with the redefinition of developmental criminology as the study of within-individual changes in antisocial behavior (Le Blanc 2015).

Second, very often the curves, particularly with longitudinal data, are truncated at around age 30. As a consequence of such an artificial cutoff point, criminologists may mistakenly think that there is no more offending after that age, that this part of the life cycle is not an interesting phenomenon to study. The nature of offending may be particular during later years of life. In addition, when studying older career criminals, criminologists may discover new unexpected risk factors for such offending and explain why they desist from property and violent crimes and switch to other forms of crime and antisocial behavior.

Third, many of the published graphs of the crime cycle do not present yearly figures. The curves are smoothed by periods varying in number of years, from a few to decades. Such a practice, which was begun by Quételet, as we saw above (Table 2.4), is inadequate. Scientists have the responsibility of being strictly precise in amount and value. Some hidden ups and downs may have specific explanations and policy utility.

Fourth, there are very often problems of comparability between published curves because of the nature of the communities (a neighborhood, a city, a country), the organization of the criminal justice system, the composition of samples (gender, ages, socioeconomic status, and so on), and the use of different measures of offending (arrests, convictions, incarcerations, self-reported, and so on). It is hazardous to compare curves even among the most recent publications with a long follow-up from childhood to late maturity. They have various measures and communities: Boston: arrest; Netherlands: convictions; Montréal: convictions; London: working class community and convictions; Pittsburg: inner-city samples and convictions. In addition, curves are drawn with prevalence or incidence (frequency) rates. It could be added, according to Table 2.1, that the curves may also be pictured with other parameters such as number of active years, variety, onset, offset, or duration. If the quantitative changes would be of interest on an age–crime curve, it could be essential to calculate change in term of degree or velocity, changes in level of participation or frequency, and so on, as well as direction, progression, and regression (Table 2.1) (Le Blanc and Loeber 1998).

Fifth, other measurement difficulties are also formulated in the last reviews by DeLisi (2015) and Britt (2019). The measurement difficulties notwithstanding, the importance of producing self-reported age–crime curves should be advocated and, particularly, curves should be displayed with other forms of antisocial behavior. In addition, there are rare conceptual and exact replications of age–crime curves by genders, normative and adjudicated delinquent samples, types of offending, and generations.

To our knowledge, only four data sets cover the criminal career of males from their childhood to around age 55 and more. First, Laub and Samson (2003) draw arrest curves with the Sheldon and Eleanor Glueck sample of 500 males recruited at the Boston juvenile court between 1939 and 1948. Second, Farrington et al. (2013a), Farrington (2019) published conviction curves for the Cambridge Study in Delinquent Development with a sample of boys from a working-class area of South London. Third, Blokland et al. (2005) report conviction curves for the age span from 12 to 72 for the 1977 Dutch population cohort. Fourth, in Montréal, curves were calculated with a school sample of adolescents and court samples of adjudicated delinquents from the 1960 and 1980 generations. Fourth, there is also a contemporary study of convictions, that is, the two Pittsburg community cohorts of inner city boys (Jennings et al. 2016) and girls (Loeber et al. 2017).

The Shape of the Age–Crime Curve in the 1960 and 1980 Generations

The dominant interpretation in criminology is that the shape of the age–crime curve is a "*brute fact*" (DeLisi 2015, p. 51). Criminologists agree that the general shape of all age–crime curves is bell-shaped with an acute upslope during adolescence, a significant drop during youth, and a slower and more regular down-slope during adulthood, at least until the 30s. After that age, individual data are exceptional. To our knowledge, for the first time, it will be possible to compare two longitudinal generations, birth cohorts of males born around 1960 and 1980 in a large city, Montréal. In addition, it will be possible to check if these curves look like some others based on comparable data.

Figure 2.1 illustrates this general shape of the curve for G60 and G80 males very well. Studies with longitudinal data on arrests and convictions confirm this general shape whatever the historical period of the second half of the twentieth century and the composition of the sample: Laub and Samson (2003) studied with arrests in court samples from Boston in the 1940s; Farrington et al. (2013a) followed a sample from a South London working class community from 1961 for convictions; Blokland et al. (2005) collected the convictions of the 1977 cohort in the Netherlands from age 12 to 72; Jennings et al. (2016) report conviction data from two Pittsburg community cohorts of inner-city youths from age 10 to 30 and recruited in the 1980s. The career span in these longitudinal studies intersects with the Montréal 1960 and 1980 generations.

A detailed reading of specific digits that constitutes Fig. 2.1 tells a more precise picture of the shape of the age–crime curve. The conviction career of the Montréal G60 birth cohorts started at age 8, it was the age of criminal responsibility according to the Juvenile Delinquency Act of Canada at that time. Very few males were active during childhood, from age 8 to 11, less than 2.5% of the 470 males at each of these ages. From age 12, the upslope was steep; very rapidly the participation increased from 17.7% at 14 to peak at 16 with 35.5% of active boys. Then, the downward slope began at 17 and, particularly, with an important drop at 18, that is, from a prevalence of 33.8% to 26.2%. After going back to the 30% at the beginning of youth, the declivity was half and quite steady between ages 20 and 30, that is, a yearly prevalence from above 30% to 15%. During the next decade, the 30s, the decline was regular but with a very restricted range, from 12% to 10% of active males. During the 40s, the participation varied a little at a lower range, from 7% to

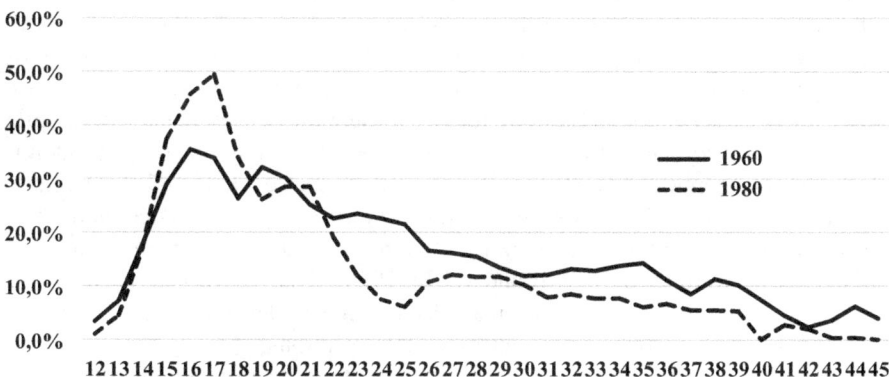

Fig. 2.1 The age–crime curve of the birth cohorts of 1960 and 1980, percentage of active males

5%. Finally, during the last decade of follow-up, the 50s, only a few males were active at each age, with ups and downs between 1.3% and 2.8%.

For its part, the conviction career of the G80 began at age 12, the new minimum age of criminal responsibility introduced by the Young Offender Act implemented in 1984. This data set ends at age 45 in 2017. At age 12 and 13 very few males were adjudicated, less than 5%. Then, the prevalence more than doubled between age 14 and 16, from 17% to 37%, and the peak was attained at 17 with a prevalence of 49%. An important drop is observable at 18, from 49% to 34%. It remained high, 20% during early youth, which is between age 19 and 22. Another level is observable as the prevalence was, for most of the ages, around 10–12% from age 23 to 30. During the 30s, the new level of low declivity was from 8% to 5%. Finally, during the first half of the 40s, the percentage of prevalence was below 3%.

In Table 2.2, it was observed that the descriptive statistics of the G80 male were clearly lower than those for G60 subjects. However, Fig. 2.1 substantially modifies this interpretation because until the end of adolescence, the G80 curve is higher than the G60 one. After that period, this last curve clearly dominates the previous curve. The reversal of the position of the generational curves is stunning. In sum, the descriptive statistics and the curves point to a generation gap. These reverse results may be explained by three categories of changes: (1) the improvement of correctional interventions for juveniles; (2) the impact of a new "welfare and justice model," as named by Corrado et al. (1992) and its consequences for juvenile justice policies and practices; (3) macro sociological changes in Québec from 1960 to the 2000s (outlined in Appendix C).

The impact of new social and justice policies for juvenile delinquents and adolescents with problem behavior may be a factor that probably accounts for the higher curve of G80 during adolescence. In Fig. 2.1, it is particularly intriguing, because in the curve of the G60 males there is a drop of 9% between the peak at age 16, 35.5%, and the level at 18, 26.2%; this is the age of the frontier between the legal age of maturity and the juvenile and adult systems of justice in Québec. The reverse position of G80 and G60 on the age–crime curve may be explained by two conditions. First, information about the juvenile criminal career was not easily available to the adult system of justice and there was a philosophy of the "second chance" among the judges and other agents throughout the juvenile and adult systems of justice, particularly with first-time offenders accused of relatively minor crimes (Le Blanc 1984a, b, c, d). Second, a longitudinal evaluation of treatments for juvenile delinquents showed that, at the end of adolescence, after leaving institutions, delinquency dropped significantly compared with before treatment and, at the same time, the boys showed statistically significant improvements in psychological and interpersonal functioning as well as making attempts to enter the conventional work market or go back to school (Le Blanc 1983a, 1985). The comparison between the age–crime curves of two generations may also provide evidence for changes in laws and policies and of the impact of macro societal evolutions.

First, radical changes in the delinquency and youth protection laws and the social and criminal justice policies for juvenile delinquents happened in between the two generations, precisely during the period between 1979 and 1984 with the implementation of a new Youth Protection Act followed by the Young Offenders Act. Let us remember that in Canada the federal government legislates on crimes and the provincial government is responsible for the application of criminal law. In Fig. 2.1, the beginning of the curves illustrate the introduction of the new law, the age of criminal responsibility became 12 instead of 8. In addition, Québec had always been more progressive and innovative than the other provinces of Canada concerning juvenile justice and correctional institutions. For example, before the introduction of this new Young Offenders Act, diversion to social services was practiced and legalized for juvenile crimes, except for a short list of the most seriously violent ones, such as homicide and rape, by the Youth Protection Act. Police arrests were then referred to a special unit of the social services and a large set of alternative measures, other than fines, probation, and institutional placement, could be applied. In court, the accused started to be represented by a public defense layer and the judges could order the previous habitual measures and new alternatives or a combination of both. Finally, the Ministry of social services implemented a strong policy of deinstitutionalization (see Le Blanc and Beaumont 1992; Le Blanc 1998 for an evaluation of the effectiveness of these new policies) in parallel with a professionalization of the personnel in the group homes and open and closed institutions (trained beyond high school in technical colleges and increasingly often at the undergraduate level in universities). As a consequence, in Fig. 2.1, the impact of these changes on the age–crime curve was that convictions were postponed to a subsequent offense during early youth, after age 18. The impact of all these changes was that the percentages of prevalence were higher for G80 males during the second half of adolescence and the peak of that curve was later, at age 17 instead 16 for G60. In summary, the young delinquents who arrived in juvenile and adult courts after the application of these new policies were older. The screening process had for a consequence that only perpetrators of the repeated and more serious crimes were sent immediately to juvenile court, whereas the delinquents also arrived later in the adult court.

Second, the comparison of the age–crime curves of the two generations also reflects important macro social change in Québec and the major city of Montréal. In Fig. 2.1, the G80 curve is always lower than the G60 one between age 21 and 45. This observation was expected because it is statistically established that the rate of juvenile and adult criminality was following a down slope from the 1980s on, particularly when the G80 subjects were adolescents during the second half of the 1990s and early 2000s in Québec and Montréal (on adult official criminality, Ouimet (2005, 2010), and on self-reported and official juvenile delinquency, Le Blanc 2006, 2010a, b).

In addition, a large variety of sociological statistical series, collected by Langlois (1999) from 1960 to 1998, show that the wellbeing of the population of Québec increased very significantly. This improvement may be the result of the adoption in the 1960s and 1970s of major social measures such as free universal health services, low cost day care and education through university, and advantageous welfare benefits. In addition, the poverty of the population diminished clearly during the second half of the twentieth century (Langlois 1999). In sum, the comparison of two generations on age–crime curves illustrates very well these important macro social, legal, and criminal justice policy changes.

The frequency curve, Fig. 2.2, follows the general shape, but with many important sudden ups or downs along the way as in the Laub and Samson (2003), Farrington et al. (2013a) and the Blokland et al. (2005) curves. These sudden variations of frequency probably represent the impact of the nature of the crimes, for example, a delinquent may be convicted of 20 thefts by breaking and entering during a short period of time at a particular age, whereas homicides are not numerous at one conviction age. It is interesting to note that the Montréal G60 and G80 down slopes proceed into three stages like the Laub and Sampson in Boston and Blokland in the Netherlands; the decline takes the form of three stages: late adolescence and early youth (age 22), youth and early maturity (age 45), and middle and late maturity.

In summary, (1) the age–crime curves of the two generations of the MTSFGCLS illustrate its universal general shape; (2) the Montréal curves are very similar to the Boston and the Netherlands ones; (3) a generation gap exists between the G60 and G80 that can be explained by macro social, legal, and criminal justice policy changes. Specific variations between these curves are discussed in the next section. Let us check if curves adopt the same shape for court and population samples, gender, and types of offending.

The Variations of the Age–Crime Curves by Delinquency Status, Genders, and Types of Offending

Figure 2.3 displays the shape of the curve of the G60 representative sample of male adolescents. It represents well the previous curve of the court sample, but it was at a very much lower participation rate; the peak is later at age 21 and the prevalence

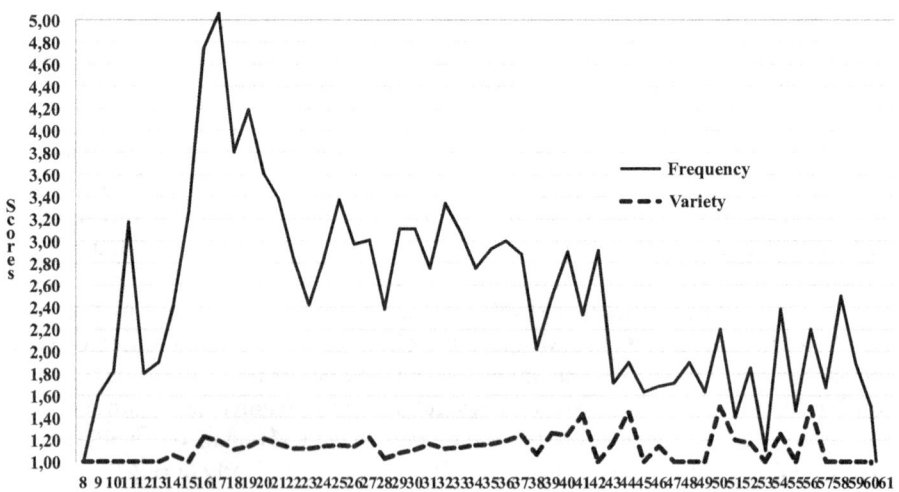

Fig. 2.2 Frequency and variety age–crime curves of the 1960 generation of convicted males

was 2.6% compared with 25.1% at the same age for the court sample. Reading this figure, it is immediately evident that the two samples are composed of different individual offenders; they represent two distinct worlds, minor and episodic delinquents in the representative sample, and aggravated delinquents, mostly recidivists, in the court sample. This disparity is called the normative gap.

Figure 2.4 compares G80 females (150) with males (506). The curve of the females is similar to the general shape but with a very much lower percentages of prevalence. For example, the maximum was a female participation of 8.3% and a peak at age 17, compared with 49% for males. In addition, from age 25 to 45 females were no longer convicted in the 2000s. This is an unexpected result because follow-up interviews at later ages up to the 30s shows alarming prevalence rates compared with males on the following difficult experiences: single-parenthood, poverty, low level of education, domestic violence, suicide attempts, psychological consultations, psychiatric hospitalizations, as well as drug addiction treatments (Lanctôt 2005; Corneau and Lanctôt 2004).

In Fig. 2.1, it was observed that the downward slope of the age–crime curves was in steps of levels of prevalence. It should be interesting to analyze the general curve in terms of crime mix. Laub and Samson's (2003) book is the only publication, to our knowledge, that reports long-term frequency age–crime arrest curves from age 7 to 70 by property, violent, and alcohol/drug offenses. Let us pursue that trail with the question that came out of the descriptive statistics: what is the position of VO and LSO crimes in relation to POs? Are they only complementary?

Figure 2.5 clearly show that the three age–crime curves have the same general shape from the beginning to the tail. However, the ordering is very distinctive from onset to the 30s: POs dominate, VOs are much lower, and LSOs are not far from but a little below VOs. In summary, VOs and LSOs are complementary to POs in the

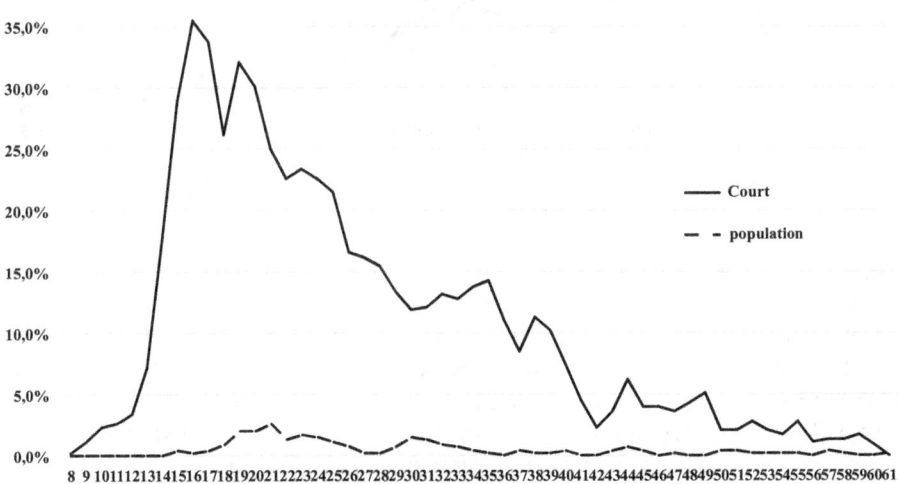

Fig. 2.3 Age–crime curve of the birth cohorts of the 1960, percentage of males active in the Montréal population and court samples

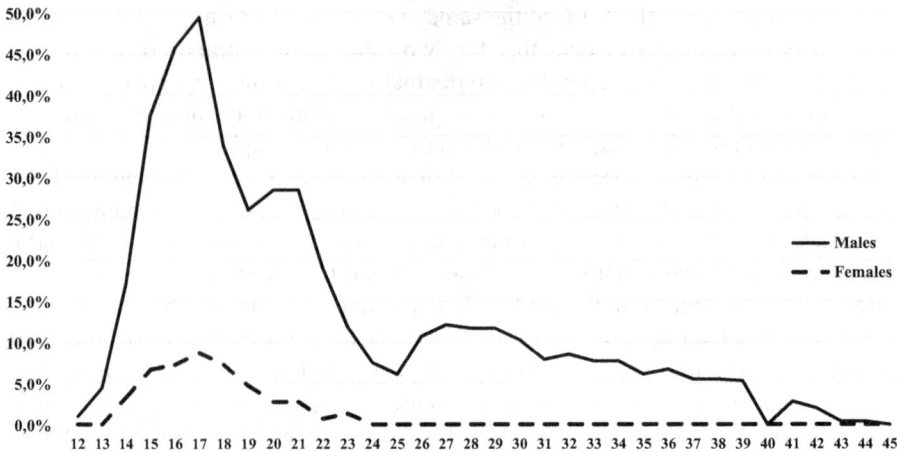

Fig. 2.4 The age–crime curves of the birth cohorts of 1980, percentage of active court females and males

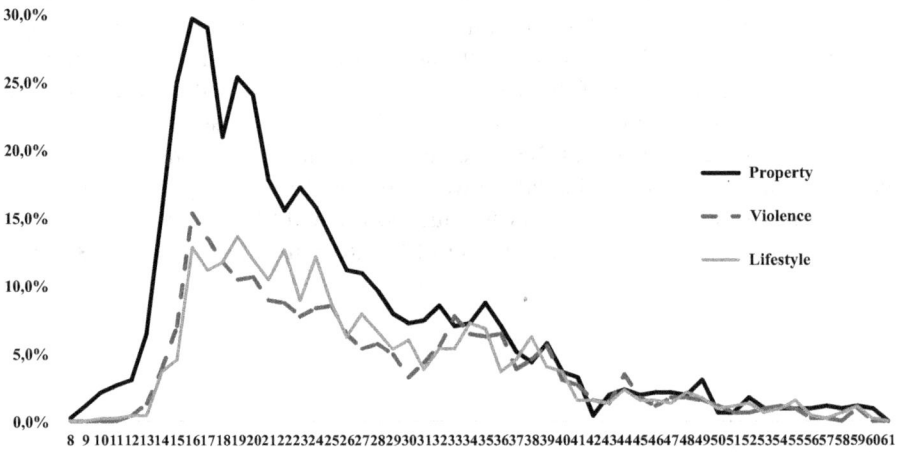

Fig. 2.5 Age–crime curves of prevalence by types of official offending, males of the 1960 generation

crime mix. Table 2.6 helps to disentangle the relative position of VOs and LSOs because the comparison of the curves is much easier with digits. First, POs are committed earlier than the VOs, as would be expected from Loeber data (2012), whereas the LSOs appear the latest. Second, the peak of the curve is at age 16 for POs and VOs and 3 years later for LSOs, at 19. The latest beginning and the older peaks were expected from the definition of this third type of offending because many of the crimes of this category need maturity or less impulsivity to manage.

According to Table 2.6, three phenomena can be noted. First, POs display the highest prevalence rate from age 8 to 32 and, for the next decades, they progressively lose

Table 2.6 The 1960 generation, yearly prevalence by types of official offending for males

Age	Property (%)	Violent (%)	Lifestyle (%)
8	0.20	0.00	0.00
9	1.10	0.00	0.00
10	2.10	0.6	0.20
11	2.60	0.00	0.20
12	3.00	0.40	0.40
13	6.40	**1.30**	0.40
14	15.10	**3.80**	3.60
15	24.90	**7.00**	4.50
16	29.60	**15.30**	12.80
17	28.90	**13.40**	11.10
18	20.90	11.70	11.70
19	25.30	10.40	**13.60**
20	24.00	10.60	**11.90**
21	17.70	8.90	**10.40**
22	15.50	8.70	**12.60**
23	17.20	7.70	**8.90**
24	15.70	8.30	**12.10**
25	13.40	8.50	**8.70**
26	11.10	6.40	**6.20**
27	10.90	5.30	**7.90**
28	9.60	5.70	**6.60**
29	7.90	4.90	**5.30**
30	7.20	3.20	**6.00**
31	7.40	4.30	3.80
32	8.50	5.50	5.30
33	7.00	7.70	5.30
34	7.20	6.40	7.20
35	8.70	6.20	6.80
36	7.00	6.40	3.60
37	5.10	3.80	4.50
38	4.30	4.50	6.20
39	5.70	5.50	4.00
40	3.60	3.00	3.60
41	3.20	2.60	1.50
42	0.40	1.50	1.50
43	1.90	1.30	1.30
44	2.30	3.40	2.30
45	1.90	1.70	1.50
46	2.10	1.10	1.50
47	2.10	1.70	1.30
48	1.90	1.70	2.10
49	3.00	1.50	1.70

(continued)

Table 2.6 (continued)

Age	Property (%)	Violent (%)	Lifestyle (%)
50	0.60	1.10	0.90
51	0.60	0.60	1.10
52	1.70	0.60	1.30
53	0.90	0.90	0.60
54	0.90	1.10	0.90
55	0.90	0.90	1.50
56	0.90	0.20	0.40
57	1.10	0.20	0.20
58	0.90	0.00	0.60
59	1.10	0.90	1.10
60	0.90	0.00	0.20
61	0.00	0.00	0.00

their undisputable dominance, even if the prevalence of these crimes is always higher. Second, from age 13 to 18 VOs show a higher participation than LSOs, whereas from age 19 to 30 it is LSOs that show a greater prevalence. Third, for the last 30 years of the OC, no type of crime is distinguished. There are 11 years when the three categories are about equal; in five instances POs and VOs are more numerous and about equal, for 4 years POs and LSOs are equal, and in three cases VOs and LSOs have about the same number of convictions. In summary, first, VOs are complementary to POs in the individual offense mix during the first half of the career. However, VOs become increasingly equal companion to POs during the second half of the potential 50 years of the offending career. Second, LSOs are not alternative offenses to POs during the criminal career; they are complementary because until the 20s their prevalence rate is about half of the participation in POs. From the 20s onward this difference diminishes to one-third between 20 and 30, then to a few percentage points during the next decade, and thereafter they are often equal. These last results have to be interpreted with statistical caution as there are only a few males active at each age toward the end of the offense career. Third, LSOs play an increasingly important role in the crime mix of males as age increases: they are never a clear alternative to POs, but their prevalence is higher than that of VOs from age 19 to 30. LSOs are not a substitute for VOs, but their role is central in the crime mix during continuation of the criminal career after youth. Our knowledge of the criminal markets lets us think that it is probable that VOs are committed to obtain results with LSOs.

The results in Fig. 2.4 and Table 2.6 confirm the proposition of a type of offending gap that constitutes a changing mix of offenses along the life span. First, POs are the spine of the offending career mix of the males of G60 and G80. Second, VOs adopt a secondary role during adolescence and then they are replaced partly by LSOs. Third, during adulthood POs progressively lose their dominance but still display the highest participation rates with a fading difference with VOs and LSOs. These observations are tested with structural equation modeling in Chap. 4.

2.2 The Official Problem Behavior Career

Chapter 1 argued that antisocial behavior was legally, theoretically, and empirically defined as being composed of two principal constructs: delinquency and problem behavior. In most modern societies a Juvenile Delinquency Law (Canada 1908, 1982, 2003) and a Youth Protection Law (Québec 1979, 2016) exist that have two components: a list of abuses and problem behaviors. In Québec, since 1979, their object was clearly delimited and their application was coordinated in the juvenile justice system and the social service system for children aged between 0 and 18 years of age (see Appendix C for more details).

Chapter 1 also shows that behavioral science, such as the MTSFGCLS data with self-reported measures, has repeatedly shown that delinquent and problem behaviors are intimately connected. However, this demonstration with official data from the juvenile justice system is much less frequent (Loeber and Le Blanc 1990; Le Blanc and Loeber 1998). The official offending (OC) data and the official problem behavior (OPB) data for the generation of 1980 are available in the MTSFGCLS. In addition, behavioral sciences postulate that the same mechanisms and processes govern the development of OPB as for the OC career (Le Blanc 2015; Lanctôt 2015).

Let us now describe the epidemiology of the OPB for the court sample composed of five birth cohorts around 1980. In Québec, the Youth Protection Act defines seven situations of abuse in article 38 (physical, psychological, sexual, negligence, and so on) and, in article 38.h problem behavior is characterized as *"serious behavioral disturbance."* It refers to *"situations in which a child behaves in such a way as to repeatedly or seriously undermine the child's or others' physical or psychological integrity and the child's parents fail to take the necessary steps to put an end to the situation or, if the child is 14 or over, the child objects to such steps"*. The Youth Protection Act do not specifies neither the nature of the *"disturbances"* nor the criteria of *"seriousness."* Nor does the Ministry of Health and Social Services of Québec in its updates of the user's manual for the professionals apply the law (university trained social workers, psychologists, criminologists, psychoeducators, etc.); only a few examples of situations that undermine the child or other person's integrity are given in the guide. The empirical study of Messier (1989) is a more helpful view of the variety of situations classified under article 38.h.

Messier analyzed the court files of 167 adolescents (boys 52% and girls 48%) for whom there was a court decision of treatment in a residential service (20% in a group home, 66% in an open unit, and 14% in a closed unit). This sample was recruited at the end of the 1980s, when the MTSFGCLS subjects of the court sample of the 1990s were going through childhood and adolescence. Of the 704 behaviors reported in the files, 32% were situations relating to parental authority, 17% to conflict at school, 16% to abuse of drugs and alcohol, 11% to violence at home, 9% to running away, 6% to theft, 4% to sexual promiscuity, and 5% to psychological distress (depression, etc.). What is more interesting is the gender gap in these types of problem behavior. Girls dominated the boys for family conflict (49% vs. 40%), running away from home (39% vs. 33%), suicide attempt (15% vs. 7%), sexual situation: prostitution (11% vs. 3%), nude dancing (3% vs. 0%), and sexual promiscuity (13% vs. 6%). Boys dominate girls on deviant friends (46% vs. 33%), verbal aggression at home (36% vs. 28%) and in school (11% vs. 6%), theft (29% vs. 18%), vandalism at home (6% vs. 3%), and sexual abuse (3% vs. 0%). Finally, the boys and girls were about equal on drug (38% vs. 40%) and alcohol abuse (31% vs. 36%), suspension from school (15% vs. 16%), frequent absconding from school (12% vs. 9%), and physical violence with family members (11% vs. 14%).

Table 2.7 displays the gender difference on OC and OPB for the MTSFGCLS court sample of the 1990s, this during childhood and adolescence. The impressive gap between females and males that was observed in previous tables and figures is still present. The participation of girls in OC is four times lower than for the boys (20% vs. 81%) and at each age the gap is sometimes even higher; however, the peak is at 16 (29.8%) and 15 (26.8%) respectively. The portrait is dissimilar for OPB. The overall participation is higher for girls (63%) than for boys (47%). In addition, the median onset age is lower for girls (14 vs. 15) even if a few boys begin between 6 and 8 years old and girls not before 9 years old. It should also be noted that the participation rate is equal at 14 (21%) and not far away at the respective peaks of the two age–problem behavior curves (29.8% for girls vs. 26.8% for boys. In summary, the gender gap that was documented for OC is also observable for OP but upside down; for OC, boys were above and for OPB, girls were superior. It should be noted that the age–problem behavior curves show the habitual shape for OC. First, for

Table 2.7 The epidemiology of official antisocial behavior, offending and problem behavior by gender for the court sample of the generation of 1980

Ages	Girls (150)		Boys (506)	
	Delinquency[a]	Problem behavior[b]	Delinquency	Problem behavior
6				0.5%
7				1.9%
8				1.4%
9		1.1%		1.4%
10		1.1%		1.9%
11		2.1%		1.4%
12	0%	3.2%	1%	4.2%
13	1%	13.8%	4.5%	10.3%
14	3.3%	**21.3%**	17%	**21.1%**
15	6.7%	**22.3%**	37.4%	**26.8%**
16	7.3%	**29.8%**	45.7%	**21.1%**
17	8.7%	5.4%	49.4%	8%
Participation (%)	20%	63%	81%	47%
Frequency median	1.5	2	6	1
Onset median age	16	14	16	15
Duration years	1	1	2	1

aAll forms of offending, as defined in Appendix B
bAppendix B defined in article 38.h of the Quebec Youth Protection Act for Children aged 0 to 18 years old

boys there is a progression until 15 for boys and a short and rapid regression there-after. Second, for girls the progression is longer, until 16, and a dramatic drop follows at 17; the participation rate is divided by six diminishing from 30% to 5%. Researchers and policy makers should also remember that the female participation rates are much lower for OC than for OPB.

3 The Epidemiology of Self-Reported Antisocial Behavior

The descriptive and boundary parameters (see Table 2.1) of an OC and OPB career are also available for SRAB. It is impossible to synthetize, from its beginnings, the enormous epidemiological literature with these parameters of SRAB. There are also numerous publications with the same parameters for drug use, and there are a few publications on other self-reported problem behaviors (SRPBs). For a general overview of this criminological literature from the 1980s onward, refer to the following sources (Blumstein et al. 1986; Le Blanc and Fréchette 1989; Loeber and Le Blanc 1990; Le Blanc and Loeber 1998; Piquero et al. 2003, 2007). In addition, review papers on specific subjects of the development of SRO and SRAB for the readers of the 2000s can be consulted (Benson 2002, 2013; Liberman 2010; Morizot and Kazemian 2015; Farrington et al. 2013a) along with some recent longitudinal books (Farrington et al. 2013a; Jennings et al. 2016).

Chapter 1 reported new conceptual replications of measures of SRAB developed by the MTSFGCLS. It concluded with the statement that the measurement of SRAB was a generalizable set of measures under this latent construct because they were reliable and validated across territories (countries, states, cities, schools, etc.), genders, ages of the life cycle, and epochs from the 1970s to the 2000s. Let us test the generalizability of SRAB with epidemiological data. Particularly, the test of the four gaps that were documented with OC: generations, genders, delinquent status samples, and types of offending.

These four gaps are investigated using the SRAB measures of participation and variety with representative and court samples of females and males from the 1970s, 1980s, 1990s, and 2000s. The criminological literature contains epidemiological data from conceptual replications at every decade from the 1960s through the 2000s. Until the 1990s most of the delinquency scales were adaptations of Nye and Short's scale (see Chap. 1). They were composed of mostly minor delinquent acts and a diversity of problem behavior, particularly sexual promiscuity, and alcohol and drug use. Reading the publications, it can be concluded that the level of SRAB was rather stable in the 1960s, 1970s, and 1980s: the ever participation of adolescents was always in the late 1980s for boys and in the middle of the 1970s for girls for representative samples of adolescents.

This is the case for the 1960s in Sweden (Elmhorn 1965) and in Montréal (Le Blanc 1969). Similar proportions were observed in the USA in the 1970s and 1980s (Gold 1970; Williams and Gold 1972; Bachman et al. 1978; Hindelang et al. 1981; Elliott and Huizinga 1983), and for some European countries (England: Farrington

1973; France: Morange 1979; Germany: Remschmidt 1978; Poland: Podgorecki 1976; Belgium: Hausmann et al. 1982). Some authors report an historical stability in USA samples: Gold and Reimer (1975) between the 1960s and the 1970s and Osgood et al. (1988) between the 1970s and the 1980s.

For this last comparison, there was only one exact replication with samples matched with the distribution of genders, ages, and socioeconomic status. Le Blanc and Tremblay (1988) used two such samples (scales described in Table 1.1, third column from the left). They report no significant statistical differences between these epochs in general, serious, and statutory SRO and drug use. It was the same conclusion for boys; however, only serious delinquency increased significantly for girls. Two other phenomena must be noted. First, among forms of SRPB, school undisciplined was more often reported than home undisciplined. In the first case, the averages over epochs were 76% for girls and 82% for boys and in the second case the averages were 64% for girls and 68% for boys. Sexual relations and drug use alternated in the third or fourth places with an ever participation mostly in the middle (40%) over historical periods. Second, even if the overall proportion of ever participation in SRD does not significantly increase over the decades, there is an interesting tendency, serious delinquency (operationalized as a mix of serious theft and physical violence in Table 1.1) increased for girls, from 3% in the 1970s, to 5% in the 1980s, and for boys the increase over time was less significant.

These SRD and SRPB observations have to be interpreted alongside the evolution of official juvenile delinquency in Montréal and Québec from 1962 to 2010 (Le Blanc 2003, 2010a, b). In the 1960s, the prevalence rates were between 30‰ and 35‰; they attained their maximum in the early 1980s, between 60‰ and 65‰, and they were followed by a general declining trajectory until the 2000s and toward the end the rates were around 35‰, as in the early 1980s. During the period from the 1970s to the 2000s, the rates of violent delinquency moved steadily from around 2‰ to around 7‰. This evolution was particularly clear for girls (Lanctôt and Le Blanc 2002; Le Blanc 2003). These data contrasted with the general stability of SRD and they mirror the increase in serious SRD. In summary, the published data from the 1960s to the 1980s in all the studies point to a possible gender gap, but not to a generation gap.

At the end of the 1980s, Elliott et al. (1989) and Le Blanc (1989) proposed adding a wider diversity of delinquent and problem behaviors, particularly more serious delinquent ones and new descriptors of SRPB. New parameters were suggested for new data gathering instruments such as frequency, age at onset, and annual participation, frequency, and variety. These recommendations were followed in the MTSFGCLS and the three school surveys of adolescents in cities from 30 countries during the 1990s and 2000s. The International Self-reported Delinquency Study conducted these studies (among a long list of publications, see Junger-Tas et al. 1994, Junger-Tas et al. 2003, Junger-Tas et al. 2010, Junger-Tas et al. 2012, and Enzman et al. 2018). The latter authors adopt a very prudent position *"Self-reported delinquency estimates should not be compared across nations."* They argue that it is not because of the methodological quality of the measure of SRD, but considering the significant variation in cultural desirability between respondents, a reporting bias was suspected by some researchers (see Chap. 1), but never sufficiently sub-stantiated with white males in North American surveys.

Only Salmi (2009), in Finland, conducted nationally representative school sur-veys of with the International Self-Reported Delinquency Study (ISRDS) research design, but yearly from 1995 to 2008. He concluded that (1) there was a decrease over time in theft and vandalism for females and males but steeper for males; (2) participation in violence was rather stable during the 6-year period, whereas it was a little more accentuated for the males; (3) the use of soft drugs and legal medicine was lower for males and there was a reversed tendency by genders, males increased a little whereas females decreased by the same amount of a few percentage points; (4) except for these SRPBs, males displayed superior prevalence rates than females almost every year.

Let us concentrate on the types of SRD and SRPB with the MTSFGCLS data sets and verify the gap hypothesis for generations, genders, delinquency official status, and types of antisocial behavior. Table 2.8 reports types of SRD and SRPB by generations from the 1970s to the 2000s and genders. Table 2.9 proposes the comparison of genders and type of sample by types of SRD and SRPB in the 1990s.

Reading Table 2.8 it is immediately clear that the gender gap is significant for all SRD scales, the figures are about 20 points more prevalent for males than for females (theft, vandalism, and physical violence), this gap is present regardless of the decade. The SDPB results are more differentiated. Males still show a higher participation than females. However, it is only by about ten points for drug use, sexual promiscuity, and school conflict, and it is not the case for home conflict, as they are about equal for both genders. In addition, we cannot discern a clear ten-dency of growth or decline across the four decades, either for males or females. There are relatively rare fluctuations from one decade to the next one. In summary, first, there is a gender gap to the disadvantage of male adolescents, particularly for SRD. Second, there is no significant generational gap for SRPB, as could have been expected from the previous scientific literature.

Table 2.9 presents the last view on the gap between genders, normative status, and forms of SRD and SRPB. The gender gap is still impressive when SRD is com-pared between a representative sample of adolescents born in the 1990s and inter-viewed in the 2000s and a court sample of adolescents born around 1980 and recruited in the middle of the 1990s. Males dominate for theft, motor vehicle theft, vandalism, and physical violence, but it is the reverse for psychological violence; females display a higher participation rate, an earlier onset, and more frequency and variety, particularly in the representative sample. Concerning the SRD frequency and variety, the statistics are in the same direction as for the participation; male results are superior to the female figures regardless of the type of sample and the form of SRD.

SRPB results are more complex. First, the participation is higher in the court sample as expected, except for conflict in school, which is equal in the two types of sample. Second, in the court sample females are more involved in alcohol and drug use, whereas the reverse is the case for males. As for participation, there are very

Table 2.8 The epidemiology of self-reported antisocial behavior in the representative samples of the MTSFGCLS from 1970 to 2000: females and males aged 14, 15, and 16 years: participation and variety by gender

(a) Delinquency

Types SRAB	Covert								Overt															
Forms	Theft (6)[a]								Vandalism (4)								Physical aggression (6)							
Samples[b]	1974		1985		1995		2006		1974		1985		1995		2006		1974		1985		1995		2006	
Gender	F	M	F	M	F	M	F	M	F	M	F	M	F	M	F	M	F	M	F	M	F	M	F	M
Participation	36	58	37	56	43	57	43	63	9	32	13	33	12	33	12	37	22	65	31	67	25	68	25	70
Variety median	1	2	2	2	0	2	1	1	0	0	0	0	0	0	0	1	0	1	0	1	0	2	1	2
75th percentile	2	3	2	3	1	2	2	3	0	1	0	1	0	0	2	2	0	2	1	2	1	3	2	3

(b) Problem behavior

Forms SRAB	Drug use (5)								Sexual promiscuity (4)							
Samples	1974		1985		1995		2006		1974		1985		1995		2006	
Gender	F	M	F	M	F	M	F	M	F	M	F	M	F	M	F	M
Participation	45	45	43	39	44	60	44	53	32	53	38	48	32	47	32	55
Variety median	0	0	0	1	0	1	2	2	0	1	0	1	0	0	0	1
75th percentile	1	1	1	2	1	2	3	3	1	1	1	1	1	2	1	2

Forms SRAB	Home conflict (3)								School conflict (6)							
Samples	1974		1985		1995		2006		1974		1985		1995		2006	
Gender	F	M	F	M	F	M	F	M	F	M	F	M	F	M	F	M
Participation	70	72	75	70	63	71	70	71	86	81	83	76	77	80	72	84
Variety median	1	1	1	1	1	1	1	1	2	2	2	2	2	2	2	2
75th percentile	1	1	1	1	2	1	1	1	3	3	3	3	3	3	3	3

[a]Number of behaviors forming the scale (see Table 1.1 and Appendix B)
[b]Appendix A describes the representative school samples: 1974, 1995, 1990, and 2006

Table 2.9 The epidemiology of self-reported antisocial behavior in the representative and court samples of the MTSFGCLS around 2000: females and males aged 14, 15, and 16: participation, frequency, variety, and onset

(a) Self-reported delinquency

Types of SRAB	Covert																Overt							
Forms	Theft (8)[a]				Vehicle theft (3)				Fraud (2)				Vandalism (5)				Physical violence (6)				Psychological violence (5)			
Sample	Representative[b]		Court[c]		Representative		Court		Representative		Court		Representative		Court		Representative		Court		Representative		Court	
Gender	F	M	F	M	F	M	F	M	F	M	F	M	F	M	F	M	F	M	F	M	F	M	F	M
Participation	66	75	78	90	60	72	48	77	20	25	73	81	48	64	48	70	66	81	85	95	91	80	69	74
Variety Median	1	2	3	5	1	1	1	2	1	1	1	2	1	1	1	2	2	2	4	4	2	1	2	2
75th percentile	2	3	5	7	1	2	2	3	1	2	2	2	2	2	2	2	3	4	6	6	3	2	4	4
Frequency Median	9	14	8	11	4	8	4	6	2	2	3	4	3	5	3	3	14	14	11	12	10	9	7	7
75th percentile	14	19	12	17	8	10	6	8	3	3	5	5	5	7	4	5	20	20	15	17	13	12	9	10
Onset Median	12	12	11	11	14	13	15	14	13	13	14	14	12	12	14	13	12	11	12	10	12	10	13	13
75th percentile	14	14	13	13	15	15	18	16	16	14	15	15	14	14	16	16	14	13	14	16	13	13	15	15

(b) Self-reported antisocial behavior

Types SRAB	Reckless								Conflict							
Forms	Drugs use (5)				Sexual promiscuity (4)				At Home (5)				In school (5)			
Sample	Representative		Court		Representative		Court		Representative		Court		Representative		Court	
Gender	F	M	F	M	F	M	F	M	F	M	F	M	F	M	F	M
Participation	68	71	94	86	86	84	100	100	79	77	98	94	88	87	87	87

(continued)

Table 2.9 (continued)

(b) Self-reported antisocial behavior

Types SRAB	Reckless								Conflict							
Forms	Drugs use (5)				Sexual promiscuity (4)				At Home (5)				In school (5)			
Sample	Representative		Court		Representative		Court		Representative		Court		Representative		Court	
Gender	F	M	F	M	F	M	F	M	F	M	F	M	F	M	F	M
Variety median	1	1	3	3	2	2	2	2	1	1	3	3	2	2	4	4
75th percentile	2	2	4	5	3	3	2	2	2	2	4	4	3	3	5	5
Frequency median	9	10	10	9	8	8	8	9	10	10	10	8	11	11	11	11
75th percentile	12	12	15	13	9	9	10	10	13	13	13	11	13	13	13	13
Onset median	13	13	13	13	13	12	13	13	12	12	10	10	12	10	12	11
75th percentile	14	15	14	15	14	14	14	14	14	14	12	13	14	13	14	13

[a] Number of behaviors forming the scale (see Table 1.1 and Appendix B)

[b] Appendix A describes the representative school sample. Among the representative males recruited in 2006, a total of 1952, 1156, or 59% were 14, 15, or 16 years of age. Among the court females, a total of 1910, 1175, or 62% were 14, 15, or 16 years of age

[c] Appendix A describes the court sample. Among the court males recruited in 1994, 506, 307, or 61% were 14, 15, or 16 years of age. Among the court females, 150, 107, or 71% were in the same age group

small variations between genders and samples for the level of frequency, variety, and onset.

In summary, the gender and the normative gaps are clearly present in the MTSFGCLS data sets for SRD, whereas for SRPB there are two scales, alcohol/drug use and psychological violence, which show that females participate more in these behaviors, particularly in the court sample.

4 Conclusion

This chapter on the epidemiology of the official and self-reported offending and problem behavior careers provide some confirmation of some of the empirical universalities, whereas other results set out important research questions. The observations from the MTSFGCLS can be summarized in terms of four similarities or dissimilarities between age–crime curve, genders, the normative status, and types of behavior.

4.1   The Shape of the Age-Crime Curves

Among the empirical universalities, first the shape of the age–crime curve was confirmed, but its peak is no longer between 25 and 30 years of age, as observed by Quételet and other researchers; it is now located at the end of adolescence. This peak was also noted for the age–problem behavior curve. Are these observations the consequence of the measure used way down the criminal justice system, conviction? Is it the impact of sociological changes between historical periods? It may be the effect of the juvenilization of the development of humans and delinquency or antisocial behavior during the second half of the nineteenth century that was noted by many behavioral scientists in psychology, sociology, and criminology. As a consequence, researchers should remember that the OPB curve displays the same shape as the OC curve until the end of adolescence, but it is legally truncated at 18 years of age. Thus, researchers should investigate in depth the parallel continuity of OD and OPB and its impact on decision making in the juvenile and adult criminal justice system and the child welfare system.

4.2   The Gender Gap

A second empirical universality was noted by Quételet; female OC is much lower than male OC and it can be added that it started earlier, it is shorter in duration, and it is also the case for its incidence, frequency, and variety that it is less severe. It may be possible that this gap is amplified by the use of court convictions as the measures of OC. In addition, this gender gap was also clearly established for SRD.

The literature review by Lanctôt (2015) continues to state that the gender gap for antisocial behavior but recognizes that "*a more complex picture emerge(s)*" (p. 299) when forms of antisocial behavior are compared. However, OPB tends to be higher for female adolescents, whereas this result does not stand for SRPB; males display higher results in SRD but not in lifestyle behavior (drug use and sexual promiscuity) and a similar level of conflict behaviors (at home and in school) (Lanctôt 2015 cites some publications outlining such variations). The explanation of the differential gender gap in OC and OPB that has been evoked by criminologists (Chesney-Lind and Shelden 1998, Lanctôt and Le Blanc 2002) is that a criminal justice gender bias exists from agents of the criminal justice system, girls have to be protected, not boys. As the reverse gap was observed for OPB, it appears essential to study the continuity with other forms of difficult situations before and after the females' short period of offending, as some data points to later behavioral and social adaptation problems.

4.3   The Generation Gap

Criminologists with a sociological training naturally postulate that the level of AB is distinct from one generation to the next because of continual positive social and technological changes. It is what they showed with state official criminal statistics in western societies. It is the same in Québec and Montréal, where this evolution manifested as an important increase from the 1960s through the 1980s and a decrease from the 1990s. The same tendency was expected for official antisocial behavior and SRAB in the MTSFGCLS data sets.

he descriptive statistics for the comparison of the 1960 and 1980 birth cohorts show a similar tendency in their respective age–crime curves. The first curve is at a higher level than the second curve for most of the criminal career, with the exception of the period of adolescence. The dissimilarity is explained by a change in the age of legal responsibility and the introduction of new practices in the criminal justice system. The impact of this difference in results between descriptive statistics and age–crime curves is that researchers and policy makers cannot rely on only one of these two types of data.

On the contrary to OC, SRAB, including SRD and SRPB, is quite stable between 1960, 1970, and 1980 for representative school samples and in the MTSFGCLS data set between 1975, 1985, 1995, and 2006; this for both genders. This relative stability for the participation in SRAB was also confirmed for the variety, the frequency, and its seriousness (Le Blanc 2010a, b).

In summary, all past and current generational figures point to the conclusion that the level of SRAB is relatively high, stable over time, normative, and universal during adolescence. This empirical law, which was formulated in 1977 still stands: "… *antisocial behavior is an epiphenomenon of adolescence, it is attached to that phase of life*" (Le Blanc 1977, p. 21). It is quite obvious that most of these behaviors are not processed by agencies of justice or should not be, even if some of them are not benign. Social tolerance, not always intentional, seems necessary as most of them have little probability of persisting since most of them disappear after adolescence.

4.4 The Normative or Delinquent Status Gap

Until the landmark experimental study on the measurement of SRD by Hindelang et al. (1981), there were many comparisons of adolescents from representative samples and delinquents, particularly living in correctional institutions (Fréchette and Le Blanc 1987). The 1981 experiment closed the question by showing major statistical differences in SRD between a community sample and samples of delinquents recruited at the police and at the juvenile court levels. In addition, with the MTSFGCLS data set, it was established, by the comparison of descriptive statistics and the age–crime curve, that the OC career was much more imposing in a court sample, a microscopic view, than in representative samples of the population, more for the males than the females, and, particularly for the generation of 1960 than for the generation of 1980. The MTSFGCLS data sets confirm unambiguously the normative gap in SRD and SRPB.

4.5 The Mix of Antisocial Behavior Gap

Two hundred and fifty years ago, Quételet showed that official crimes against property are much more numerous than crimes against persons regardless of the age for the longitudinal OC mix and in the SRD mix (covert versus overt offending). In addition, as he observed, as age increases the proportion of official offenses against persons increases among offenses of all categories. A new construct was proposed to consider many of the other offenses that were not against property and persons, the lifestyle involvement in delinquency and criminal markets. Laub and Samson (2003) limited themselves to alcohol and drugs that are rather restrictive compared with the diversity of other offenses. Cusson (2005) develops the notion of delinquent lifestyle as a festive life: glorification of crime, living during the night (going to bed late and waking up late), a regular cocktail of sex, alcohol, and drugs, wasting vast amounts of money, etc. It was operationalized (Appendix B) as driving under the influence of alcohol, using and selling drugs, buying and selling stolen goods, active in the sex market, etc. It was observed that, with the passing of age, these behaviors were progressively replacing offenses against persons as companions of offenses against property, the spine of the OC mix. Future research must pursue, deepen, and replicate these results with other data sets and, particularly with qualitative interviews with delinquents 40+ years of age and new analysis of the OC mix.

Chapter 3
The Developmental Mechanisms of Antisocial Behavior and Crime, a Process View

1 Introduction

According to Morris and Giller (1987), Worsley, in 1849, described the progression form petty delinquencies to greater and more heinous crimes. In spite of all similar assertions since this distant era, criminologists were far from unanimous on the escalation and aggravation questions as evidenced in the Cohen (1986) and Loeber (1987) reviews. Le Blanc and Fréchette (1989) and Le Blanc (2002) document two potential reasons for disagreement. One of the reasons was the conceptual confusion between progression, escalation, aggravation, and offense switching. Another reason was the excessive empiricism and, particularly, the setting up of an appropriate procedure of analysis to deal with these phenomena.

Le Blanc (2015) stated that one of the central tasks of developmental criminology is the identification of the mechanisms that produce the age cycle of antisocial behavior and crime. It was conceived as a system of moving forces working together to create the age curves for all forms of antisocial behavior. Loeber and Le Blanc (1990) classified the forces that perform quantitative and qualitative changes along the life course. This distinction is essential for developmentalists in psychology (Lerner 1986) and it also appears to be necessary in developmental criminology. Therefore, two series of mechanisms were proposed and empirically documented (Le Blanc and Fréchette 1989; Loeber and Le Blanc 1990; Le Blanc and Loeber 1998) and they are redefined in Table 3.1 as the operating forces of the developmental system of official offending (OO) and self-reported antisocial behavior (SRAB). Table 2.1 defines the forces that are created with the criminologically agreed static or descriptive parameters: participation or prevalence, frequency (lambda) or incidence, variety, seriousness, and crime mix and the boundary or dynamic parameters are: onset, offset, duration, career span, and crime switching.

The quantitative mechanism is called activation–deactivation. It was never investigated before our 1989 work, according to Jennings and Hahn Fox (2019); even if the importance of the onset of crime has been well known by criminologists since

© Springer Nature Switzerland AG 2021
M. Le Blanc, *The Development of Antisocial Behavior and Crime*,
https://doi.org/10.1007/978-3-030-68429-7_3

Table 3.1 Analytical tools for the study of the developmental mechanisms of antisocial behavior and crime

Quantitative changes
Activation
• Launching: an earlier onset produces immediately high participation in antisocial behavior
• Diversification: an earlier onset sustains a greater variety of antisocial behavior
• Explosion: an earlier onset confirms a prompt higher frequency of antisocial behavior
• Stabilization: an earlier onset supports a lengthier career span of antisocial behavior
Deactivation
• Slackening: a declining participation in antisocial behavior with a later age at onset
• Declivity: a decrease in frequency of antisocial behavior with a later age at onset
• Specialization: a diminution of the variety of antisocial behavior with a later age at onset
• Vanishing: a later onset of antisocial behavior implies a shorter career span
The cycle of activation–deactivation: their sequence
• Velocity: changes from a year to the next.
Qualitative changes
Developmental sequence: a set of hierarchical stages in the antisocial behavior repertory in terms of seriousness or antisocial behavior mix
Individual
change: uplifting and downlifting on an antisocial behavior sequence: escalation–de-escalation
• antisocial behavior switching: the changes in the content of an individual mix that make it more or less versatile along the life course
Simultaneity: two antisocial behavior mixes are beginning at the same time
Innovation: the addition of a new antisocial behavior mix to an existing one
Retention: maintaining a previous antisocial behavior mix while introducing a new mix
Elimination: dropping an antisocial behavior mix
• Aggravation: the changes in an antisocial behavior that make it more serious during the life course
Simultaneity: two antisocial behaviors with different degrees of seriousness are introduced at the same time
Innovation: the addition of a new, more serious antisocial behavior to an existing one
Retention: maintaining a less serious antisocial behavior while introducing a more serious one
Elimination: dropping an antisocial behavior

Lombroso (1895). The mechanic of activation refers to the impact of the onset of antisocial behavior on its frequency, variety, and duration and to their interaction that produces a general system effect. The quantitative developmental changes during the life course, the acceleration–deceleration system, are defined in terms of progression and regression in antisocial behavior. This system is composed of four gears of acceleration. Their existence will empirically demonstrate: launching, diversification, explosion, and stabilization. First, the launch gear manifests at the beginning of the development and is observable by the fact that an earlier onset produces a higher participation in antisocial behavior. Second, there is the diversification gear or a higher variety of antisocial behavior when the onset is earlier. Third, the explosion gear sustains the development of antisocial behavior and it appears as a prompt high frequency or a change in velocity over time. Fourth, stabilization is observable when an earlier onset of antisocial behavior produces a lengthier career. In summary, all these gears of acceleration are increasingly effective with the power of an earlier age at onset. Globally, acceleration operates, first with a push, in these ways, and second, through contemporary and causal (statistical or from time 1 to time 2) interactions between the parameters along the life course.

The phenomenon of deactivation is similar but in the opposite direction. The decline of antisocial behavior is also manifested in the form of four gears. First, the hindering is observable when a later onset of antisocial behavior is followed by less subsequent participation. Second, the declivity of antisocial behavior is the decrease of its frequency with age. Third, the specialization is illustrated by a diminution of variety of antisocial behavior with age (it is not the repetition of the same type of crime as often in research). Fourth, the vanishing of antisocial behavior is the result of a later onset that produces a shorter career. Globally, deactivation operates, first, through these four gears, and second, via the contemporary and causal interactions between these gears. The impact of these interactions are investigated in Chap. 4.

The qualitative changes refer to something new, something that is different from what went before, and something that is more complex according to the ontogenetic principle state by Werner (1957, p.126).

> ... whenever development occurs it proceeds from a state of relative globality and lack of differentiation to a state of increasing differentiation, articulation, and hierarchic integration.

There are two forms of qualitative changes: switching and aggravation. First, the antisocial behavior switching manifests by changes in the content of the antisocial behavior mixes. They become decreasingly versatile along the life course. Second, the changes in the nature of OO and SRPB with time are subdivided into a developmental sequence that comprises a certain number of hierarchical stages and individual changes in terms of uplifting/downlifting at the various stages (Le Blanc and Fréchette 1989).

The qualitative mechanism was called escalation; it was revived by the landmark review on criminal career by Blumstein et al. (1986). In 1989, the term aggravation–deaggravation was used and it referred precisely to the identification of a gradual sequence of progressiveness or regressiveness in the seriousness of behaviors during the life course. In subsequent papers (Loeber and Le Blanc 1990; Le Blanc and Loeber 1998), this conceptualization was updated based on existing literature. The importance of this qualitative mechanism was later confirmed by reviews (Le Blanc 2002; Piquero et al. 2003; Jennings and Hahn Fox 2019). Table 3.1 adds another type of aggravation, SRAB switching with age.

These quantitative and qualitative developmental cycles have a breaking point as antisocial behavior follows a general reverse U-shaped cycle; it is important to identify the moment when growth stops and decline starts. That is an age when the progressive quantitative and qualitative sequence becomes a regressive course.

In Chap. 2, the development of OC and SRAB was approached on the basis of unidimensional characteristics of a synthetic nature, its career span, age the first behavior was committed, etc. Le Blanc and Fréchette (1989) proposed a method of combining the descriptive and developmental parameters. It is the association of descriptive and developmental characteristics to constitute processes that show that the development is not a matter of chance. The procedure for the construction of the mechanisms is the one used to work out measurements in natural sciences, particularly in physics. Duncan (1984) described it as follows: a list of fundamental elements, physical quantities, for example, is compiled, then the variables are defined according to the combinations of these basic elements, in such a way that the variables are represented mathematically by the product of the fundamental elements adjusted by integral calculus. By way of analogy, Le Blanc and Fréchette (1989) proposed defining the processes that encourage the development of antisocial behavior and crime as the result of the relationship between two or more descriptive and developmental parameters that are the basic elements of antisocial behavior. The advantage of this procedure is twofold. First, it affords clarity concerning the elements in question in the operative definition of concepts such as activation, deactivation, switching, aggravation, and deaggravation. Second, it can be reproduced, that is, it is possible for another researcher to construct the same measurements and thus find out whether or not he or she arrives at the same results. By applying this procedure the basic processes that support the development of OC and SRAB are illustrated.

In criminology, there is a vast literature on the level of agreement between official records and self-reported measures of offending. Farrington et al. (2014) edited a special number of the journal *Criminal Behavior and Mental Health* on that question. They concluded their introduction with a list of seven generalizations from longitudinal research in four countries:

1. Self-reports of offending show that many more (over 20 times as many) crimes are committed compared with offenses that lead to convictions.
2. The vast majority of males have committed an offense that, in theory, could have led to a conviction.
3. Generally, the most frequent offenders according to self-reports are those most likely to be convicted.
4. Self-reports of offending predict future convictions.
5. Most offenders are versatile; very few are specialists.
6. Criminal careers last longer according to self-reports than according to official records of convictions.
7. The age at onset of offending is a few years earlier in self-reports than in convictions, providing an opportunity for early intervention to prevent persistence and escalation in offending.

In this chapter we try to add three new generalizations to this list. First, the proposed developmental processes can be identified with official offending and self-reported data. Second, as was done in Chaps. 1 and 2, it will be possible to replicate the above processes with two generations of convicted males 20 years apart. Third, the quantitative and qualitative processes can be reproduced with categories of official offenses and with the vast array of forms of antisocial behavior that are validity measured.

2 The Mechanism of the Quantitative Changes in Antisocial Behavior and Crime: Activation–Deactivation

In criminology, the precociousness has long been the foundation for the understanding of the development of the criminal and his or her criminal activity. Lombroso (1895) was the first to report data on this subject and to draw our attention to the importance of this parameter. This variable was often measured in longitudinal studies of OC and it was later proposed as required in every SRAB questionnaire (Elliott et al. 1989; Le Blanc 1989).

In 1986, Blumstein et al., in their mathematical model of the criminal career, made this information the foundation of its study and the conception of criminal policies. At all stages of the criminal justice system, from police to correctional agencies, these are data that are essential in decision-making (Gottfredson and Gottfredson 1985; Le Blanc 1998). The main criminal career criminologists followed that proposition (Piquero et al. 2003, 2007); it is also recognized by the recent review by Doherty and Bacon (2019). The developmental criminologists made the onset of antisocial behavior the backbone of the antisocial behavior career (Le Blanc and Fréchette 1989; Loeber and Le Blanc 1990; Le Blanc and Loeber 1998; Le Blanc 2015). This section focuses on its role in the quantitative development of OC and SRAB.

2.1 The Quantitative Changes During an Official Offending Career

Le Blanc and Fréchette (1989), using the 1970s court sample of males of the MTSFGCLS, observed that participation, frequency, variety, seriousness, and duration in OO and SRO (self-reported offending) diminished regularly with the increase in the age at onset. It was the highest when it started during childhood and the lowest when it began during adulthood. At the end of the offending career, a saturation phenomenon was observed when the onset was no longer driving participation, frequency, variety, seriousness, and duration; they declined before termination.

The solidity of these conclusions had two weaknesses, even if some converging observations were reported in subsequent publications (Loeber and Le Blanc 1990; Le Blanc and Loeber 1998; Piquero et al. 2003). The first deficiency of the original study was the short follow-up window on the official career, from late childhood through middle youth. The pursuit of the tests of the impacts of the developmental mechanisms are done for the life span from age 8 to 61. The second deficiency was that the proofs were not exactly replicated with another court sample and SRAB.

This subject of the developmental mechanism of offending was revived in 2019 by two reviews. In the first review, Mazerolle and McPhedran concluded that, in the voluminous literature on the versatility versus specialization question, the convergent conclusion was that a small degree of specialization exists during the offending career. However, their argument was that, from a longitudinal point of view, offending is versatile for a good part of the career, but it becomes more specialized as age increases when this phenomenon is measured by the variety of offenses rather than as a degree. The second review, by Jennings and Hahn Fox, found very few publications, after Le Blanc (2002), on acceleration–deceleration or escalation–de-escalation. They suggest for future research: (1) the analytical strategy of unpacking the career span by decades of life; (2) the study of these phenomena with some new advances in statistical models, such as bivariate probit and random logistics regression models; and (3) the use of new research designs to increase the robustness of the existing conclusion. These proposals are applied to the life span from 8 to 61.

Table 3.2 reports the results for OO and the first generation from two points of view: the age at onset, on the left, and the age at offset, on the right. The first part of Table 3.2 is an upgrade of Tables 5.1, 5.2, and 5.3 in Le Blanc and Fréchette (1989). Let us start by a comprehensive view of activation–deactivation, that is, the correlations between the age at onset and the age at offset with the number of years delinquents are active during their career, the variety and frequency of their offenses, and the duration of the career (offset − onset). These statistically significant Spearman correlations at least at $p = 0.0001$ are displayed at the bottom of Table 3.2.

All the correlations with the age at onset are negatives with the number of years of participation (−0.48), the variety or the number of types of offenses for which they were convicted (−0.41), the frequency or the number of offenses in their crime mix (−0.33), and the duration or career span in terms of the distance between onset and offset (−0.37). However, these new correlations are higher, by between 4 and 10 decimal points, than their counterparts in Le Blanc and Fréchette (1989).

These observations are also valid for the court sample of the 1990s. They are a little lower but very similar, respectively −0.33, −0.29, −0.27, and −0.23 for a follow-up from age 12 to 45 compared with the period of age 8 to 61 in the first court sample. When the age at offset of the career correlates with the descriptive parameters, the correlations are positive and very similar, for the court sample of the 1970s. These linear and replicated results give credence to a question that was brought up in Chap. 2: does the length of the age span under study have an impact on the results from a longitudinal analysis of an OC? These conclusions tell researchers that the age span of the sample does not significantly affect the validity of the results but only their degree.

In summary, the analysis of the correlations confirm, for two generations of adjudicated males 20 years apart, that an early age at onset produces a launching effect (an augmented number of active years of participation during a career), a diversification action (increased variety), an explosion influence (more frequency), and a stabilization motion (longer career span). On the other hand, the positive correlations of the descriptive parameters of the OO with the age at offset illustrate the same mechanism. An early offset preceded by a low participation (slackening), a reduced variety (specialization), a rare frequency (declivity), and a short career (vanishing). Let us see how these activation–deactivation forces manifest by periods of the life span.

Table 3.2 Quantitative changes in official offending, males of the court sample of the 1970s: median of years active, variety, frequency, and career span by the ages at onset and offset

	Statistics By Age of Onset						Statistics by Age of Offset				
Age of onset	Nb males	Active[1]	Variety	Frequency	Duration	Age of offset	Nb males	Active[1]	Variety	Frequency	Duration
8	1	12	4	94	20						
9	4	13	11	46	28						
10	8	17	9	43	29						
11	5	11	8	27	27						
12	9	8	6	15	26						
13	24	8	7	19	23	13	1	1	1	1	1
14	62	7	6	16	21	14	5	1	2	2	1
15	70	7	6	15	20	15	12	1	2	2	1
16	77	6	6	16	21	16	10	1	2	2	1
17	35	6	6	14	22	17	8	2	2	4	1
18	18	4	4	6	10	18	11	2	2	6	2
19	30	5	6	8	19	19	10	2	2	4	1
20	22	4	4	8	17	20	5	3	4	7	3
21	12	4	3	8	12	21	7	3	3	4	3
22	6	3	4	13	11	22	7	3	3	5	6
23	7	4	4	5	6	23	9	2	3	4	3
24	5	3	4	6	6	24	5	2	2	4	7
25	3	4	2	6	8	25	9	3	5	10	7
26	1	3	3	4	28	26	7	7	6	16	10
27	1	2	5	5	27	27	8	5	3	7	12
28	1	1	1	1	1	28	12	5	5	11	13
29	1	6	5	27	12	29	8	4	4	6	11
30						30	6	7	5	10	13
31						31	5	7	7	22	16
32	3	1	1	2	11	32	14	7	7	32	15
33	3	3	4	6	5	33	8	4	3	6	16
34	2	1	1	1	1	34	19	7	5	13	19
35	1	1	1	1	1	35	17	8	6	18	20
36	1	10	6	18	24	36	11	7	6	19	21
37	1	2	3	7	1	37	11	9	7	28	22
38	1	5	7	9	9	38	25	8	7	19	21
39						39	27	10	8	36	23
40	2	1	1	2	1	40	23	12	8	30	24
41						41	13	8	8	27	25
42	1	1	5	5	1	42	5	7	6	13	26
43	3	2	3	4	2	43	8	5	5	9	24
44						44	7	5	6	14	28
45						45	6	7	6	11	29
46	2	3	2	3	5	46	5	7	7	16	25
47	2	2	3	3	5	47	7	8	9	26	31
48	1	1	1	1	1	48	5	8	8	14	33
49	2	1	2	20	1	49	16	7	6	17	36
50	1	1	2	6	1	50	6	4	4	6	33
51	1	1	1	1	1	51	5	8	6	15	35
52						52	5	7	7	8	34
53	1	1	1	1	1	53	7	10	8	28	36
54						54	7	8	7	12	39
55	1	1	1	1	1	55	8	6	4	11	36
56						56	5	7	5	13	40
57						57	2	9	6	29	44
58						58	4	8	8	16	43
59						59	6	8	9	25	41
60						60	4	8	6	21	44
Correlation[3]	431	- 0,38 p = 0,01	- 0,33 p = 0,01	- 0.33 p = 0,01	- 0,33 p = 0,01			0,36 p = 0,01	0,28 p = 0,01	0.28 p = 0,01	0,36 p = 0,01

1. The number of years a male was convicted for an offense.
2. The career span is claculate in the following wau: age of offset minus age of onset.
3. The Spearman corrlation (it is very similar with the Pearsoin correlation).

The age–crime curves of OO in Chap. 2 showed a peak or a turning point at age 16, that is, when the yearly increases began to decrease. Table 3.2, for the birth cohorts of 1960, shows that the activation forces become deactivation energies from the above turning point. A general linear reduction of OO, except for scattered exceptions here and there, manifests by a diminution of the years of participation in OO (from over 10 during childhood to 1 and 2 during middle adulthood and beyond) and its variety (from around ten to below five types of offenses), frequency (from over 15 to below five during middle adulthood), and the career span (from over 20 before the 20s to a few years after 40 years old). The other side of the coin tells us that an early offset is associated with few years of participation, a few offenses of one or two types, and a short career span.

A few specific results must be mentioned. (1) The correlation between the ages of onset and offset is very low and not statistically significant for the two generations of delinquents (1960: 0.08; 1980: 0.06). This result may indicate that an early onset introduces a launching impact but not necessarily a continuity effect or a desistance one. This hypothesis is checked in the following chapters. (2) The correlations of the age at offset with participation, variety, frequency, and career span are positive and highly statistically significant; $p = 0,0001$), particularly for the court males of the 1990s (for 1960: 0.38, 0.36, 0.29, 0.82; for 1980: 0.80, 0.69, 0.62, 0.97). This result may also be the consequence of a shorter follow-up for this second generation, as suggested earlier. A later offset may be a sign of saturation with OO that precedes termination, as was empirically illustrated in Le Blanc and Fréchette (1989). (3) The deactivation duration is much more lengthy than the activation period is early for the two generations of court males; it takes the form, for most of the ages, of some individuals that are not productive in terms of variety, frequency, and career span. These results seem to indicate that some male delinquents convicted during adolescence wait a long time before reentering into OO. A phenomenon that was not expected from data on a shorter follow-up nor it is a reflection of imprisonment or other life causalities (see Piquero et al. 2001). However, the age–crime curves by types of OO (property, violence, and lifestyle), reported in Chap. 2, tell us that after 30 years of age, property crimes lose their great dominance over violent and lifestyle offenses. In fact, during adulthood (after age 30) these two latter forms of OO occupy a more important role in the OO mix. In summary, deactivation or progressive desistance is a natural phenomenon during a career. It manifests by the forces of slackening (declining participation), declivity (decrease frequency), specialization (reduction of variety), and the vanishing of OO (shorter career span).

Let us conclude this section on quantitative changes with data that are never reported in criminology to our knowledge, that is, the velocity of the OO or the yearly changes. In addition, these data will be compared with other longitudinal studies. Table 3.3 report such figures for the Montréal G60 and G80 court samples and the community samples from a working class community of South London, UK (Farrington et al. 2013a, b), and Pittsburg inner city multiracial youngest and oldest cohorts (Jennings et al. 2016). The value in each cell of Table 3.3 represents the calculus of the percentage of increase or decrease in the number of participating males in OO from one specific age to the next one. Let us start by the four means at the bottom of Table 3.3. The velocity calculations are (1) the overall mean of the

Table 3.3 Quantitative changes: longitudinal velocity of prevalence, comparison of court males between generations, 1960 vs 1980, and longitudinal studies: Montréal, London, and Pittsburg

Ages	Montréal[1] 1960 Ages 8-61	1980 12-45	London GB Ages 10-56	Pittsburg Cohort Ages 10-30 Youngest	Oldest
8					
9	0,9				
10	1,2				
11	0,3		0,3	0,3	0,0
12	0,8	3,5	0,7	1,9	1,3
13	3,8	12,5	1,6	1,9	2,3
14	10,5	20,4	2,0	3,3	3,8
15	11,2	8,3	-0,2	-0,5	2,9
16	6,6	3,7	0,0	1,2	0,6
17	-1,7	-15,6	2,1	-2,3	-2,2
18	-7,6	-7,7	-0,5	2,3	-0,3
19	5,9	2,4	-0,5	0,9	-0,4
20	-1,9	0,0	-1,5	-3,6	-1,5
21	-5,1	-9,5	-1,8	0,0	-2,0
22	-2,5	-7,1	1,0	0,2	-0,7
23	0,8	-4,4	-2,3	-2,1	1,3
24	-0,8	-1,4	0,5	1,0	-0,9
25	-1,1	4,6	0,0	-1,6	-1,5
26	-4,9	1,4	-2,3	-0,2	-1,0
27	-0,4	-0,4	-0,3	0,7	1,6
28	-0,7	0,0	0,2	-1,2	-0,7
29	-2,1	-1,4	0,2	1,0	-1,0
30	-1,5	-2,4	-0,5	-1,9	0,0
31	0,2	0,6	-0,2	0,3	0,0
32	1,1	-0,8	-0,3		
33	-0,4	0,0	0,2		
34	1,0	-1,6	0,3		
35	0,5	0,6	0,2		
36	-3,2	-1,2	-1,0		
37	-2,6	0,0	0,5		
38	2,8	-0,2	-0,3		
39	-1,1	-0,2	-0,7		
40	-2,8	-2,3	0,8		
41	-2,9	-0,8	-0,5		
42	-2,2	-1,6	0,5		
43	1,3	0,0	0,3		
44	2,6	-0,4	0,0		
45	-2,2	3,5	-0,3		
46	0,0		-0,2		
47	-0,4		-0,7		
48	0,7		-0,5		
49	0,8		0,2		
50	-3,0		0,7		
51	0,0		0,2		
52	0,7		-0,8		
53	-0,7		-0,2		
54	-0,4				
55	1,1				
56	-1,7				
57	0,2				
58	0,0				
59	0,4				
60	-0,8				

(continued)

Table 3.3 (continued)

61	-0,9				
Total mean[2]	2,06		0,91	1,35	1,24
Progression[3]	4,41		1,34	1,27	1,97
Regression[4]	2,52		0,72	1,68	1,11
Reversion[5]	1,37		0,40	1.5	1,45
12-45					
Total Mean	3,31	3,54			
Progression	8,23	9,68			
Regression	2,14	3,28			
Reversion	1,44	1,92			

1. For purpose of comparison there are two sets of means G60 court sample: those calculated on the total life span from age 8 eight to 61 and those for the career span from age 12 to 45 for the comparison with G80 court sample.
2. The over all mean of the yearly changes over the total official career.
3. The mean of the progressions until the breaking point.
4. The mean of the regressions after the breaking point.
5. The mean of the reversions that is a change in direction during a strecht of progressions or regressions.

yearly changes over all the OCs, (2) the mean of the progressions until the breaking point on their age–crime curves, (3) the mean of the regressions thereafter, and (4), the mean of the reversions that is a change in direction during a stretch of progressions or regressions. Reading the means in Table 3.3, two conclusions can be drawn.

First, as expected, the four means are much lower for the three community samples of London and Pittsburg than for the two court samples of the MTSFGCLS. It is also the case for the ranges of velocities, from 2 to −2 in London, from 3.5 to −3.6 in Pittsburg and the Montréal court samples: G60 from 11.2 to −7.6 and G80 from 20.4 to −15.6. The difference between the court and community samples reflects somewhat the normative gap that was also illustrated in Chap. 2. In addition, it is lower in the two socioeconomically disadvantaged communities of London (Farrington et al. 2013a, b) and Pittsburg (Jennings et al. 2016) and even more in the racially mixed communities of the latter city, not forgetting that the velocity distributions are composed of birth cohorts a decade apart, born in the 1960s in London versus the 1970s in Pittsburg.

Second, the results for OO between age 12 and 45 in the two Montréal court samples are dissimilar. The delinquents of the five birth cohorts around 1980 show higher velocity results than the cohorts around 1960. The total mean is 3.54 in the 1980 group vs. 3.31 in the 1960 one; the progressions are respectively 9.68 vs. 8.23; the regressions are 3.28 vs. 2.14; and the relatively few reversions are 1.92 vs. 1.44. These differences are around 1.25 change. They can be interpreted as somewhat important because each of them is about one-third of their maximum. They confirm that the career of G80 delinquents developed a more concentrated and explosive course that was more centered during adolescence and early youth. This concentration of the OO can be explained, as we already noted in Chap. 2, by important changes in juvenile laws (delinquency and child welfare) and juvenile and adult criminal justice policies. The impact of economic and sociological changes should not be forgotten.

Table 3.4 offers a synthetic view of the activation–deactivation mechanism. First, childhood is particularly activating for participation, variety, frequency, and duration. This is manifested by the highest values for every parameter of OO. Second, the early and late adolescence and early and middle youth are periods of continuity because the level of the parameters is quite similar. Third, late youth and the maturity phases are moments of deactivation because the parameters are the lowest. They indicate the slackening of participation, declivity in frequency, specialization, or reduction in variety, and vanishing by a shorter career span.

2.2   The Quantitative Changes During a Self-Reported Antisocial Behavior Career

Longitudinal studies that gathered official and self-reported data on offending for five decades of the life span are unusual. There are two, the Cambridge Study in Delinquent Development (Farrington et al. 2013b; Farrington 2019) and the MTSFGCLS G60 population and court samples. These studies present descriptive data on onset and its association with prevalence, continuity, and the overlap between OO and SRO. Only the second study conducted analysis on the developmental mechanism of activation–deactivation with these two measures.

Table 3.4 A synthetical view of quantitative changes for the males of the court sample of the 1970s: ANOVA of mean participation, variety, frequency, and career span by phases of the life span[a]

Phases of life	Participation	Variety	Frequency	Career span
Chidhood 8-11 (18)[2]	13,3	8,8	53.3	27,5
Adolescence Early 12-14 (95)	7,5	6,6	22,3	23,1
Late 15-17 (182)	6,6	6,3	21.3	20,8
Youth Early 18-21 (82)	5,1	5	16,2	18,2
Middle 22-25 (21)	4,2	4	11,2	14,5
Late 26-29 (4)	3	3,5	9,5	22,3
Maturity early 30-39 (12)	2,7	2,7	5,7	10
Middle 40-49 (13)	1,8	2,4	2,8	6
Late 50-61 (4)	1	1,2	2,3	1

1. All the tests for the comparison of means were statistically signifiant at p = 0,0001: homogeneity of variances, Anova, and robustness of equality of means.
2. In parenthesis the number of males in this group.

In Le Blanc and Fréchette (1989) analyzed quantitative changes with a time window that spread only from childhood to early youth and it was limited to only 11 specific crimes graded by seriousness. In their book, Tables 5.1, 5.2, and 5.3 showed very well the activation phenomenon in the forms of the launching, diversification, explosion, and stabilization gears that moved the SRD career of the males convicted for the first time in the 1970s. This activation was high for a few years during childhood and early adolescence, and then deactivation manifested during late adolescence and early youth. Another conclusion was that the activation–deactivation phenomenon was observable in a representative sample and a court sample of boys born around 1960. These data had two deficiencies. The first one was the restricted range of the self-reported offenses, it covered only 11 crimes, representing crimes of all levels of seriousness, and there were no problem behaviors. In this section, the measures of forms of SRAB that was validated in Chap. 1 are used (see Appendix B). The second drawback was the short follow-up; it will be extended to age 30 instead of the early 20s. Two questions will be addressed: are these results reproduced in the sample of court males recruited during 1990s? Are these results reproducible for all forms of SRAB?

To answer these questions, the data are presented in Table 3.5. In this table, the reader will find a first column with each form of SRAB, the next one displays their ages at onset, and, in the last column on the right, their ages at offset. In the middle five columns are displayed the sets of results at each interview. The first line presents correlations and the second line shows means. Let us remember that 16, 18, 24, and 30 are average ages (the standard deviations are around 2 years) of the convicted males when they responded to the SRAB questionnaire. The data in this table support a common and positive response to the above two questions: definitively "yes."

In response to the first question, the reader has to look at the correlations at the first interview, around the average age of 16, in the vertical boxes for participation, variety, and frequency. The correlations are all highly statistically significant. In addition, they are much higher than in the three subsequent columns for ages 18, 24, and 30. For some forms of SRAB, they are still high at 18, 24, and 30, that is, theft, fraud, vandalism, psychological violence, conflict at work, and sexual activity. These correlations vanish at 30, but they are also high at 18 and 24 for motor vehicle theft, physical violence, authority conflict in the home and at school, and drug use. The career span also correlates highly, significantly, and negatively correlated with onset for all forms of SRAB. In summary, it can be concluded that all the gears of acceleration are propelling all forms of SRAB, including SRD, such as theft, fraud, motor vehicle theft, and physical violence, this early on during childhood and adolescence as expected.

In response to the second question, the reader must look at all the second lines for each form of SRAB. They report the means of participation, variety, frequency, and duration at each interview. The first values, at around age 16, are much higher than the values at the other following three interviews. This is the case for all forms of SRAB. The values are declining from interview to interview; this tendency may be interpreted as the fact that the involvement in SRAB is disappearing, and that the abandonment of each SRAB is progressive. In addition, participation, variety, and frequency

Table 3.5 Quantitative changes in self-reported antisocial behavior, types of SRAB for the 1990 court sample of males

Types SRAB		Initiation (Age onset)[2]	Launching – Slakening (participation) 0 – 1				Diversification – Specialization (variety) 0 – 7				Explosion – Deceleration (frequency) 0 – 28				Stabilization (duration) offset – onset 5 – 35	Stopping (age offset)[2]
Age[1] T1T2T3T4			16	18	24	30	16	18	24	30	16	18	24	30		
Covert	Theft	11.2	-32[3]	-19	-19	-19	-29[3]	-17	-16	-21	-25[3]	-16	-11	-18	-48	22.6
			75[4]	*66*	*48*	*40*	*2.9*	*2.3*	*1.3*	*.98*	*12.9*	*11.2*	*9.3*	*8.8*	*11.8*	
	Motor vehicule	14.7	-39	-29	-03	-08	-37	-25	-05	-08	-33	-24	-17	-16	-32	22.2
			63	*65*	*61*	*26*	*1.1*	*1.1*	*.71*	*.30*	*5.7*	*5.6*	*4.5*	*3.6*	*7.9*	
	Fraud	14.1	-38	-24	-14	-17	-36	-22	-14	-19	-35	-22	-14	-19	-33	23
			64	*58*	*63*	*41*	*.96*	*.81*	*.82*	*.56*	*4*	*3.5*	*4.6*	*4*	*9.2*	
Overt	Vandalism	13.1	-38	-21	-13	16	-35	-19	-12	-12.	-10	-17	-11	-11	-47	17.7
			42	*28*	*16*	*14*	*.63*	*.40*	*.20*	*.20*	*4.1*	*3.6*	*3.3*	*3.1*	*7.4*	
	Physical violence	10.4	-29	-21	-13	-08	-25	-17	-08	-08	-23	-16	-07	-13.7	-41	22
			84	*70*	*47*	*32*	*3*	*2.2*	*1.1*	*.66*	*13.7*	*11.5*	*9.9*	*9.1*	*11.8*	
	Psychologcal violence	13.8	-47	-24	-18	-17	-39	-10	-16	-15	-34	-17	-15	-14	-47	21.2
			58	*46*	*32*	*24*	*1.4*	*1.1*	*.62*	*.47*	*8.5*	*7.6*	*7*	*6.3*	*8.4*	
Conflict	In home	10.4	-26	-10	-10		-22	-12	-07		-21	-12	-10		-52	19
			77	*66*	*54*		*1.7*	*1.3*	*.91*		*8.3*	*7.1*	*6.7*		*10.4*	
	At school	8.3	-32	-14			-28	-19			-29	-21			-71	17
			87	*84*			*2.8*	*2.3*			*11.2*	*9.1*			*8.5*	
	At work	17.8		-32	-20	-27		-22	-20	-25		-23	-19	-17	-27	24
				72	*59*	*56*		*1.5*	*1.1*	*.79*		*9.1*	*8.7*		*7.5*	
Life style	Drug use	13.2	-44	-32	-36	-35	-46	-34	-26	-30	-45	-29	-24	-24	-46	25
			82	*92*	*82*	*8*	*.08*	*1*	*2.6*	*.2*	*10.2*	*11*	*10.8*	*9.4*	*12*	
	Sexual activity	13	-63	-57	-31	-31	-61	-54	-30	-25	-57	-47	-31	-29	-17	27
			.08	*.08*	*.03*	*.03*	*.08*	*.03*	*.03*	*.04*	*2.2*	*2.2*	*2.1*	*2.1*	*7.5*	
	Risky driving	15	-40	-08	-08	06	-38	-13	-12	-09	-35	-07	-11	-24	-44	23.3
			.74	*.72*	*.8*	*.8*	*1*	*1.2*	*-06*	*-04*	*3.9*	*6.6*	*5.3*		*8*	
	Disorderly	13.6	-23	-13	-13	-09	-24	-12	-09	-08	-24	-11	-09	-09	-.09	23
			.38	*.38*	*.53*	*.36*	*.38*	*.38*	*.53*	*.36*	*2.7*	*2.6*	*2*	*1.7*	*11*	
	Gambling	15.6	-66	-11			-55	-11			-46	-14			-58	24
			.73	*.61*			*1.2*	*.61*			*3.9*	*1.7*			*8.9*	

1. Median age at time of each interview.
2. The median age of onset and offset.
3. Pearson correration that are statistically significant at least at p = 0.05 are outline in grey.
4. Means are reported.

decelerate and the correlation of onset is negative with duration.[1] In summary, with time SRAB participation hinders, variety shows specialization or diminution of variety, frequency explosion, and vanishing of duration. It should be noted that if the speed of the gears decreases much faster between age 18 and 24 than between 24 and 30. It may be explained by the time lapse, 6 years, whereas it is only 2 years from age 16 to 18. The same phenomenon has been reported in other studies (Le Blanc and Loeber 1998; Piquero et al. 2003; Farrington et al. 2013a, b; Jennings et al. 2016).

In summary, the results on quantitative changes in SRAB strongly support two conclusions. (1) All forms of SRAB display a cycle of the shape of the age–crime curve; that is, a reverse U shape with a long extended right arm. In fact, for a few years during childhood or the first half of adolescence there is a sharp increase in the quantity of SRAB, then a decrease occurs during the second half of adolescence and youth. (2) A generic mechanism of quantitative development (activation–deactivation) is in operation for all forms of SRAB. It applies to males convicted in juvenile court for two generations recruited 20 years apart, born around 1960 and 1980.[2]

These conclusions also apply for the behavioral patterns identified in Chap. 1, delinquency (covert, overt) and problem behavior (conflict, and lifestyle). They apply for males and females of a population sample recruited in 2006–2007. Table 3.6 displays the correlations between onset and participation, variety, and frequency for the above four behavioral patterns. Virtually all the correlations are statistically significant. The developmental gears of acceleration are observable not only for convicted delinquents, but also for boys and girls of the population.

In conclusion, the developmental mechanism of activation–deactivation was initially identified in samples of males that were representing the population and court cases aged 8–20 (Le Blanc and Fréchette 1989). It is now reproduced for convicted males of two generations, the 1960 and 1980 birth cohorts, with official crime data from age 8–61 and SRAB data from childhood through early maturity. Criminology can consider the activation–deactivation phenomenon a generalization for genders, official crime, SRAB, and generation.

3   The Mechanism of Qualitative Changes in Antisocial Behavior and Crime: Aggravation–Deaggravation

Qualitative changes involve measuring distinctions based on the nature of antisocial behavior and crime. In criminology, it was most often the grading of the seriousness of offenses. In developmental psychology, Wohlwill (1973) defines developmental

---

[1] We correlated participation, variety, frequency, and duration or career span with offset instead of onset for all forms of SRAB and they were positive instead of negative and at a similar level compared with onset.

[2] The same analyses were conducted for G90 convicted girls and the same results were found. They are not displayed because the initial sample consisted of only 150 girls. In addition, two factors diminished dramatically the number of cases at each follow-up interview, the attrition and the very low prevalence of girls for all forms of SRAB.

Table 3.6 Quantitative changes for self-reported antisocial behavior, behavioral patterns for the court sample of males and females of the 1990s

Behavioral patterns	Covert[a]		Overt		Delinquency		Conflict		Lifestyle		Problem behavior	
	Boys	Girls	Boys	Girls	Boys	Girls	Boys	Girls	Boys	Girls	Boys	Girls
Participation	−0.15[a]	−0.04[b]	−0.27	−0.13	−0.24	−16	−0.28	−0.24	−0.10	−0.18	−0.25	−0.24
Variety	−0.26	−0.19	−0.34	−0.30	−0.34	−0.28	−0.30	−0.31	−0.19	−0.21	−0.30	−0.29
Frequency	−0.29	−0.11	−0.39	−0.34	−0.36	−0.13[b]	−0.44	−0.21	−0.07[c]	−0.14	−0.47	−0.09[b]

[a]The behavioral patterns identified in Chap. 1
[b]These correlations are not statistically significant
[c]The Pearson correlations are statistically significant at least at 0.05, most of them at 0.0001

changes as (1) a particular sequence of behaviors and (2) the progression and regression of persons on such a successive order of behaviors. In developmental criminology, this course is called aggravation–deaggravation and the sequence has been investigated using three methods: (1) the analysis of the switching from one offense to the next one; (2) the changes in the crime mix over time; (3) the escalation of a developmental pathway. Whatever the method, two criteria were used to measure a progression and a regression: the onset and offset ages and the offense seriousness.

3.1   Offenses Switching or Changes in Behavioral Mixes

S. Glueck and E. Glueck (1930) were the first longitudinal criminologists to consider changes in offending patterns. They showed that property offenses were more common during adolescence and violent offenses more frequent during adulthood. This aggravation result was replicated in several studies, cities, and countries (Le Blanc and Loeber 1998). The landmark book by Wolfgang et al. (1972) on the OO in Philadelphia males introduced a new perspective, with the investigation of the transition between offenses as a Markov process. In his review of this type of study, Le Blanc (2002) concluded that despite many technical difficulties, they are helpful because they illustrated the large random component in the development of offending studied crime by crime. Generally, the results of over 20 studies favored the escalation hypothesis for a certain number of delinquents (the proportion varies from study to study), although stability and random mobility were more dominant. The most recent study of the sequence of offenses investigated the lifelong official crime sequences during a follow-up from age 8 to 56 in London, UK. (Basto-Peireira and Farrington 2018). The most common sequences of two, three, four or more convictions involve types of stealing. As the studies of crime switching were trying to understand the sequence of every crime during a long career for a group of individuals, the usefulness of this analytic strategy for theory development and policy and practice recommendations is remote because of the microscopic nature of the results.

In 1986, Blumstein et al. proposed the concept of crime mix to account for the combination of different types of offenses that individuals commit or are convicted for at a particular point in time or during a specific period of a criminal career. Le Blanc and Fréchette (1989) analyzed self-reported data on 14 crimes graded by seriousness and identified the different mixes during early and late adolescence and youth. They concluded that burglary was an universal component of the mixes whatever the phase of life; that automobile theft was the type of crime that was most often associated with other offenses; that the aggravation of the crime mixes was clear: first, minor offenses disappeared at an early age (petty larceny, shoplifting, and common theft); second, more serious crimes were more prevalent during late adolescence and youth (aggravated theft, sexual aggression, drug trafficking); third, that the number of individualized configurations of offenses increased with age, that is, mixes that characterized only one individual; fourth, that there was a tendency toward specialization as age increased (defined as a reduction in the degree of variety of offenses). In short, among the 1970 wards of the court, burglary appears as a crucial form of criminal activity. Basto-Peireira and Farrington (2018) were also observing the presence of stealing. Based on the Montréal and London longitudinal studies, it can be concluded that burglary and other forms of stealing can be qualified first as a " *common activity*" for delinquents (it involves a much greater number of subjects than the other categories of offenses); second, as a " *polyvalent activity*," capable of not only being associated with any other category of crimes but also maintaining a very strong affinity for all of them; and third, as a " *catalyzing activity*," which, although tied to certain categories of offenses, seems the most capable of being associated with the most dangerous forms of official criminal activity.

3.2   Age at Onset–Offset Versus Seriousness

There are two ways to appreciate the aggravation–deaggregation phenomenon: the onset–offset ages and the seriousness of the offense. The use of the age at onset–offset is justifiable for measuring this phenomenon because there is a vast criminological literature on its central role in the development of an antisocial behavior and crime career (reviews: Le Blanc and Loeber 1998; Piquero et al. 2003; Doherty and Bacon 2019). Concerning criminal offenses, official and self-reported, the timing of onset has been describe over and across generations, samples, cities, countries, and systems of justice. Some conclusions are reproduced and universal according to the review by Le Blanc and Loeber (1998). From the MTSFGCLS, five conclusions are considered generalizable.

1. The beginning of SRO and SRAB take place in late childhood.
2. The onset data show a gradual unfolding of increasingly more serious behaviors in several domains of SRAB with age; this is the case for conduct problems, offending, and different forms of antisocial behavior. This phenomenon was illustrated for lack of discipline at school and home, aggression, theft, vandalism, drugs, and sex in the MTSFGCLS (Le Blanc and Loeber 1998, Table 3).
3. Specific behaviors from the above categories are inserted in between behaviors of other forms of SRAB (for example, Le Blanc and Girard 1998).
4. The onset of all forms of antisocial behaviors often takes place in waves in the sense that some antisocial behaviors are often associated with the onset of other antisocial behaviors, for example, school and family rebelliousness during childhood, aggression, theft, and vandalism during early adolescence, as well as sex and drug use in middle adolescence.
5. An early age at onset is a marker of the future quantity of SRO and SRAB, prevalence, variety, and career span, the launching gears of quantitative change during the life course (Sect. 3.2, Table 3.2).

Concerning the age at offset, none of these five conclusions is documented.

Quételet (1835) noted that some criminals progress from property to person crimes. This observation has been recurrent in criminology during the twentieth century and even now (Jennings and Hahn Fox 2019). This type of aggravation of offending, as it was called (Le Blanc and Fréchette 1989; Le Blanc and Loeber 1998) was based on some estimation of the seriousness of offenses that was obtained through three categories of methods in the literature.

The first category involved the judgment of experts: (1) academic researchers estimated the severity of offenses, for example, Glueck and Glueck (1930); (2) a group of experts from the criminal justice system grades official criminal offenses (Gorsuch 1938); (3) criminals and noncriminals estimate the gravity of offenses (Van Der Westhuizen 1981) or experts grade antisocial behaviors (Maxwell 1999). The second category implies an independent criterion such as the nature or length of sentences by criminal courts, for example, the Crime Severity Index of Statistics Canada (Wallace et al. 2009). The third category of the gradation of offense seriousness took the direction of estimates of crime seriousness by samples of a population. In 1922, Clark developed a scale from the gradation of 15 juvenile offenses based on the judgments by university students, faculty members, and other persons engaged in social and educational work. This type of scale was revived in the landmark and most comprehensive study of the gradation of crime seriousness by a population sample (Sellin and Wolfgang 1964; replicated in Canada by Akman and Normandeau 1968; replicated by Wolfgang et al. 1985). See also Carlson and Williams (1993) for a new method, the Q-Sort. In a new study, it was established that the population is more moralist than consequential and thereafter, this type of measure is not useful for criminal policy (Andriensen et al. 2018). Blumstein et al. (1986), in their salient statement on the criminal career, restored the interest of criminology in the notion of aggravation, which they called escalation. In the MTSFGCLS, the point of departure was the Sellin and Wolfgang estimates applied to the G60 male court sample (Le Blanc and Fréchette 1989). The conclusions of the study (2005) with these data were (1) that seriousness was a distinct measure compared with variety and frequency; (2) it was a good predictor of the subsequent levels of gravity during adolescence and youth. However, the Gagnon analysis and the Kazemian et al. (2008) comparison of the Montréal and London samples showed that social and self-control were weak predictors of deaggravation.

3.3   A Developmental Sequence or Pathway

Studies of SRAB showed that there was clearly a developmental sequence for some types of antisocial behavior, such as conduct problems (Patterson et al. 1992), problem behavior (Elliott 1994; Elliott and Menard 1996), violence (Loeber and Hay 1997), disruptive child behaviors (Loeber et al. 1992; Loeber et al. 1993; Loeber and Wilström 1993), drug use (Le Blanc and Loeber 1998; Kandel 2002), and types of car crimes (Slobodian and Browne 1997). In the MTSFGCLS, it was expected to demonstrate such sequences for all the types of SRAB described in Table 1.1 of Chap. 1.

Rolf Loeber became interested in antisocial behavior developmental pathways after a meta-analysis (Loeber and Schmaling 1985). They are defined as " … the orderly behavioral development between more than two problem behaviors …" (Loeber 2019, p. 160). Two pathways were described. First, the overt pathway or confrontational acts has three steps, minor aggression followed by physical fighting and later by serious violent crimes. The covert pathway or concealing acts begins before age 15 and its steps are, first, shoplifting, and frequent lying, second, property damage (vandalism, fire setting), third, moderate delinquency, and fourth, serious delinquency (auto theft, burglary). The third pathway, called authority conflict, was added later. It starts with stubborn behaviors before age 12; it is followed by defiance and disobedience and it ends with authority avoidance (truancy, running away from home, staying out at night). In the Pittsburg Youth Study (above references) it was established that these steps took place systematically rather than randomly for boys and that the data confirmed a three-pathway model rather than a single pathway. These results were replicated prospectively by Loeber et al. 1998a) and by other studies (Gorman-Smith and Loeber 2005; Loeber et al. 1999; Tolan et al. 2000). In summary, the developmental pathways seem conceptually sound. However, they are based on a limited number of behaviors at each step, the life span of the data is rather limited from youth on, the hemimorphy of some behavior is not considered, and there are no mention of pathways of de-escalation. In this section, pathways are compared with the results of the MTSFGCLS.

In addition, it must be remembered that qualitative changes, defined in Table 3.1, can be analyzed in terms of uplifting–downlifting on a developmental sequence, moving up and down across the stages of seriousness or graded offense mixes as established by Le Blanc and Fréchette (1989) for delinquency, and Loeber et al. (1998a) for problem behaviors. Uplifting implies changing behaviors that are part of the person's repertoire. It takes, first, the form of innovation, the introduction of a new behavior in the repertoire, and retention, maintaining a less serious type of behavior while moving to more serious behaviors. Then, it can be a synchrony of the development of different types of antisocial behavior that is manifested by simultaneity, attaining the same level of seriousness in two or more types of behavior, and adjacency, the embedding of antisocial behavior of different types (Le Blanc and Kaspy, 1998, analysis for delinquency and problem behavior). It is a strong fact for offending rather than a contentious issue according to Jennings and Hahn Fox (2019), which is not the case for the deaggravation hypothesis (see also Le Blanc 2002).

3.4   The Qualitative Changes in Self-Reported Offending

Marcel Fréchette, coauthor of the 1987 French book, had the brilliant idea of building a figure with 14 self-reported official offenses on vertical and age on horizontal, and, inside the graph, data on age at onset, career span, and age at offset for each of these offenses. Reading this figure gives the authors the idea that there was a developmental sequence of offenses and an individual uplifting of their onsets and downlifting on their offsets. The Sellin and Wolfgang (1964) measure of seriousness (replicated in Canada by Akman and Normandeau 1968), was displayed beside each of the offenses in the figure. Le Blanc and Fréchette (1989, Fig. 5.4) concluded that there were five stages in a developmental sequence for the 14 offenses ranked by seriousness. These offenses were selected because they were conceptually distinct, frequent in criminal statistics reports, could be graded by a rigorous measure of seriousness, and easy to remember by the 1970s court males during an interview.

This figure was interpreted as displaying the following stages of aggravation from late childhood to early youth that were characterized by a particular SRO mix of offenses: (1) the emergence was represented by petty theft from 7 years old to 12; (2) the exploration combined shoplifting and vandalism between 8 and 12; (3) the explosion lumped together common theft, burglary, personal larceny, and public mischief between 13 and 16; (4) the conflagration amalgamated personal attack, aggravated theft, drug trafficking, and sexual offenses from 16 and 18; and (5) the outburst incorporated fraud and homicide after 18.[3] These authors also calculated that 14% of the delinquents regressed on these graded SRO mixes during their career (from childhood to youth), 15% were stable, and 71% were progressing, whereby 34% did so by three stages or more.

More recently, the MTSFGCLS reinterviewed the adjudicated males around the average ages of 32 (T4), 41 (T5), and 54 (T6). These interviews were conducted at different time intervals, at 5, 9, 9, and 13 years respectively. Some factors of attrition diminished the total number of subjects from T4 to T6, such as deceased, impossible

Table 3.7 The qualitative changes in self-reported official offending, court males of the 1970s

SRO stages	Seriousness[a]	Age T1–15, T2–17, T3–23[b]		Percentage inactive[c] and age at suspension[d] Five years before last interview					
		Onset	Offset	T4–32[b]		T5–41		T6–54	
Outburst									
Fraud (6)[a]		19.4	21	92.1[c]	26.8[d]	94[c]	37[d]	98.3[c]	42[d]
Conflagration									
Drugs trafficking	**(17.2)**	16.5	21.6	94.5	26.7	98	36	87.9	47
Sexual offense	**(14.3)**	17	17.5	99.2	26.7	100	36	100	42
Personal attack	**(13.21)**	16.4	19.2	86	26.7	98	35	93.1	46
Aggravated theft	**(11.54)**	16.4	19.6	98.8	26.8	98	35	98.3	42
Motor vehicle theft	**(6.7)**	15.2	16.9	95.3	26.8	94	36	98.3	42
Explosion									
Public mischief	**(0.7)**	15.8	18.9	89.4	26.8	100	35	91.4	42
Personal larceny	**(7.1)**	14.7	16.2	87.8	26.7	98	35	100	42
Burglary	**(6.43)**	14.3	18.2	87.3	26.7	92	36	96.6	45
Common theft	**(5.07)**	13.6	16.2	94.6	26.8	95.9	35.5	98.3	45
Exploration									
Vandalism	**(1.8)**	12.2	13.3	95.1	26.7	94	36	96.6	46.5
Shoplifting	**(2.2)**	11.5	14.5	93.7	26.7	91.5	36	93.1	45
Emergence									
Petty larceny	**(1)**	7.6	11	91.4	26.8	87.2	36.2	87.9	44

[a]The Sellin and Wolfgang measure adapted for Canada
[b]Average age at each interview
[c]Percentage of males that suspended their SRO the last 5 years at each interview
[d]Average age of males who suspended their SRO before the last interview

---

[3] During the T2 interview a SRO homicide was reported (confirmed by news paper articles). This SRO offense was left out of other interviews because no adult wanted to respond to that question as expected.

to locate, or intermittent attrition (for a period in-between interviews), and partial or total suspension of SRO. With these contexts in mind, let us look at the two aspects of the qualitative changes in SRO: first the changes in the offenses mix between periods of life course and, second, the continuity over time in participation.

Table 3.7 presents the qualitative changes in SRO mix from the first to the sixth interview. Thirteen offenses and their Sellin and Wolfgang seriousness scores are listed in the left column. The offenses are ordered by their age at onset based on the first three interviews. In most cases, this age gradation is similar to the ordering by their seriousness index. It should also be noted that the offsets are later for the most serious SRO. In the right section of Table 3.7, for the interviews at ages 32, 41, and 54, first the percentage of subject that suspended their official offending during the last five years before their last interview and, second, he agerage age of the males when they did so. Some observations should be remembered.

At T4, age 32 or the late youth and early maturity period, more than 90% of the subjects were inactive for 9 out of 14 SRO and this was since age 27. Among these offenses were some of the most serious ones: sexual offense, aggravated theft, and drug trafficking. On the other hand, the delinquents were more active in personal attack, public mischief, personal larceny, and burglary.

At T5, age 41 or the late early maturity and early middle maturity periods, the most serious offenses had virtually disappeared during the 5 preceding years: drug trafficking, sexual offense, personal attack, aggravated theft, and personal larceny. On the other hand, the less serious offenses were committed more frequently: petty larceny, common theft, burglary, and fraud. In addition, it was also the case for a more serious offense, motor vehicle theft. These data clearly show a deaggravation from the previous T4 interviews.

This decline in seriousness is also evident at the T6 interview, around 54 or the late maturity period. The males had perpetrated the most serious property and violent crimes less frequently and had increased their involvement in drug trafficking. In addition, they reported two new forms of offenses, buying and selling stolen goods and false statements to governmental agencies (income tax, welfare, unemployment, banks, etc.), which were introduced in the interview. At least 10% of the respondents admitted these forms of offenses. Future study with groups of males of mature age should include these offenses in their SRO questionnaire. The data on the drug trafficking and selling stolen goods may point to the construct of criminal markets that was introduced earlier (for example, managing prostitutes, operating a massage facility, collecting and counting money for organized crime, etc.).

These qualitative changes show a deaggravation in the seriousness in the SRO mix. In Table 3.8a, it can be observed that the adjacent continuity in SRO from T1 to T2 is 57%, with more progressions (32%) then regressions (5%). However, between late adolescence and early youth, the level of continuity is not far from before, 50%, but the position of the progressions (13%) and the regressions (33%) is reversed. If they were involved in SRO during the first half of youth, they had 74% continuity until age 40, whereas after that age their participation regressed (59%). Farrington et al. (2013a, b) in the Cambridge study and Jennings et al. (2016) for the Pittsburgh study also document a high level of continuity in SRO during adolescence and youth.

Table 3.8 Self-reported antisocial behavior mix, switching from late childhood to late youth, escalation and de-escalation of court males of the 1990s

(a) SRAB mix changes from late childhood to early adolescence						
SRAB	Late childhood mix					
Early adolescence mix	Before 12[a]		12–14		Total	
Before 12	21	8.6	5	2	26	10.6
12–14	89	36.3	83	33.9	172	70.2
15–17	16	6.5	31	12.7	47	19.2
Total	126	51.4	119	48.6	245	100

(b) SRAB mix changes from early to late adolescence[b]								
SRAB	Early adolescence mix							
Late adolescence mix	Before 12		12–14		15–17		Total	
12–14	21	8.8	85	35.6	8	8.3	114	47.7
15–17	4	1.7	66	27.6	27	11.3	97	40.6
After 17	1	0.4	16	6.7	11	4.6	28	11.7
Total	26	10.9	167	69.9	46	19.2	239	100

(c) SRAB mix changes from late adolescence to early youth[b]								
SRAB	Late adolescence mix							
Youth transition–E mix	12–14		15–17		After 17		Total	
15–17	82	24.2	54	15.9	12	3.5	148	43.7
After 17	101	29.8	59	17.4	31	9.1	191	56.3
Total	183	54	113	33.3	43	12.7	339	100

(d) SRAB mix changes from youth transition to early youth[b]						
SRAB	Youth transition–D mix					
Early youth mix	17–19		21–24		Total	
17–19	21	14.8	0	0	21	14.8
21–24	26	18.3	46	32.4	72	50.7
25–31	5	3.5	44	31	49	34.5
Total	52	36.6	90	63.4	142	100

(e) SRAB mix changes from early to late youth[b]								
SRAB	Early youth mix							
Late youth mix	17–19		21–24		After 25		Total	
17–19	30	12.3	0	0	0	0	30	12.3
21–24	15	6.2	64	26.3	7	2.9	86	35.4
After 25	0	0	59	24.3	68	28	117	52.3
Total	45	18.5	113	50.6	75	30.9	243	100

[a]In each category the frequency is presented on the left and the percentage on the right
[b]All Chi-squared and measures of association are statistically significant at least at 0.05

In addition, Table 3.8b illustrates the dominant roads of ternary continuity. From T1 to T3 and T2 to T4, the continuous participation is at a level of 46–47%, whereas it is lower for the later starters, 26% and 11% respectively. Ternary continuity between T3, T4, and T5 is much lower (22%), whereas the majority (52%) of the court males had suspended their SRO for the last 5 years when they were interviewed at T6, in their early 50s. This drop was also evident on the age–crime curves in Chap. 2.

In summary, these results illustrate that the aggravation hypothesis in SRO is clearly confirmed. However, the data in Tables 3.7 and 3.8 are insufficient to confirm the deaggravation in SRO. In addition, the steps of the Loeber covert pathway are evident in Table 3.7: from minor property crimes to increasingly serious ones during adolescence and youth. The overt pathway is not the same because there are more minor violent behaviors during childhood in the Loeber behavioral definition of this pathway.

3.5   The Qualitative Changes in Official Offense Mixes

The developmental theory of antisocial behavior and crime states that sequential stages exist in OO and SRAB; these stages take two forms of switching during the life span: first, a differentiation in behavioral and offense mixes over time and an increase–decrease in gravity.

To investigate these questions, the unpacking strategy proposed by Jennings and Hahn Fox (2019) was chosen to determine if the aggravation–deaggravation phenomenon is age-graded. The unpacking of the life course follows what is generally accepted by behavioral scientists. The nine categories are (1) childhood from age 9 to 11, (2) early adolescence from 12 to 14, (3) late adolescence from 15 to 17, (4) early youth from 18 to 21, (5) middle youth from 22 to 25, (6) late youth from 26 to 29, (7) early maturity from 30 to 39, (8) middle maturity from 40 to 49, and (9) late maturity from 50 to 61, the last age included in the longitudinal data set of OO. These categories are displayed on the right of the onset section in Table 3.9 for G60 and Table 3.10 for G80; the last column in the offset section in these tables displays the periods. The OO mixes begin the onset and offset sections of these tables.

Tables 3.9 and 3.10 are very complex, but they were constructed with the same structure. The left-hand section of these tables displays the onset data and the offset data are presented in the right-hand section. The first column in these two parts lists the names of the categories of OO and they are ranked according to their median age at onset or offset. These age data are increasing from the type of offenses with lowest age at onset to the type of offense with the highest; they are in reverse order for the offset data, from earliest to latest. The onset and offset age spans are divided by double lines according to the age-periods of life that were specified above. The second column in each section displays the rank of these categories of OO based on the Statistic Canada Crime Severity Index (Wallace et al. 2009, and adapted yearly after that date). At the bottom of the tables, the same data are reported for the whole career and for covert (POs), overt (VOs), and lifestyle (LSOs) offending.

In the next sections on the sequence of official offense mixes, four questions are investigated with Tables 3.9 and 3.10. (1) Can age-specific offense mixes be observed? (2) What are the difference between the onset and the offset offense mixes? (3) Is there a developmental sequence of offense mixes? (4) Are there similarities or dissimilarities between offense mixes of the 1960 and the 1980 generations?

Table 3.9 The qualitative development of male official offending for the 1960 generation: offense mixes

		Age of Onset					Age of Offset				
	Offense[1] Sever.[2]		Minim.	Median	Mean	Offense[1] Sever.[2]		Minim.	Max.	Median	Mean
Early maturity	Threats[3]	16	31	38	40	Motortheft[4]	11	14	56	17	18	*Early youth*
	Conspiracy		15	35	34	Public diso.	3	14	49	17	18	
	Rape	19	15	35	34	Larceny	10	13	54	22	24	
	Drug traffic	2	15	31	32	Breaking	13	13	59	23	25	
Late youth	Homicide[4]	20	17	27	31	Robbery[4]	17	15	36	23	23	*Middle Youth*
	Drugs posses.	1	14	26	28	Stolen goods	18	11	58	24	26	
	Physical agr[4]	18	12	26	29	Murder	5	18	39	25	26	
Middle youth	Murder[4]	21	18	25	25	Prostitution	15	16	33	25	25	
	Prostitution	15	16	25	25	Simple thef	1	9	60	26	28	
	Sexual agres[4]	18	15	25	30	Sexual aggr	18	18	51	26	31	
	Fraud[4]	7	14	23	26	Fraud	7	14	60	27	30	*Late Youth*
	Driving alco.	4	13	23	26	Arms, tool	5	15	59	27	29	
	Mischief[4]	6	9	23	25	Homicide	20	17	46	27	31	
Early youth	Arms, tools,	5	14	21	25	Mischief	6	13	50	28	29	
	Stolen goods[4]	8	11	21	24	Driving alc	6	23	61	29	30	
	Robbery[4]	17	15	20	21	Drug posse	1	14	59	32	33	
	Theft enter[4]	13	8	18	16	Physical ag	18	19	59	34	35	
Late adolescence	Motor theft[4]	11	12	17	16	Drug traff	2	15	59	35	35	*Early maturity*
	Larceny	10	10	17	20	Conspiracy		15	60	36	37	
	Simple theft	1	9	17	20	Rape	19	15	50	35	36	
	Public disord	3	10	16	17	Threats	16	32	56	39	40	
	Covert		8	16	18	Covert		12	60	29	30	
	Overt		10	19	23	Overt		13	59	34	35	
	Lifestyle		10	19	23	Lifestyle		13	60	33	33	
	Total		12	15	16	Total		13	60	37	26	

1. All the offenses categories are composed of convicted crimes of various level of seriousness.
2. The rank of the offenses seriousness base on the Canadian crime severity index from the less to the more serious.
3. The threats category was more clearly specifies in the revision of the Criminal code in the nineties and, particularily, all crimes against persons.
4. The Canadian Criminal Code distinguishes some levels of seriousness for all these categories of offense either in term of the monetary value, the nature of the physical harm or type of operandy.

Table 3.10 The qualitative development of officially offending males of the 1980 generation: offending mix: offense onset and offset

Age of Onset

	Offenses[1]	Sever.[2]	Minim. age	Median age	Mean age
Middle late youth	Murder	21	16	31	30
	Drugs poss.	1	15	22	25
	Driving alcohol	19	15	21	23
	Drug traffic	2	15	21	24
	Fraud	7	14	21	23
	Threats	16	13	21	23
Early youth	Prostitution	15	15	18	23
	Sexual aggress.	18	14	18	23
	Rape	19	13	18	19
	Mischief	6	12	18	20
	Conspiracy	4	12	18	18
Late adolescence	Public disorder	3	14	17	18
	Homicide	20	14	17	19
	Physical aggress	18	13	17	19
	Arms, tools,	5	13	17	18
	Theft breaking	13	12	17	18
	Simple theft	1	12	17	19
	Stolen goods	8	12	17	24
	Robbery	17	15	16	17
	Motor theft	11	13	16	17
	Laerceny	10	12	16	17
	Covert		12	16	17
	Overt		12	16	17
	Lifestyle		12	16	17
	Total		12	15	16

Age of Offset

	Offenses[1]	Sever.[2]	Minim. age	Maxim. age	Median age	Mean age
Late adolescence	Robbery	17	15	18	16	16
	Larceny	10	13	39	17	18
	Motor theft	11	13	37	17	17
	Public disorder	3	14	36	17	18
	Homicide	20	15	26	17	19
Early youth	Rape	19	13	33	18	19
	Sexual agress.	18	14	40	18	22
	Prostitution	15	15	39	18	23
	Stolen goods	8	12	41	19	21
	Theft breaking	8	13	42	20	22
	Arms, tools,	5	13	40	20	23
Middle youth	Conspiracy		13	41	20	21
	Mischief	6	13	42	21	23
	Physical agress.	6	13	43	22	25
	Simple theft	1	14	44	22	22
	Driving alcohol	19	16	41	22	25
	Drugs traffic	2	15	41	23	25
	Fraud	7	14	44	24	25
Late youth	Threats	16	13	42	27	27
	Drugs	1	15	44	28	28
	Murder	21	16	41	31	30
	Covert		12	44	22	24
	Overt		13	43	21	24
	Lifestyle		12	44	21	24
	Total		13	44	22	26

1. All the offenses categories are composed of convicted crimes of various level of seriousness.
2. The rank of the offenses seriousness base on the Canadian crime severity index from the less to the more serious.
3. The threats category was more clearly specifies in the revision of the Criminal code in the nineties and, particularly,
4. The Canadian Criminal Code distinguishes some levels of seriousness for all these categories of offense either in terms of the monetary value, physical harm or type of operandy.

3.5.1   The Sequence of Official Offense Mixes

Can age-specific offense mixes can be observed? Reading Table 3.9, the general conclusion is startling for the launch of the OOs. Each age period displays a particular mix of OOs that are begun and terminated and their hierarchy is very similar. A mix of five offenses is ordered with the median age at onset. (1) Half of the court males (median) were convicted during the end of adolescence and some of them were adjudicated during childhood (minimum age at onset column) for simple theft, personal larceny, public disorder, and motor vehicle theft. (2) During early youth, half of the males were involved in theft by breaking and entering, robberies of various kinds, buying and selling stolen goods, and using arms, tools, or a disguise; some of them initiated these offenses for the first time during late adolescence. (3) The third offense mix characterizes middle youth, it is composed of mischief, driving under the influence of drugs or alcohol, fraud, sexual aggression, participating in a prostitution market, and murder; in addition, some of them introduced the first four offenses during early adolescence and the last two during late adolescence. (4) Later, during late youth, the fourth offense mix was composed of physical aggression, drug possession, and homicide; for some of these convicted males the first two offenses were committed for the first time during early adolescence. (5) The last and fifth offense mix was initiated during the 30s, and is composed of soft drug trafficking, rape, conspiracy, and threats; the last three offenses were first initiated around age 15, but the medians were in the 30s, a sign of recidivism.

The OO was ended through four offense mixes, the right section of Table 3.9. (1) First, half of the adjudicated males stopped motor vehicle theft and public disorder at the end of adolescence and some a little earlier. However, the maximum age at offset for these offenses was in the 50s. (2) The second desisted offense mix, during middle youth, was composed of personal larceny, theft by breaking and entering, robbery, buying and selling stolen goods, murder, and participating in a prostitution market. Some offenders terminated these offenses during adolescence, whereas some offenses were not stopped until the 30s (robbery, murder, and participating in a prostitution market) or some not until the 50s (personal larceny, theft by breaking and entering, and buying and selling stolen goods). (3) The third offset offense mix was dropped during the end of youth; it was composed of the most numerous types of offenses: simple theft, sexual aggression, fraud, arms, tools and disguise, homicide, mischief, and driving under the influence of alcohol or drugs. For most of these offenses, it was during late youth (median) and for some offenders it was during adolescence. It is interesting to note, contrary to the previous mixes, that for most of these offenses the maximum age of conviction was in the 50s and even during the early 60s. (4) Finally, the last mix grouped as drug possession, physical aggression, drug trafficking, conspiracy, rape, and threats was ended during the 30s (medians), early maturity. Some of these offenses were terminated during adolescence, whereas for all of them the maximum age of conviction was at the end of the 50s.

In Table 3.9, some additional phenomena need to be mentioned. First, for every offense the gap between the medians and the means is in general 1 or 2 years; this indicates that the career of each offense is not far from normally distributed and rather short, even if the overall career span is rather long as calculated in in Chap. 2. Second, when the minimum ages at onset are compared with the median ages, the gap, for most of the offenses, is around 10 years. This may indicate that the OO may be composed of episodes. The analysis of trajectories will lighten that phenomenon. Third, the maximum ages at offset, for almost all 20 of the offenses and offending mixes, are in the 50s. This may be an indication that the criminal career is intermittent for whatever reason: incarceration, drug or alcohol treatment, adverse economic and marriage situations, health problems, etc.

What are the differences between the onset and the offset offense mixes? The onset offense mixes are less versatile than the offset mixes. In the first case, each mix is composed of around four offenses distributed over the five periods of life, whereas in the second case there are around five offenses in the mixes that are part of only four periods of life. In summary, the launching of the offending career is much more diffuse and slower, whereas its termination is more rapid and more types of offense are ceased at the same time. That observation is in concordance with the shape of the age–crime curves analyzed in Chap. 2.

In addition, some onset mixes are more focused on certain objects, for example, the late adolescence and the early youth mixes are more dominated by types of offenses against property, while later mixes contains more types of offenses against persons, an observation that has been recurrent in criminology since Quételet. This conclusion does not point to an age specialization in offense mixes because in later mixes offenses against property are replaced by lifestyle crimes such as participating in a prostitution market, drug trafficking, and possession. On the contrary, the offset mixes are more diversified in terms of the blending of offenses against property and persons. These observations let us think that convicted male offenders progressively construct their career and, later, they suddenly discontinue a good number of types of offenses at the same time. These conclusions are very similar to those formulated in Chap. 2 after the analysis of the age–crime curve for covert, overt, and lifestyle offenses.

Is there a developmental sequence of offense mixes? the content diversity of the onset and offset offense mixes notwithstanding, three noteworthy sequences are observable in Table 3.9. The first conclusion is that there is a clear hierarchy in the age sequence of the offense mixes. Each launching and ceasing period displays a particular set of offenses. This specificity manifests, first, by the fact that offense mixes initiated earlier in life are also those stopped earlier (for example, most of the forms of stealing) and the reverse is also true (for example, rape, threats, and drug trafficking).

The second conclusion concerns the content of the offense mixes, the usual hierarchy of property crimes followed by offenses against persons is clear. The onset mixes of late adolescence and early youth are dominated by offenses against property, whereas the offense mixes of later periods are dominated by offenses against persons (sexual and physical aggression, homicide and murder) and lifestyle behavior (drug possession, drug trafficking, participation in a prostitution market). For their part, the offset mixes follow a similar reverse pattern: the late adolescence and early and middle youth mixes are dominated by offenses against property, whereas the later offset mixes are composed of offenses against persons and lifestyle. In addition, there are common onset and offset sequences among the offenses against property and persons during the life periods. For example, among offenses against property, simple theft is initiated before, in order, theft by breaking and entering, robbery, and fraud, and, among offenses against persons, sexual and physical aggression appears before homicide, murder, and rape.

The last type of sequence of aggravation–deaggravation is the seriousness hierarchy of offense onsets and offsets. Before beginning the analysis, it is essential to remember the measure of seriousness for the mix of offenses used in Tables 3.9 and 3.10. First, it was impossible to grade all the OOs for which there was a conviction. In the available police file only the name of the convicted offenses was available. It would have been an enormous task to go back to all court files to code the level of physical and economic harm to victims such as in the Sellin and Wolfgang measure of seriousness. In addition, to our knowledge, a scoring system of the seriousness of a wide range of antisocial behaviors does not exist. Second, Statistic Canada (Wallace et al. 2009) developed and updated yearly a severity index, a classification of the seriousness of criminal offenses based on the incarceration rate and the length of prison sentences for each crime.

In Table 3.9, all the offense mixes are given a severity rank from 1 to 21. When there were some levels in a particular offense, for example, murder of first or second degree (many such offenses have a note beside their name in the tables), the chosen weight was the central value. It is of common knowledge in behavioral sciences that in general the early antisocial behaviors are less serious than the later ones. Two conclusions can be advanced from these foggy severity scores. First, these scores of the age periods of onsets increase. They are generally higher for the late youth and maturity periods than for the late adolescence and early youth periods. Second, it is the reverse for the offset data. The severity scores are lower for the late adolescence and middle youth period compared with the late youth and early maturity periods.

Even if these results may not be considered totally satisfactory because of this weak measure of seriousness, the aggravation–deaggravation hypothesis was sustained for the males of the court sample of the 1970s, with data for 14 self-reported OOs ranked using the Sellin and Wolfgang seriousness measure (Le Blanc and Fréchette 1989). In addition, there is an indirect confirmation with the longitudinal analysis, from childhood to the 40s, of self-reported crime perpetration data. The G60 males described their preparation, complicity, use of violence, tension, and motivation for each SRO. It was also observed that the motives for offenses perpetrated during childhood and adolescence were more hedonistic, whereas for youth offenses they were more utilitarian (Le Blanc 1996). In addition, Kazemian and Le Blanc (2004), with a career span from childhood to the 40s, identified two patterns of perpetration of crimes: the organized pattern was mainly characterized by a predominance of planning, use of instruments, utilitarian motives, and little co-offending; the disorganized pattern involved little preparation, more co-offenders, hedonism and thrill-seeking motives, and more use of alcohol and drugs before, during, and after the offense. In addition, the organized pattern of crime perpetration became more organized with age, whereas the disorganized pattern grows increasingly disorganized. These results do not indicate whether offenders become more or less organized with age; they rather suggest that the same pattern of offense perpetration tends to show increased (organized pattern) or declining (disorganized pattern) signs of organization at later ages in comparison with earlier stages of the offending career. In summary, there was an aggravation in the patterns of perpetration of offenses and five individual trajectories in performing OO. The greatest proportion of the males of the 1970s court sample adopted the trajectory from organized to disorganized offense patterns from adolescence to adulthood (40%). We would think that moving from property offenses to violent and lifestyle offenses would correspond to the evolution of the age–crime curves displayed in Chap. 2.

Are there similarities or dissimilarities between G60 and G80 offense mixes? When the age–crime curves of the two generations were compared in Chap. 2, their disparities were accounted for by changes in the law, particularly moving the age of criminal responsibility from age 8 to 12, and the introduction of less punitive policies in the adolescent and adult criminal justice systems, such as diversion from court and deinstitutionalization. The impacts of these changes are translated in Table 3.8. The offending mixes for G80 are less numerous at onset, three mixes instead of five, and at offset, three mixes instead of four for G60. The career span of G80 is more condensed because it starts later, age 11, and it is also truncated at 45. As a consequence, the offense mixes of this generation show a greater diversity; the offenders are much more versatile, the fact that no offending mix is specialized in offenses against property or persons notwithstanding. This conclusion supports the large volume of literature on that question (Mazerolle and McPhedran 2019).

In Table 3.10 most of the offenses of G90s began (median) during late adolescence, 10 of the 21 (6 are against property), and early youth, 9 out of 21 (4 lifestyle offenses and 2 sexual aggression). In the first case, 4 offenses were launched during late adolescence for the two generations (larceny, motor vehicle theft, simple theft, and public disorder) and the six others (robbery, buying and selling stolen goods, theft by breaking and entering, arms, tools, and disguise, physical aggression, and homicide) were initiated later for G60, during early youth. There are no significant resemblances for the offense mixes of the other periods of onset and offset. In addition, the blend of offenses against property and persons is greater for G80 regardless of the age period. The same phenomenon is observable concerning the offsets. In addition, all offenses were terminated at the end of the 30s for G80 in comparison with the 40 for G60. This conclusion may be explained by the fact that G80 follow-up was truncated at 45. When the comparison of OO mixes for G60 and G80 was performed on the same basis, a follow-up from age 12 to 45, the above observations were not modified (this table can be obtained from the author).

In Table 3.10, two previous conclusions are not clearly verified for G80. First, the progression from offenses against property to offenses against persons has disappeared inside the offense mixes. Second, each generation makes its own mix of offenses at each period of the life span. Changes in the laws and policies may explain these disparities, but some sociological changes may also be responsible for such evolution.

3.5.2   The Uplifting and Downlifting of the Sequence of Official Offense Mixes

Identifying the sequential specificity of the OO mixes is only the first step in the analysis of qualitative changes. It is essential to assess the flow of individuals along the sequential onset and offset mixes. To our knowledge, Le Blanc and Fréchette (1989) were the latest researchers to analyze the progression from a mix of adjudicated property crimes to a mix of convicted offenses against persons. They also investigated the up- and downlifting question with self-reported interview data on 14 official crimes graded by seriousness for G60. They concluded that 40% of the offenders moved from a mix of offenses against property to a combination of offenses against persons during adolescence or youth and between these two periods. As a consequence, 60% of the males maintained either a property or a person offense mix during their career from age 8 to 30. When the 14 self-reported official crimes were classified into five offense mixes, then regressions on the sequence of mixes accounted for 14%, stability for 16%, and progression for 70%. Let us see what happens when the sequences of the onset and offset offense mixes described from Table 3.10 are considered.

A court male was classified in the late adolescence onset offense mix if he was convicted of at least one of the four offenses in that combination during that period. This same procedure was followed for the early, middle, late youth, and early maturity onset offense mixes. It was the same for the offset offense mixes.

For the G60 males, 46% were members of only one onset offense mix during their career, 37% two, 13% three, 3% four, and 1% five. Let us remember that each mix is composed of at least four types of offenses. The analysis of upliftings by the comparison of adjacent mixes shows that only the late adolescence mix was statistically followed by the early youth mix ($X^2 = 7.99$; $p = 0.005$; Tau = 0.13; $p = 0.004$). However, the other adjacent sequences were not statistically confirmed (early to middle youth, middle to late youth, and late youth to early maturity). These upliftings seem to be more random. The high versatility of the offense mixes may explain these results.

The offset sequences of blend of offenses were less numerous (four versus five). Forty-one percent of the G90 males terminated their career by only one offset mix, two 32%, three 19%, and four 1%. Contrary to the onset upliftings, which are more often at random, the offset downliftings are statistically sequential. The late adolescence mix is followed by a middle youth mix ($X^2 = 3,33$; $p = 0.07$; Tau = 0.08; $p = 0.09$), the middle and the late youth mix succeed each other ($X^2 = 12.47$; $p = 0.000$; Tau = 0.16; $p = 0.002$) and, at last, the late youth mix is before the early maturity mix ($X^2 = 4.91$: $p = 0.03$; Tau = 0.10; $p = 0.04$).

In summary, in this section on qualitative changes in OO, it was established that age-specific offense mixes are observable at each period of the life span; that there was a sequence of offense mixes based on onset ages and a comparable one with the ages at offset; that the content of these sequences was very similar but in reverse order; the offenses that appeared earlier in the life of the convicted males are also those that disappeared earlier and the reverse was also illustrated for the later mixes. In addition, there was indication that the sequences were graded in terms of seriousness. However, even if these conclusions apply to the G60 and G80 males, the sequence for these latter offenders was more compacted; the offense mixes were composed of a greater diversity of offenses when they were launched and terminated. Versatility was the norm in all cases and generations.

In the analysis of OO, there are only behaviors that can be assimilated with Loeber's covert and overt developmental pathways. They are clearly observable in the escalation and aggravation courses and also in the de-escalation and deaggravation processes. However, the two categories of behaviors come in between each other among the less and the more serious behaviors.

3.6   The Qualitative Changes in the Self-Reported Antisocial Behavior Mixes

In this section, the previous conclusions on the qualitative mechanisms of the development of the OO and SRO will be tested with the data from the self-reported antisocial behavior career, from its initiation during childhood to the 30s with G1980. The tests will not be conducted with all the specific behaviors; they are to numerous (see Chap. 1 and Appendix B for the content of the 14 scales). The following scales were retained in the analysis of the quantitative changes: delinquent behavior (theft, motor vehicle theft, fraud, physical violence, and vandalism); and problem behavior (conflict with parents, intimates, in school and at work; sexual activity, drug use and trafficking, disorderly conduct, gambling, risky driving, and psychological violence). In the next two sections, first, the mixes of these scales will be sequenced on the periods of life, defined earlier on, based on their ages at onset and offset and, second, the up- and downlifting will be calculated on the observed sequences of initiation and cessation of SRAB.

As, to our knowledge, a method of gradation for all the types of SRAB that are measured in this book do not exist, a seriousness criterion to order all the SRABs could not be employed. Instead, the ages at onset and offset will permit the ordering of the SRAB scales. The age at onset is a legitimate criterion, even if this measure may be left censored by the age at the first interview. However, at the first interview, the questions were labeled with the adjective "ever" in the questionnaires. The age at offset, on the contrary, is right censored by the age at the last interview (the average age was 30 for the 1990s court adolescents). In addition, some scales are legally censored, for example, the age of legal responsibility is age 12 for this generation or the age of compulsory schooling is 16.

Table 3.11 Developmental sequence in male self-reported antisocial behavior for the 1980 generation: behavior onset, offset, and severity

Developmental stages	Age of onset[2]		Rank onset-offset		Age of offset[3]		Developmental stages of offset
	Conflict intimate[1]	24	15	1	Conflict school	17	Transition adolescence-youth
Youth trabsition	Conflict at work	18	14	2	Vandalism	18	
	Gambling	16	13	3	Conflict parents	19	
	Motor veh. theft	15	12	4	Psychol. violence	21	Early youth
Late adoles.	Risky driving	15	11	5	Physical violence	22	
	Fraud	14	10	6	Motor veh. theft	22	
	Phychol. volence	14	9	7	Theft	23	
	Disorderly conduct	14	8	8	Risky driving	23	
	Drug use & traffic	13	7	9	Fraud	23	
	Vandalism	13	6	10	Disorderly conduct	23	
Early adoles.	Sexual activity	13	5	11	Conflict at work	24	
	Theft	11	4	12	Gambling	24	
	Conflict parents	10	3	13	Drug use & traffic	25	
	Physical violence	10	2	14	Sexual activity	27	
Late childhood	Conflict school	9	1	15	Conflict intimate	31	Late Youth

1. This scale was measured for the first time at the third interview at an average age of 24; this scale and all others are right-hand censored at the last interview, around 30 years of age.
2. The ages of onset and offset are rounded average at 0,5.
3. These ages of offset are the oldest that were reported at time 2 (average 18), time 3 (average 24) or time 4 (average 30) interviews; it is not presume that these SRAB had definitively stopped.

3.6.1 The Sequence of Self-Reported Antisocial Behavior Mixes

Table 3.11 presents the qualitative changes in the SRAB mixes for the convicted males interviewed during the 1990s. The first column on the left and the last one on the right are divided into the periods of life that were defined earlier on. In the onset section, SRAB scales are listed according to their rounded median. The offset section on the right displays the same data. In between the two sections, the SRAB scales are ranked in order. In Table 3.11, the term youth transition is used in the hierarchies of onsets and offsets because it is in good part the same age group and the same period of human development. It is the turning point period in the development of SRAB.

In the onset section, the central column, the SRAB scales are ordered from 1, conflict in school, to 15, conflict with intimates. In the offset section, the central column, the scales are in reverse order from 1, conflict in school, to 15, conflict with intimates. It can be noted that there are some SRAB scales that start at the same age (conflict with parents and physical violence at age 10, sexual activity, drug use, and vandalism at age 13, disorderly conduct, psychological violence, and fraud at age 14, and motor vehicle theft and risky driving at age 15). Overall, for three of the six SRAB scales, their components start at the same age at onset (arousing: sex and drug use; strolling: vandalism and disorderly conduct; and exciting: motor vehicle theft and risky driving. For the other behavioral patterns, one of its components precedes the other: for conflict, at school before in the home; for covert, theft before fraud; for overt, physical before psychological violence.

The late childhood mix is composed of, in order, conflict at school, physical violence, conflict with parents, and theft, that was initiated between age 9 and 11. It is a large array of behaviors, lack of discipline in school and at home, fighting and threatening or overt behaviors, and theft or minor covert behavior. The next period, early adolescence, for ages 13 and 14, involves the introduction of six forms of SRAB: in order, sexual activity, vandalism, drug use, disorderly conduct, psychological violence, and fraud. This is the period of the greatest diversification of SRAB, six types compared with two, three, or four at the previous and next onset stages. Late adolescence is the moment to start more serious offending, motor vehicle theft and risky driving and an adult lifestyle behavior, gambling. Finally, youth transition is the time to begin more adult lifestyle SRABs, lack of discipline at work and conflict with a spouse.[4]

On the right-hand section of Table 3.11, the ages at offset column, the same scales are ranked from the earliest to the latest age of cessation. It is to be noted that these ranks are mostly the exact reverse of their rank for the ages at onset. As is noted for the onsets, cessation for some SRAB scales is simultaneous: physical violence and motor vehicle theft at age 22, theft, risky driving, fraud, and disorderly conduct at age 23, and conflict at work and gambling at age 24. Contrary to the results for the onsets of these behavioral mixes, only theft and fraud, covert behavior, stop at the same age. It can be concluded, from the ages at onset and offset columns, that there are modifications in the SRAB mix as age increases in the form of a reverse U shape, as antisocial behavior as in official crime.

Let us look at the stages of de-escalation in offset, the fact that offsets were truncated by the moment of the last interview, at an average age of 30, notwithstanding. The offset SRAB stages are less numerous, three, when there were four onset mixes. Two periods are clear and restrained in terms of SRAB mixes. First, the transition from adolescence to youth, from age 17 to 19, is composed mainly of forms of SRAB that were began early, lack of discipline at school and in home, and, in addition, a minor form of childish offense, vandalism. Second, the last stage, late youth, after age 25, manifests with SRAB scales that cannot be expected to have ceased definitively, sexual activity and conflict with the spouse. In between these two extreme periods, early youth appears to be the time to stop most of SRABs, 11 out

---

[4] The questions of this scale were introduced at the age 24 and 30 interviews. The same behaviors may have been practiced with a girlfriend during adolescence.

of 15. In order, first, physical and psychological violence and motor vehicle theft at age 22; second, theft, risky driving, fraud, and disorderly conduct at age 23; third, undisciplined at work and gambling at age 34, and last, drug use at age 25.

In summary, each developmental stage of aggravation and deaggravation on the sequences of onsets and offsets produces a particular SRAB mix. These mixes evolve from childhood types of behaviors, for example, lack of discipline in home and at school and minor theft, to more serious categories of SRAB behaviors, motor vehicle thefts and risk driving, and to adult lifestyle behaviors, conflict at work and with the spouse. Thereafter, these SRAB mixes are modified step by step during aggravation.

Again, the four conclusions of the analysis of the sequence of onsets and offsets of the OO and SRO are confirmed. They are age specific; the onsets of SRAB mixes are spread out over a longer length of time and more numerous than the offset mixes; an increased aggravation–disaggregation is observable; an SRAB behavior launched earlier disappeared faster.

3.6.2   The Uplifting and Downlifting on the Sequence of Self-Reported Antisocial Behavioral Mixes

The next question is how G90 males make their way along these hierarchical stages of SRAB mixes. The following procedure was employed to classify each court male according to his onsets or offsets on the SRAB mixes. First, if a person reported, at least, an age at onset before 12 on the first SRA mix, lack of discipline in school and at home, physical violence, or theft, he was declared a late childhood starter. If the male reported the onset of the next mix of behaviors but between age 12 and 14, he was identified as an early adolescence beginner, and so on. Second, to respond to the question about the paths used by the subjects along the developmental stages of uplifting and downlifting on the SRAB mixes, a step-by-step comparison was realized as an indication of switching; for example, comparing the late childhood SRAB mix with the early adolescence one, and so on, all the way for the other periods of life up to youth transition and then down to the late youth mix. Table 3.12 a, b, c, d, and e presents the switching with cross-tabulations.

Table 3.12a illustrates the transition from the childhood mix, that is, minor conflict with parents and teachers, minor aggression, and theft, and the early adolescence mix, which involves a diversity of SRAB, not necessarily very serious; that mix involves first sexual activity, drug use, vandalism, disorderly conduct, intimidation, and trickery. First, 51.4% of the males started their SRAB with the late childhood mix before age 12 and for 48.6% of them it was activated later, between age 12 and 14. Conversely, 10.6% of the boys initiated prematurely the early adolescence mix, before 12, and 70.2% at the anticipated ages, from 12 to 14, whereas only 12.7% delayed the introduction of this mix until ages 15 to 17. In addition, nearly half of the boys waited until 12 and 14 for the onset of the childhood mix, 48.6%, whereas 70.2% of the males started the early adolescence mix at the expected ages.

Table 3.12 Self-reported antisocial behavior mixes, switching from late childhood to late youth, court males of the generation of 1980

(a) SRAB mixes: changes from late childhood to early adolescence[a]						
SRAB	Late childhood mix					
Early adolescence mix	Before 12[b]		12–14		Total	
Before 12	21	8.6	5	2	26	10.6
12–14	89	36.3	83	33.9	172	70.2
15–17	16	6.5	31	12.7	47	19.2
Total	126	51.4	119	48.6	245	100

(b) SRAB mixes: changes from early to late adolescence[a]								
SRAB	Early adolescence mix							
Late adolescence mix	Before 12		12–14		15–17		Total	
12–14	21	8.8	85	35.6	8	8.3	114	47.7
15–17	4	1.7	66	27.6	27	11.3	97	40.6
After 17	1	0.4	16	6.7	11	4.6	28	11.7
Total	26	10.9	167	69.9	46	19.2	239	100

(c) SRAB mixes: changes from late adolescence to early youth[a]								
SRAB	Late adolescence mix							
Youth transition	12–14		15–17		After 17		Total	
15–17	82	24.2	54	15.9	12	3.5	148	43.7
After 17	101	29.8	59	17.4	31	9.1	191	56.3
Total	183	54	113	33.3	43	12.7	339	100

(d) SRAB mixes: changes from youth transition to early youth[a]						
SRAB	Youth transition mix					
Early youth mix	17–19		21–24		Total	
17–19	21	14.8	0	0	21	14.8
21–24	26	18.3	46	32.4	72	50.7
25–31	5	3.5	44	31	49	34.5
Total	52	36.6	90	63.4	142	100

(e) SRAB mixes: changes from early to late youth[a]								
SRAB	Early youth mix							
Late youth mix	17–19		21–24		After 25		Total	
17–19	30	12.3	0	0	0	0	30	12.3
21–24	15	6.2	64	26.3	7	2.9	86	35.4
After 25	0	0	59	24.3	68	28	117	52.3
Total	45	18.5	113	50.6	75	30.9	243	100

[a]All Chi-squared and measures of association are statistically significant at least at 0.05
[b]In each category the frequency is presented on the left and the percentage on the right

Second, inside the Table 3.12a, a few phenomena should be noted. The greatest number of boys (36.3%) uplifted from the childhood mix to the early adolescence mix; a few, 8.6%, were premature, starting the two mixes before 12. In addition, a few, 6.5%, were overdue as they initiated the childhood mix between 15 and 17 and some, 2%, downlifted as they inversed the childhood mix and the early adolescence mix. In summary, two main paths dominated the transition. First, the uplift path included 59% of the boys that moved from the childhood to the early adolescence mix and only 6.5% to the late adolescence one. Second, the existence of a simultaneous initiation of these two mixes should be noted, 42.5%.

Table 3.12b describes the switch from the early to late adolescence mixes, which is from a great diversity of forms of SRAB to more serious and exciting behaviors, such as motor vehicle theft and risky driving. As was noted previously, most of the males (69.9%) started with this mix between 12 and 14, but only 10.9% introduced this mix into their repertoire earlier during childhood, before 12, and 19.2% later, between 15 and 17. What is more interesting, is the fact that 47.7% of the boys began with that mix earlier, between 12 and 14, whereas a good number of males, 40.6%, did so at the anticipated ages of 15–17. Very few adopted that mix later, after age 17. In summary, two types of switch dominated the hierarchical transition from the early to the late adolescence mixes. First, two simultaneous transitions account for a good number of boys: 35.6% initiated the early and late adolescence mixes between 12 and 14 and 11.3% did the same between 15 and 17. Second, three uplifts are notable, particularly from early to late adolescence (27.6%), from early (8.3%) or late (4.6%) adolescence to youth transition. In addition, very few court males reversed their course; that is, starting the late adolescence mix before the early one (8.3%).

Fourth, the last introduction of a new mix is the youth transition one, that is, SRAB that are more characteristic of adult lifestyle behaviors, conflict at work or with a spouse (Table 3.12c). This initiation most often happened, as expected, after age 17 (56.3%), but frequently prematurely between 15 and 17 (43.7%). It was followed, in order, by the early (54%) and late (33.3%) adolescence mixes. These two mixes appeared simultaneously during late adolescence (15.9%) or after 17 (9.1%). The uplift from previous stages, early or late adolescence, accounted for 71.4% of the males' moves; it was the most significant proportion compared with all previous tables.

Let us look on the other side of Table 3.12, that is, the changes in the SRAB mixes during the three stages of offset. Tables 3.12d reports the downlift from the youth transition mix composed of forms of SRAB that were first initiated during the males' SRAB and Table 3.12e presents the stage of cessation of 10 out of 15 forms of SRAB. The offset of the youth transition mix is delayed between 21 and 24 (63.4%), rather than when expected, between 17 and 19 (36.6%). For its part, the early youth mix was initiated when it was anticipated by the males between 21 and 24, or later from 25 on (34.5%). In Table 3.12d, two switches are dominant, simultaneity of cessation, starting the two mixes at the same age between 17 and 19 (14.8%) and, most often, 21–24 (32.4%) as well as uplifting from the youth transition mix (21.8%), or, more frequently, from the early youth mix (31%).

The last step of downlifting on the hierarchy of mixes, from the early to the late youth mix, is described in Table 3.12e. The late youth mix downlifting ceased at the anticipated time, after the age of 25 (52.3%). However, sexual activity and conflict with a spouse may have not been reported at the last interview, but at a later interview it may be proven the contrary. It may be the same for alcohol and drug use and trafficking, gambling, conflict at work, and other behaviors that are often associated with the adult lifestyle. The late youth mix is more often ceased after 25 (52.3%) than earlier (35.4%), and less often before 21 (12.3%). Only two transitions are of interest because of the number of males adopting them. First, the simultaneous switches are highly dominant with 66.6% of the males, between 17 and 19 (12.3%), 21 and 24 (26.3%), or after 25 (28%). Second, the uplift switch from early to late youth accounts for only 24.3% of the active court males.

In summary, developmental stages of uplifting and downlifting on a set of SRAB mixes were identified in concomitance with stages of human development. This phenomenon was illustrated with measures of four stages of onset (late childhood, early and late adolescence, and youth transition) and three stages of offset (youth transition and early and late youth). Three conclusions emerged with the G90 males. (1) Most of them were switching to the adjacent stage, rarely jumping over the next stage, and even less often reversing to an earlier stage. (2) Many court males simultaneously initiated two adjacent SRAB mixes regardless of the comparisons in Table 3.11. This phenomenon was observed for the uplifting and downlifting. (3) The most impressive result is the sudden and massive collapse of 10 out of the 15 forms of SRAB in a short period, from age 21 to 25.

In this section on the qualitative changes in SRAB, the Loeber three developmental pathways can be pointed out. The authority conflict pathway began during late childhood with oppositions to parents and school authorities and progress to conflict with intimates and bosses during the youth transition period, whereas they disappear after the middle of youth. The overt pathway is initiated during childhood and diversified and aggravated during adolescence, with physical and psychological violence, and it disappears during the first half of youth. Finally, the covert path is introduced at age 11 with theft and aggravated with motor vehicle thefts and risky driving during late adolescence.

4 Conclusion

Thirty years ago Le Blanc and Fréchette paid attention to two developmental puzzles that were replaced on the criminological table in the landmark book on criminal careers by Blumstein et al. (1986). That is, the developmental mechanisms of quantitative changes, escalation–de-escalation, and qualitative changes, aggravation–deaggravation, during an official offending and antisocial behavior career. Since that time there have been rather few studies on these questions, as attested by recent reviews in the last handbook by Farrington et al. (2019).

In this chapter, a few steps were taken toward generalizations. First, the quantitative developmental mechanisms initially identified in samples of males who were representing the population and convicted males aged 8 to the early 20s were confirmed with more confidence, as a longer life span period was used and a replication with the G80 convicted males was performed. What is more interesting is that the results also apply to a vast array of antisocial behaviors. Criminology can consider the activation–deactivation phenomenon a significant generalization because it is confirmed for self-reported and official crime and self-reported antisocial behavior. The results confirm the action of the quantitative gears of activation, launching, diversification, explosion, and stabilization, and the mechanisms of deactivation, slackening, declivity, specialization, and vanishing. What is needed now is to test these generalizations in other communities and countries, and in females.

Second, in the sections on qualitative developmental changes on OO, SRO, and SRAB, it was established that age-specific offenses and mixes are observable at each period of the life span; that there was a sequence of offense mixes based on the age at onset and a comparable one based on the ages at offset; that the content of these sequences was very similar but in reverse order; the offenses and the antisocial behaviors that appeared earlier in the life of the convicted males were also those that disappeared earlier. In addition, there was indication that the sequences were graded in terms of seriousness.

However, even if these conclusions apply to the 1960 and 1980 generations of convicted males, the sequence for these last offenders was more compacted; the offenses and SRAB mixes were composed of a greater diversity of offenses when they were launched and terminated. Versatility was the norm in all cases. Most of the aggravation and deaggravation switching was to the adjacent stage, rarely jumping over the next stage, and even less often reversing to an earlier stage. Many males initiated simultaneously two adjacent mixes of forms of SRABs. This phenomenon was observed for the uplifting and downlifting. The most impressive result is the sudden and massive collapse of 10 out of the 15 forms of SRAB in a short period, from age 21 to 25. The aggravation-disaggregation mechanisms still have to be tested with an improve measured of seriousness, in other communities and countries, and females. Concerning Loeber's three developmental pathways, which were hidden beneath hierarchical sequences of official crime, self-reported offending, and self-reported antisocial behavior, they have to be considered interdependently instead of autonomously.

In summary, if replications of the developmental processes exposed in this chapter are still to be conducted, the escalation–de-escalation and aggravation–deaggravation results are very solid as they apply to data from three independent measurement procedures: the official register of crimes, self-reported data from interviews on the perpetration of crimes, and self-reported data on a vast diversity of antisocial behaviors.

Chapter 4
The Antisocial Behavior and Crime Autodynamic, a System View

1 Introduction

Criminology is well equipped to measure antisocial behavior and crime (ABC) with official and self-reported instruments, to describe their epidemiology, and to identify the developmental mechanism that produces their course as detailed in the previous chapters.

Alfred Blumstein was trained in operational research and he imported system morphology and methodology into criminology. He led the Task Force on Science and Technology of the President's Commission on Law Enforcement and Administration of Justice (Blumstein 1967) that produced the first system analysis flowchart of criminal justice. In 1972, I had the honor of translating one of his papers on criminal justice as a system for a French book (Le Blanc and Blumstein 1972). His morphological view became the foundation of the MTSFGCLS conception of behavioral development and the organization of causal factors. Drawing from the system perspective, the developmental perspective in psychology and the chaos–order paradigm in hard science, Le Blanc integrated progressively their methodological principles (Le Blanc and Janosz 1998) into social and self-control theory (Le Blanc 1997, 2006, 2019), the development of offending (Le Blanc and Fréchette 1989; Le Blanc 2009), and it was proposed that it should be applied to all forms of antisocial behavior and crime (Le Blanc 2015).

In this chapter, ABC is defined as a self-regulating phenomenon. It is conceived as a closed system that is *"partly"* autonomous in its development as it is postulated, *"all other things are remaining equal outside of that system."* However, ABC, official or self-reported, has never been studied as a self-organizing phenomenon and existing theoretical and empirical knowledge in criminology have proposed no instrument to describe its autodynamic, its systemic developmental process.

M. Le Blanc, *The Development of Antisocial Behavior and Crime*, https://doi.org/10.1007/978-3-030-68429-7_4

2   System Functioning, Principles, and Empirical Explorations

The system action is characterized with the help of nine consensual axioms, and some of the MTSFGCLS empirical explorations with crime are reported.

2.1   Theoretical Developmental Axioms of System Action

A system, in computer science, is a set of *"function compositions or mechanisms"* (for example, the relationship between onset and variety and all others that were established in Chap. 3) and these *"simple functions are combined to build more complicated ones."* And, as in mathematics, *"each function is passed as the argument of the next, and the result of the last one is the result of the whole"* (en.wikipedia.org/wiki/Software composition). There are nine theoretical statements about the development of any forms of antisocial behavior that were adapted to crime.

1. From developmental psychology (Lerner 1986), it is retained that the level of ABC of an individual is specific to a particular time and space. This is the axiom of *contextuality* for every sociological and psychological phenomenon. In this chapter, this axiom is tested for generations, types of sample, and forms of ABC.
2. In addition, it could be stated that changes in one type of ABC will affect changes in any other types, as noted in Chap. 2, particularly the age–crime curves. There is a *coevolution* of the changes at the various layers of the ABC domain (for example, covert, overt, authority conflict, and lifestyle behaviors or property and violent crimes).
3. The fundamental developmental course reflects the *orthogenic principle*. This is the increase in complexity that can be represented by the quantitative, escalation and de-escalation, and qualitative changes, aggravation and deaggravation, as described in Chap. 3. However, some criminologists still dispute the application of that principle to the development of individual criminal activity. They would argue that crimes are committed mostly at random, whereas developmentalists claim that there are developmental stages of offending, that is, the increased seriousness and diversity of ABC mixes.
4. The evolution toward more complexity is governed by two principles: sensitivity to the initial condition and probabilistic epigenesis. Criminologists report *the sensitivity to the initial condition* when they demonstrate that past criminal activity explains in part subsequent offending. The impact of the initial ABC is also represented in the vast body of literature on the importance of the age at onset (Le Blanc and Loeber 1998; Doherty and Bacon 2019) and the results in Chap. 3. The initial condition is referred to as the " Butterfly effect " in the chaos–order paradigm (Gleick 1987); he gives the example of the airflow from a butterfly in part of the world that becomes a storm in another part of the world.

5. The principle of *probabilistic epigenesis* states that there are some normative developmental stages, but that the outcome of individual behavioral development is only probable, never certain. This axiom is illustrated in reviews of individual antisocial behavior and crime (Loeber and Le Blanc 1990; Le Blanc and Loeber 1998; DeLisi 2015; chapters 3, 4, 5, and 6 in Farrington et al. 2019). Some individuals pass through all stages, some will not; some individuals will start at the initial stage and some at later ones. Developmental ABC sequences are hierarchic rather than embryonic, as shown in Chap. 3.

6. The development is *interactional*, as proposed by many criminologists (for example: Thornberry 1987; Le Blanc 2009) and developmentalists in psychology (Lerner 1986). The interactions can take various forms. (1) The reciprocal interdependencies among types of ABC at a specific point in time; (2) the causal relationships between types of ABC over time, such that behaviors that will become alternatively independent and dependent variables; (3) the state dependencies or direct continuity for each manifestation of ABC.

7. The system methodology recognizes that all systems *are open, complex, fractal, self-organized, preserver of energy, structured randomness, nonlinear, and with inner rhythms* (Gleick 1987; Briggs and Peat 1989). These notions are adopted in developmental psychology (Lerner 1986) and the author imported them into developmental criminology (Le Blanc and Janosz 1998).

8. In hard science, *chaos* refers to a relative state of disorder, uncertainty, nonlinearity, and unpredictability. However, the confusion that is involved with a chaos state is that it is never pure randomness or chance. In a chaotic state, according to Peak and Frame (1994), *"statements clarifying the limits and likelihood of future behaviors can still be made for a chaotic process."* (p. 158). With this meaning of the concept of chaos in mind, it can be specified that ABC will be in a state of chaos when there is a low probability of committing all types of ABC; as a consequence there is a high level of uncertainty about which ABC will follow the previous one. This situation is common in the hierarchical domain of ABC during late adolescence, when the behavioral syndrome of ABC attains its peak.

9. The last axiom is the *self-organization* of systems of living and human beings. It is a basic principle of developmental theories in psychology (Lerner 1986). Developmentalists recognize the importance of this process when they state that the individual is active in his development. The individual gives form to his experience by activating or deactivating the action of environments. Self-organization, according to Abraham (1995), means that human beings:

> … can control their own control parameters, giving them the capability to make bifurcations within their own dynamical schemes and complex dynamical systems. Sentient beings can thus learn their own response diagrams, so to speak, can learn to navigate them, and can imagine extrapolations of those diagrams and test a new universe of self (p. 41)

This principle, or an example in the marihuana use subsystem, implies that individuals can modify the parameters of use by altering the quantity, the nature of the substance, etc. Individuals are not obliged to try marihuana even if they drink alcohol and smoke cigarettes; possible bifurcations are possible in their drug use system. Individuals can learn from their experience, they can stop using acid after a particularly bad trip. Developmentalists also accept that these characteristics of development are integrated into the analysis of behavior, particularly by the theoretical and empirical behaviorism approaches (Lerner 1986).

2.2   The MTSFGCLS Empirical Explorations

Le Blanc and Fréchette (1989) had the intuition to draw a system model of crime (Figs. 5.8 and 5.9). Age at onset was the initial condition; participation, variety, and frequency were active developmental parameters; and age at termination was the dependent variable. It was observed that these variables entertained statistically significant simple and partial correlations between each other. No statistical model testing, such as path analysis, was applied until 10 years later.

Le Blanc (2009), using longitudinal data from the G60 sample of court males on self-reported offenses (SRO) and drug use (these measures are described in Appendix B), tested a theoretical model that operationalized the previous developmental axioms. Figure 4.1 is limited to the statistical empirical relations between crime and drug use from ages 15 to 40. In such a model, there are launching, contemporary, and causal effects between SRO and drug use. The launching effects, the association between the age at onset with the subsequent measures of SRO and drug use, are the equivalent of the impact of the initial condition. The contemporaneous

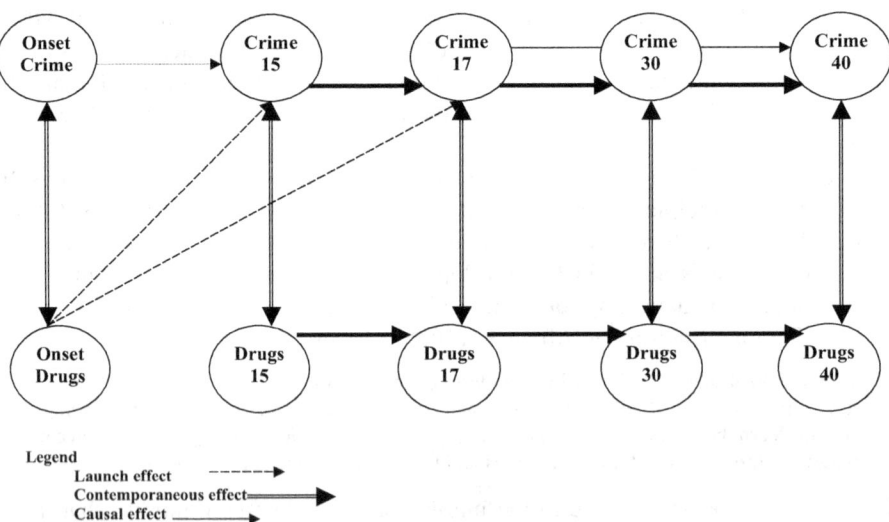

Fig. 4.1 The autodynamic of antisocial behavior and crime: an empirical system view of self-reported crime and drug use for the sample of court males of the 1960 generation

effects are the correlations between the two variables at each point in time, ages 15, 17, 30, and 40. The causal effects take two forms. First, it is the continuity in SRO or drug use; that is the case when the same behavior, SRO or drug use, is significantly related at adjacent or subsequent times. The second form of continuity is the correlation between SRO at a particular time and drug use at a subsequent time and the reverse. The final results of a longitudinal path analysis are displayed in the bottom part of Fig. 4.1; it is the empirical system model of SRO and drug use.

A few observations from Fig. 4.1 become a hypothesis for further investigations with ABC as an autodynamic system. (1) Contemporaneous effects should be expected at each period of life, even for the initial conditions of the onset of the forms of ABC. (2) Continuity in behavior over time should be awaited; it may more often take the form of an association between two adjacent times, but it may also involve many continuous times. (3) The anticipated general impact of the initial condition, onset, may not be observed across all forms of ABC. (4) As the onset of drug use correlated with the first two levels of crime, at ages 15 and 17, and that it was not the case for the association between the onset of SRO and the following levels of drug use, this kind of result is not expected to be replicated with other forms of ABC.

Having in mind these exploratory results and that there are, to our knowledge, no other publications in criminology with a system view of the development of ABC, let us go back to the basic themes of this book, the replication of results to formulate generalizations. The following questions will be investigated. Is the system model of crime similar for the two generations, 1960 and 1980? Is the system model comparable for forms of crime (covert, overt, lifestyle)? What are the characteristics of the global system model of ABC? Is this system model comparable for all forms of ABC?

3   The Crime System Autodynamic

The crime system is represented by the five parameters that were used in previous chapters: age at onset, participation (the number of years an offender is active during a time period), variety (the number of different offenses an offender was convicted for), frequency (the number of times offenses are repeated), and duration or career span (the number of years the career, or offset minus onset), the dependent variable.[1] Path analyses were computed using the Mplus package (Muthén and Muthén 2007).

---

[1] The model was also tested with age at offset as the dependent variable. The duration and offset path analysis results were similar and the correlations between these variables were higher (0.90).

3.1   A Global Look at the Crime System

Figure 4.2 presents the global crime model proposed by Le Blanc and Fréchette (1989). On each link between the parameters, a letter indicates nine statistical associations that will be commented on. Table 4.1 lists the results from the path analysis with the males of the two generations, the global crime system and its subsystems (covert, overt, and lifestyle crimes). The rows in the left-hand column indicate the analyses that were conducted: by generations and forms of crime. The next three columns display the three usual fit indicators (the left value is the minimum accepted level and the right one the more severe criteria) and their statistical significance: Chi-squared ($X^2 < 0.05$), root mean square error approximation (RMSEA: <0.08 and more severe 0.05), and the Comparative Fit Index (CFI: 0.90 >more severe 0.95). The last column on the right presents the level of explained variance for each parameter and a letter that refers to direct links between parameters that were not statistically significant.[2]

The first two lines offer a comparison of the global crime system of the two generations. In each case, the fit data respect the most severe criteria. In addition, a link in Fig. 4.2 was removable, g; the early onset does not increase the frequency level and the only indirect link that remained statistically significant was that a higher crime frequency was associated with a higher variety and a longer duration. However, the explained variance differed between the two generations 20 years apart. For G60 males, the duration explained that the variance was lower, 45% compared with 71% for G80, but the follow-up was longer (age 8–61 versus 12–45). Maybe the truncated effect mentioned in Chap. 2 is still manifested here. Whatever the impact of this difference, the similarity of crime system functioning stands, even if offending is more concentrated on a shorter period for G80. On the contrary, the

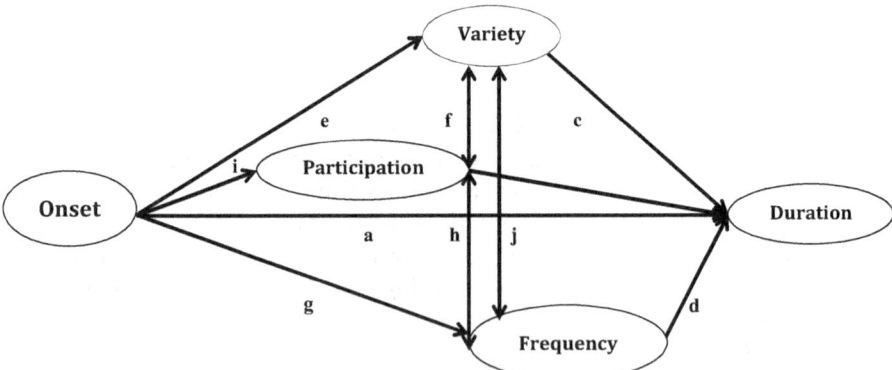

Fig. 4.2 The crime system for the males of the generations of 1960 and 1980, total system and subsystems for covert, overt, and lifestyle offenses

---

[2] All the statistics, particularly the direct and indirect correlations and the statistical significances in all the analyses, are available from the author.

Table 4.1 The males' global crime system, path analysis with onset, participation, variety, frequency, and duration by the 1960 and 1980 generations and types of offenses (covert, overt, and lifestyle)

Analysis	X^2 < 0.05	RMSEA < 0.08 (0.05)[b]	CFI > 0.90 (0.95)[b]	Explained variance %	
1960 generation total career	0.22[a]	0.00	1	Participation[c] Variety Frequency Duration Remove[d]	14 72 57 45 g
1980 generation total career	0.09	0.06	1	Participation Variety Frequency Duration Remove[d]	6 67 66 71 g
1960 generation covert	0.37	0.01	1	Participation Variety Frequency Duration Remove[d]	10 59 52 47 d, g, j
1980 generation covert	0.36	0.01	1	Participation Variety Frequency Duration Remove	5 54 64 64 g, j
1960 generation overt	0.06	0.07	0.99	Participation Variety Frequency Duration Remove[d]	16 64 47 53 c, e, g
1980 generation overt	0.20	0.03	1	Participation Variety Frequency Duration Remove[d]	5 45 62 64 c, d, g
1960 generation lifestyle	0.87	0.00	1	Participation Variety Frequency Duration Remove[d]	17 65 77 53 d, g
1980 generation lifestyle	0.87	0.00	1	Participation Variety Frequency Duration Remove[d]	17 65 77 53 d, g
1960 generation covert, overt, and lifestyle	0.00	0.04	0.99	Table 4.2	

(continued)

Table 4.1 (continued)

Analysis	X² < 0.05	RMSEA < 0.08 (0.05)ᵇ	CFI > 0.90 (0.95)ᵇ	Explained variance %
1980 generation covert, overt, and lifestyle	0.00	0.06	0.97	Table 4.2

ᵃThe Chi-squared level of statistical significance; the minimum accepted is at least $p = 0.05$
ᵇThe left value is the minimum accepted and the right one the more severe criteria
ᶜThe four variables in the model: participation (number of years), variety (number of different offenses), frequency (number of times convicted), and duration (the career span: offset minus onset)
ᵈThe letters represent a link that was removed from the model because it was not statistically significant, for example "g" indicates that the correlation between onset and frequency was removed from the calculation of the path analysis

Table 4.2 The global crime system, proportion of variance for onset, participation, variety, frequency, and duration for the males of the G60 and G80 generations and by type of crime

	Participation			Variety			Frequency			Duration		
1960 generation total career	14			62			57			45		
1980 generation total career	6			67			66			61		
1960 generation covert	10			59			52			47		
1980 generation covert	5			54			64			64		
1960 generation overt	16			64			47			53		
1980 generation overt	5			45			62			64		
1960 generation lifestyle	17			65			47			53		
1980 generation lifestyle	14			72			57			45		
1960 generation covert, overt, and lifestyle	14	16	18	59	64	65	53	47	67	51	55	52
1980 generation covert, overt, and lifestyle	6	5	5	54	46	62	65	62	61	63	62	64

frequency variance was higher for G80, 66% vs. 57%, and it was the reverse for variety, 67–72%. In sum, the fit results of the global crime system are replicated for two generations of convicted males 20 years apart; even if there were, during that period, very important improvements in the laws, criminal justice policies, and sociological indicators for Québec (see Appendix C).

When the subsystems of covert, overt, and lifestyle crimes are considered, the model fit results are still totally satisfactory for two of its three indicators: RMSEA and CFI, whereas Chi-squared values were not statistically significant. The explained variance of duration for types of offenses is in the low 50s as it was for the global system. In Table 4.1, the variety and frequency parameters alternated to the second or third position, but frequency attained a higher level for lifestyle crimes. In addition, there is another similarity between the total system and the subsystem. First, the g link, from onset to frequency, could be removed because it was not statistically significant. Second, some other direct relations were removable from the model; they are indicated by a letter in Table 4.1; it was most often the link d, from frequency to duration, and more rarely the correlation c, variety to duration, and j, the reciprocal link between variety and frequency.

The overall results in Table 4.1 confirm that the global crime system and its three subsystems regulate the flow of offending in a very similar way, particularly through the central interactions between the parameters of onset and variety. An earlier onset associated with a greater variety sustains a longer duration. The results in Table 4.1 confirm four of the above axioms of the system perspective: (1) the contextuality of the crime systems regardless the particularities for each generation and type of crimes; (2) the fractal nature of the global crime system because of similar results for the subsystems: covert, overt, and lifestyle; (3) the impact of the initial condition because of the launching role of onset; and (4) the self-organization because the fits of the crime system and subsystems were good and, particularly, because the levels of explained variance of the career span were 50% and 60%; these figures are high in social science and criminology.

Let us conclude the analyses of the global crime system with the interactions between the three subsystems by types of offenses. In Fig. 4.1, there are two layers, crime and drugs, that represent the global ABC system. Let us imagine that Fig. 4.2 is composed of three layers, the covert, overt, and lifestyle subsystems. In addition, there would be arrows between all parameters of each layer with all the parameters of the other two layers. Drawing and reading all the arrows of such a complex multilayered model would be extremely difficult. The path analysis results of the tridimensional crime system are presented in the last two rows in Table 4.1. The fit results are very satisfactory for its three indicators and the two generations. Printing all the figures for all direct and indirect links between the 15 parameters would cover many pages.[3] Let us make a presentation of the most interesting features of this complex tridimensional and fractal crime system. In the G60 system, 62% of the 68 correlations are statistically significant compared with 40% for G80. These associations, except for a few of them, are between the same variables for the two generations.

First, the three onset measures are significantly and positively associated with each other and negatively with their measures of duration, whereas these last parameters also correlate significantly between each other. However, there are no cross-over correlations between the onset of a subsystem and the duration of the other two systems. In summary, the activation process is internal, the early onset in a subsystem produces a higher level of participation, variety, frequency, and duration in this subsystem, and it is only partly external because the onset in a subsystem reinforces the role of onset in other subsystems without any direct influence on the levels of most of the parameters in other subsystems.

Second, the contemporary correlations identified earlier are also maintained in each subsystem. The participation parameters of the three subsystems are statistically associated with each other and with their measures of variety, frequency, and duration. However, they display no correlation with the other parameters of another subsystem, for example, the participation in the covert subsystem is not associated with the levels of frequency, variety, and duration in the overt and lifestyle

---

[3] All these results can be obtained from the author.

subsystems. The subsystem parameters seem to reinforce each other internally without stimulating other parameters in other subsystems. Crossover between systems does not exist, that is, for example, from participation in covert to variety in overt crime.

Third, generally the onset in a subsystem, for example, covert, is not associated with any of the parameters of the overt and lifestyle subsystems. It appears that the output of a subsystem, duration, is internally produced.

These three observations are confirming two other axioms of the system functioning. First, coevolution is parallel between the covert, overt, and lifestyle subsystems because of the internal relations between the parameters and the impacts of the intersubsystem are non-existent. Second, the global crime system matched itself to the orthogenic axiom; the global crime system is a complex integration of the interacting subsystems.

Table 4.2 lists the explained variance for the global crime system (rows one and two), its subsystems (rows three to eight), and the complex multilayered system (rows nine and ten); all these data are reported by generations. They confirm, first, the contextuality of the functioning of the global crime system because the values are most often higher for G80 in all its rows and they also vary by form of crime. Second, the multilayered system is a little more efficient than the global system but not by much (the last two rows compared with the first two rows). For example, the explained variance of duration is 45% for the G60 system and 52% for the multilayered system. For G80, it is 61% compared with 64%. All other comparisons between the global system, the subsystems, and the complex systems are within a similar range. Two questions need to be investigated in light of this section on the global crime system. Can these conclusions be confirmed with longitudinal data? Particularly, can the launching, continuity, and desistence phenomena be observed in the systems and subsystems?

3.2   A Longitudinal Look at the Crime System

The career span of each generation was initially divided into nine periods and preliminary path analysis of the crime system showed that these analyses were statistically inappropriate because of an extremely large number of criminal career descriptors (45) and the relatively small number of offenders in some life course periods such as childhood (8–11), early (30–39) and middle maturity (40–49), and, particularly, late maturity (50–61). These conditions caused insufficient power to estimate path analysis models. The nine periods were then divided into three. (1) The first period is childhood and adolescence, from ages 8 to 17 for G60 and from 12 to 17 for G80. (2) The second phase is youth, from ages 18 to 29 for the two generations. (3) The third period is maturity, from ages 30 to 61 for G60 and to 45 for G80. The criminal career parameters (participation, variety, and frequency) were calculated as the mean for each period. The resulting crime and subsystems models were still complex. As a consequence, they are not drawn because Fig. 4.2 would be

Table 4.3 The male crime system, longitudinal path analysis with onset, participation, variety, frequency, and duration by generations and types of crimes

Analysis	X^2 < 0.05	RMSEA < −0.08 (0.05)[b]	CFI > 0.90 (0.95)[b]	Explained variance %		Adolescence[c]	Youth[c]	Maturity[c]
1960 generation total career[a]	0.000[a]	0.000	1	Participation		29	18	14
				Variety		80	87	87
				Frequency		61	59	83
				Duration				59
1980 generation total career	0.000	0.000	1	Participation		46	14	33
				Variety		69	86	90
				Frequency		81	77	68
				Duration				74
1960 generation covert	0.000	0.000	1	Participation		31	15	15
				Variety		85	90	92
				Frequency		55	52	73
				Duration				58
1980 generation covert	0.000	0.000	1	Participation		53	19	25
				Variety		82	88	92
				Frequency		81	75	57
				Duration				69
1960 generation overt	0.000	0.000	1	Participation		29	26	13
				Variety		87	88	82
				Frequency		67	65	63
				Duration				63
1980 generation overt	0.000	0.000	1	Participation		43	7	27
				Variety		82	88	94
				Frequency		70	78	88
				Duration				72
1960 generation lifestyle	0.000	0.000	1	Participation		23	28	12
				Variety		91	93	92
				Frequency		66	84	88
				Duration				63
1980 generation lifestyle	0.000	0.000	1	Participation		38	10	26
				Variety		86	70	85
				Frequency		87	65	83
				Duration				70
1960 generation covert, overt, and lifestyle	0.007	0.04	0.99		Covert	Overt	Lifestyle	
				Participation	14	16	19	
				Variety	59	64	65	
				Frequency	53	47	77	
				Duration	51	55	52	
1980 generation covert, overt, and lifestyle	0.000	0.06	0.97	Participation	6	5	5	
				Variety	54	46	62	
				Frequency	65	62	71	
				Duration	63	62	64	

[a]The Chi-squared level of statistical significance; the minimum accepted is at least $p = 0.05$
[b]The left value is the minimum accepted and the right value the more severe criteria
[c]The nine life periods are regrouped into three. For the 1960 generation, the periods are childhood and adolescence, from 8 to 17, youth from 18 to 29, and maturity from 30 to the 60s. For the 1980 generation, the periods are adolescence from 12 to 17, youth from 18 to 29, and maturity from 30 to 45

expanded with two sequential sets if the variables and all the links in between all the parameters over time. Table 4.3 displays the path results by generations, for the total career, and for the forms of crimes (the list of all the statistics for all the links would cover many pages; it can obtained from the author).

The fit results for the longitudinal career, the three forms of crime, and the two generations are all highly statistically significant (X^2, RMSEA, CFI). The right-hand section of Table 4.3 presents the explained variance results for participation, variety, frequency, and duration by periods of the life course. Reading the list of percentages, it becomes immediately clear that the lowest percentages of variance are observed for participation and the highest for variety, and this is the case regardless of the period, adolescence, youth, and maturity, and the object, total, covert, overt, and lifestyle crimes. It should also be noted that the variance results are higher for G80 than for G60 and it is also the case for the three forms of crime. This observation, in the case of duration, the dependent variable, takes the form of an advantage of around ten points for G80 over G60 and for all measures of crime. Can these results reflect the fact that the official crime data of G80 are truncated at the two extremes; the career starts legally at age 12 instead of 8 and is terminated at age 45 instead of 61 for the G60 convicted males? All these results of the longitudinal analysis confirm the above global results in Sect. 0. Previously, it was stated that in a longitudinal crime system there are five types of links between the parameters: the launching, contemporary, continuity, causal relations, and withdrawal.

1. The launching gear, the impact of onset on participation, variety, frequency, and duration that were identified in Chap. 3 are also observed in the path results. The onset is associated with the level of participation and degree of variety during adolescence, youth, and maturity, and the length of duration for G60. Such a generalized impact of onset on all parameters of the criminal career is not present for the G80 males. Only the level of participation and variety during adolescence are propelles, whereas variety during maturity and duration are sustained by onset. For the males of the two generations, the frequency during adolescence is not launched. It is difficult to explain the dissimilarities in the launching gear between the generations. One possibility would be the lower variability of the onset variable for G80 males; many of them only begin during early adolescence, whereas a good number of G60 subjects start between ages 8 and 12.

2. The contemporary relations, the associations between participation and variety and variety and frequency, at each point in time, are similar for G60 and G80 in Fig. 4.3. However, participation and frequency are not significantly related. These results mean that the level of participation at an age period is associated with the degree of variety at the same time and this one is correlated with the level of frequency regardless of the period. These associations at each period of the career constitute the heart of the functioning of the crime system.

3. Continuity in the career was expected to manifest in three ways. First, it was anticipated in the form of the association between the same parameter at adjacent points in time. It is never the case for the level of frequency of the two genera-

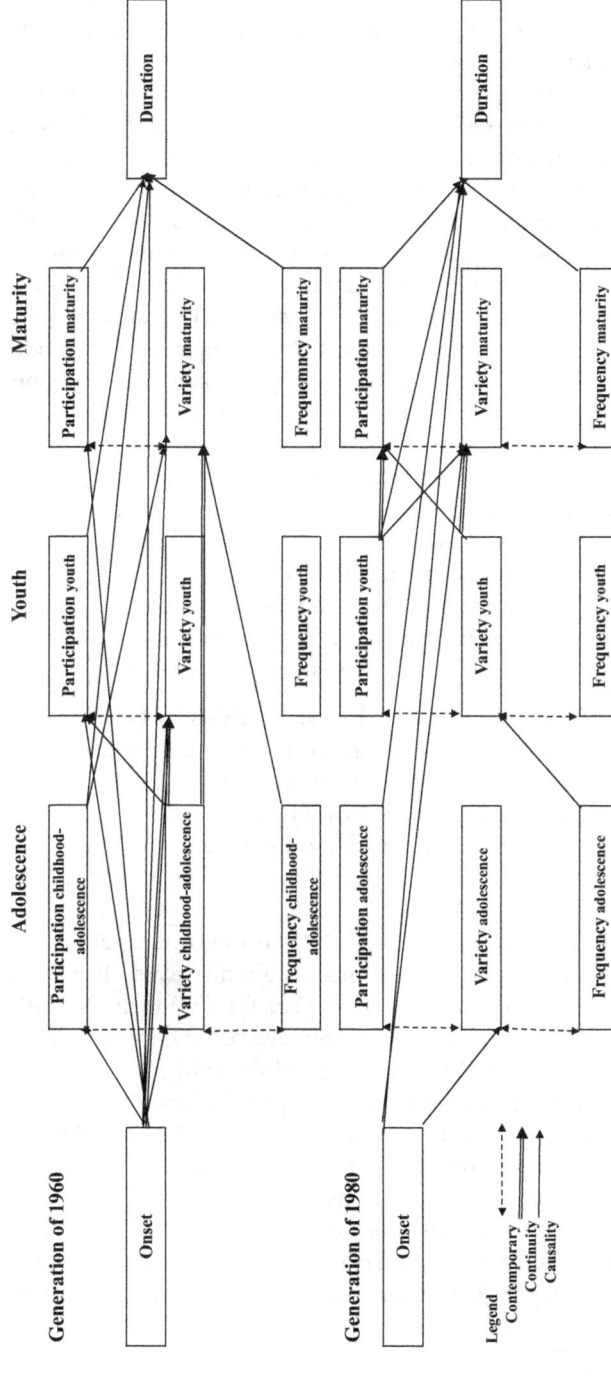

Fig. 4.3 The males' official offending system, longitudinal path analysis for the 1960 and 1980 generations

tions. It is the case for the G80 variety during adolescence, youth, and maturity. It is also observable between G60 variety during youth and maturity. The variety of offending manifests as the principal support of the criminal career. Second, it was believed that an early onset was a condition that favored continuity; it is partly the case, as the age at onset predicts the participation and variety during youth and adulthood for G60. In the case of G80, its impact is important later for the level of participation and variety during maturity. Third, it was expected that an early age at onset was significantly associated with the length of the career; this was a supplementary keep push for its duration for G60 and G80.

4. Causal relationships were awaited in the hub of the crime system, between the parameters of adolescence, youth, and maturity. For G80, the causal associations between participation and variety are present from youth to maturity; there is only one between adolescence and youth, from frequency during adolescence to variety during youth. For G60, there is only one causal association between a high frequency during childhood and adolescence and variety during maturity. Causal impacts are also observed for the two generations between a high participation and frequency during maturity and a short duration. Regardless of all specific launching, contemporary, and causal associations, the career will continue if a male had an early onset and if he was active for a greater number of years and had many convictions during maturity.

5. Finally, for the two generations, the withdrawal from the crime career will happen early if the onset was late and participation rare during the career span, and, particularly, if the level of frequency was low during maturity.

Table 4.3 also report the results of the path analysis by types of crimes, covert, overt, and lifestyle. The fit indicators are also statistically significant. In addition, the above observations for each generation were the same for the three types of crimes of each generation.[4] The only dissimilarity is that the initial push from the early onset of lifestyle crimes involves not only participation and variety, but also frequency. Everything else in the generational models is part of the forms of crime models.

Finally, in the last two rows of Table 4.3, the results of the path analysis with the longitudinal multilayered generational models are displayed. The fit data are very satisfactory. The explained variances are higher for G60 than for G80 concerning participation, variety, and frequency. It is the reverse for duration. This figure replicates the above cross-sectional results for the global crime model.

The launching gear is propelles by links that are the same as in the global model. The continuity is articulated around the level of variety. The causal relationships are different between one generation and the other one. For G60, they originate mostly from childhood and adolescence, whereas for G80 they reinforce the heart of the model, which is between participation and variety during the central periods of youth and maturity, withdrawing for a career the same mechanism for the two generations: late onset, low frequency, and participation before termination.

---

[4]All the results can be obtained from the author.

In summary, the path models for the analysis converge to indicate that the crime system adopts the nine characteristics of a complex system specified at the beginning of this chapter. The crime system for G60 and G80 males and their forms, covert, overt, and lifestyle, display many common elements. However, the theoretical links are not always statistically significant in all the models. The launching action is clear with the constant impact of onset. The heart of the system is repeatedly observed with the action of participation, frequency, and dominantly with variety. All the reported results may be affected by the statistical power of the data, the size of the sample, around 500 offenders, and the large number of variables, particularly in the longitudinal analyses with three periods, childhood and adolescence, youth, and maturity. All the deficiencies of the calculated path analysis notwithstanding, it is a strong fact that crime is a system.

4 The Antisocial Behavior System

In Chap. 3, it was established that the quantitative and qualitative developmental mechanisms of antisocial behavior and crime were similar and generalizable because of the comparable results by types of measures, self-reported and official, forms of these behaviors (covert, overt, and lifestyle), and the two generations, G60 and G80. In the above section, it was demonstrated that crime could be conceived as a system and that its functioning, globally and longitudinally, was very similar for the two generations and the types of crime. Can these conclusions be confirmed with self-reported antisocial behavior (SRAB)? Le Blanc (2015) formulated that hypothesis. To our knowledge, no empirical response to this question has ever been published.

The SRAB system differs from the longitudinal crime model in two ways. First, there are also four age periods, though in a shorter life span, from early adolescence through early maturity. The periods are represented by the average age at each interview, that is, 16, 18, 24, and 35. Second, the measures of SRAB are more numerous than the crime measures (see Chap. 1 and Appendix B) and they were conceived initially as part of two main domains: delinquency (two scales: covert and overt) and problem behavior (two scales: three lifestyle scales: strolling, arousing, and exciting behaviors, and three conflict scales: with parents, in school, and at work. The delinquency domain, an equivalent of crime (as a convicted violation of the criminal code in this book), is divided into two forms, covert or property crimes, and overt, crimes against persons in the forms of physical and psychological violence. The problem behavior domain was illustrated as a network in Fig. 1.2. The scales are listed in the left-hand column of Table 4.4. The onset is a retrospective question in the form of *"ever done"* at the first interview and *"done since last interview"* at each subsequent age. The offset measure is truncated with the last interview at an average age of 30. It cannot be recognized as a total termination because the life spans considered do not exceed early maturity, the 30s. The age at offset must be regarded as an indication of suspension. The path analysis method was computed for the overall SRAB system, the delinquency and problem behavior subsystem, and the particular systems corresponding to a specific scale.

This section is an exploration of the relevance of the system view with SRAB. The results are not definitive for two reasons. First, the number of behavioral parameters had to be reduced to obtain a satisfactory model fit. As a consequence, frequency had to be left out because it was secondary in previous crime systems analyses and the analyses with all the descriptive behavioral parameters. Second, the number of free parameters was often over a hundred in models and the sample was composed of the 506 G80 males with normal attritions over time. In this statistical context, it is prudent to think that, as was expected from the crime system results, the path analysis fit data, columns two, three, and four in Table 4.4, show the existence of fractal genuine systems of SRAB, that is, the legitimate subsystems of delinquency (row 1: covert row 2 and overt row 3), problem behavior (row 4: lifestyle row 8 and conflict row 9), and all the specific subsystems composing all these categories. The last row confirms that the overall SRAB system is composed of delinquency and problem behavior.

In addition, all these SRAB systems seem to conform to the axioms defining what a system view is. It would be beyond one' means to analyze in detail each path analysis result (12 in Table 4.4: these data are available from the author). Le Blanc and Loeber (1998) suggested that all types of deviant behavior are part of a general antisocial behavior syndrome. This theoretical position has never been tested to our knowledge. However, there is a vast literature on the relations between alcohol or drug use and crime (see Rankin White 2015, 2019), but rarely studies with other specific forms of SRAB. The analysis of the global system of SRAB, that is, the integration of many forms of delinquency and problem behavior into a global developmental system of antisocial behavior, is theoretically and empirically urgent in this context.

The last row of Table 4.4 is a starting point in this direction. The fit data are satisfactory even with over 100 free parameters. The explained variance data tell us that the addition of the delinquency and problem behavior is more efficient for explaining the later age at suspension, offset, of delinquency (84%), than for problem behavior (67%). As a consequence, delinquency has a stronger autodynamic; it is more internally produced than problem behavior, which seems more externally powered by factors outside the realms of antisocial behavior.

The longitudinal view of crime (Sect. 0), pointed to five phenomena in this global system: launching, contemporary, continuity, causal effects, and suspension. Let us see if they appear as part of the SRAB system. Table 4.5 presents data to comment on these four phenomena.

The launching gear that was observed in the crime systems is active in the following ways. (1) The onsets of self-reported delinquency (SRD) and problem behavior (SRPB) are significantly associated. In Chap. 3, it was observed that they tend to be initiated around the same period of life, the second half of childhood. However, SRPB is initiated before SRD, at age 8 compared with age 10. (2) According to Table 4.5, the onset of SRPB stimulates participation in SRD at ages 16 and 18 and variety at ages 16, 18, and 35. On the other hand, the onset of SRD

Table 4.4 The antisocial behavior system, longitudinal path analysis with onset, participation, variety, and offset for the males of the 1980 generation

Antisocial behavior scales	X2 > 0,05[1]	RMSEA < -0.08 (0,05)[2]	CFI > 0,90 (0,95)[2]	Explained variance %				
					Adol1[3]	Adol2[3]	Youth[3]	Adu[3]
Delinquency Covert & overt	0,000	0,000	1	Participation	5	7	7	6
				Variety	17	27	29	40
				Offset				85
Covert Theft & fraud	0,000	0,000	1	Participation	10	8	5	9
				Variety	37	44	44	56
				Offset				82
Overt Physical & psychological violence	0,000	0,000	1	Participation	10	9	12	8
				Variety	22	35	44	44
				Offset				61
Problem behavior	0,000	0,000	1	Participation	1	3	5	24
				Variety	13	23	10	29
				Offset				49
Strolling Vandalism & disordely conduct	0,000	0,000	1	Participation	9	6	53	19
				Variety	58	64	9	19
				Offset				18
Arousing Substance use	0,000	0,000	1	Participation	24	16	16	10
				Variety	43	44	39	66
				Offset				92
Exciting[5] Motor veh. Theft & dangerous driving	0,000	0,000	1	Participation		22	6	13
				Variety		54	41	88
				Offset				85
Life style Strol. Arous. & Excit.	0,000	0,000	1	Participation	8	8	5	26
				Variety	30	34	24	26
				Offset				60
Conflict School & work	0,000	0,000	1	Participation	4	3	5	8
				Variety	54	39	57	65
				Offset				72
Conflict with parents[5]	0,000	0,000	1	Participation	9	8	3	
				Variety	44	51	71	
				Offset			80	
Conflict School, work, & parents	0,000	0,000	1	Participation	4	4	6	19
				Variety	26	29	33	66
				Offset				71

Table 4.4 (continued)

Family violence	0,04	0,000	1	Participation	14		8		4		7	
				Variety	79		86		64		55	
				Offset							47	
					De[4]	P[4]	D	Pr	D	Pr	D	Pr
Total system Delinquency & Problem behavior	0,000	0,03	0,97	Participation	25	7	7	3	4	3	4	31
				Variety	17	50	73	34	27	47	40	37
				Offset							84	67

1. The Chi square level of statistical significance: the minimum accepted is at least p = 0,05.
2. The left value is the minimum accepted and the right value the more severe criteria.
3. The nine life periods of the life span are regrouped into four for the generation of the 1980: Adol1: the first half of adolescence from twelve to fourteen; Adol2: youth from fifteen to seventeen; Youth: eighteen to twenty nine; Adu: maturity from thirty to forty-five.
4. The explained variance for delinquency and problem behavior of each period of life.

Table 4.5 The antisocial behavior system, longitudinal path analysis with onset, participation, variety, and offset for the males of the 1980 generation

Self-reported delinquency		Self-reported problem behavior	
Participation 15[a]	Participation SRPB 15	**Participation 15**	Onset SRD
Participation 18	Variety 15 Onset SRD Onset SRPB	**Participation 18**	Variety 15
Participation 24	Variety 15	**Participation 24**	Variety 18
Participation 30	Participation 18 Variety 18	**Participation 30**	Participation 24 Variety 18 Variety 24
Variety 15	Participation 15 Onset SRD	**Variety 15**	Participation 15 Onset SRPB Variety SRD 15
Variety 18	Variety 15 Participation 15 Variety PB 18 Onset SRPB	**Variety 18**	Variety 15 Participation 18 Participation SRD 18
Variety 24	Variety 15 Variety 18 Participation 15 Participation 24	**Variety 24**	Variety SRD 24 Participation SRD 24
Variety 35	Variety 24 Participation 35 Onset SRPB	**Variety 35**	Variety 15 Variety 24 Variety SRD 35 Onset PB
Offset SRD	Participation 15 Participation 35 Participation PB 18 Participation PB 24 Participation PB 35	**Offset SRPB**	Participation 18 Participation 30 Variety 15 Variety 24 Variety 30 Participation SRD 18 Participation SRD 24 Participation SRD 35 Onset SRD

PB problem behavior, *SRD* self-reported delinquency, *SRPB* self-reported problem behavior
[a]All the direct links in this table are statistically significant at least at $p = 0.05$ and most of the time at $p = 0.000$

energizes only SRPB participation and variety at age 16. In summary, the initiation of SRPB seems to be a precondition for SRD at the beginning of the career and an activator along the way to stimulate the continuity of SRD. The onset of SRD seems to drive the initial participation in SRPB. (3) The onset of SRD and SRPB do not have direct links with their own offset, whereas only the early onset of SRD is associated with the later suspension of SRPB.

The continuity in the SRAB system manifest in four ways.

1. The contemporary bidirectional links between the parameters of participation and variety in the crime system are also observable in the SRAB system. However, they are not statistically significant at all ages. It is interesting to note that it is at the beginning of the career, ages 16 and 18, for SRPB and the reverse for SRD, at ages 24 and 30. These results confirm the launching importance of SRPB.
2. The longitudinal continuity in each parameter is relatively rare for participation in SRD and SRPB and frequent for variety; for example, variety at age 16 predicts its level at age 18, in the same way from age 18 to 24, and from age 24 to 35. This continuity in SRD and SRPB represents their internal stability, which guarantees chronic behaviors.
3. There is another form of continuity, the causal reinforcements that manifest when participation at age 16 is significantly associated with variety at age 18 and so on for the other ages and the reverse situations with variety on participation. In the SRD and SRPB systems, there are, respectively, five and four stepping stone sequences. The causal links form a sort of chain in each system that sustains chronic SRD and SRPB.
4. A last way of building continuity in the SRAB system is by intersubsystem direct links outside of the above cases with the onsets of the subsystems. The intersystem relation takes the form of parameters of SRD that correlate with parameters of SRPB and the reverse. There is only one such case for SRD, the variety of SRPB at age 18 influences the degree of variety of SRD at the same age. However, there are more associations of SRD parameters with SRPB variables. First, the variety of SRD at ages 15 and 35 are related to the variety of SRPB at the same ages. Second, the participation in SRD at ages 18 and 24 is related to the variety of SRPB at ages 18 and 24.

The last phenomenon that was observed in previous system analyses is the source of suspension measured by the age at offset. In Chap. 3, it was observed that the suspension of SRD was earlier, at an average age of 23, than for SRPB, at age 25. In summary, according to Table 4.5, SRPB starts earlier and is suspended later. SRPB is a sort of background for SRD. However, the onset of SRD correlates with the offset of SRPB, but it is not the case for the reverse. The subjects were still active in SRD at the last interview, age 35, if they had participated at ages 15 and 35, and if they had participated in SRPB at ages 18 and 24. On the other hand, males were still active in SRPB at age 35 if they had participated in SRPB at age 18 and had a high variety at ages 18 and 24 and if they had participated in SRD at ages 18 and 24.

In summary, for the first time in criminology, the hypothesis that a comprehensible diversity of self-reported antisocial behaviors functions as a developmental system is confirmed. This system is fractal and multilayered. It is structured in multiple strata as expected in Fig. 1.1: first, delinquency and problem behavior; second, respectively, covert and overt and lifestyle and conflict behaviors; third, a diversity of lifestyle and conflict categories of behaviors.

5   Conclusion

This chapter on the system view confirms that antisocial behavior and crime are authentic systems. They manifest contextuality because the variance figures, Tables 3.3, 3.4, and 3.5, follow a common pattern without being equal. The coevolution is revealed because subsystems are considered in layers, for example, covert, overt, and lifestyle. They were complex systems with interacting parameters that are producing their energy and they were composed of subsystems that function in similar ways. The launching, as the sensitivity to the initial condition, and continuity mechanisms were clearly manifested by interactions between participation, variety, and frequency over time and the dominant role of variety. The most intriguing result was that the termination mechanism did not seem to be the result from most of the measured parameters. Only the last ones in time, the diminution of participation and frequency during maturity, were entertaining a negative link with offset.

The best hypothesis that can explain all the above results is that all antisocial behavior and crime systems are chaotic developmental mechanisms. With the meaning of the concept of chaos in mind, it can be imagined that antisocial behavior and crime are in a state of chaos or doubt and there is then a low probability of committing or not any types of ABC. As a consequence, there is a high level of uncertainty about which ABC will follow the previous one. This situation is common in antisocial behavior and crime during late adolescence when the behavioral syndrome of ABC attains its peak. Finally, it is evident that ABCs are self-organized systems, anything being equal outside them.

In a nutshell, to attain greater generalizability of these conclusions about autodynamic systems, the results of the system view must be replicated with females and other generations, the fact that all the questions that were investigated in the previous chapters need to be tested in other communities and countries notwithstanding. At the end of this system journey, criminologists must not forget that systems of antisocial behavior and crime are extremely complex and the analyses in this chapter are only a first exploration of this view.

Chapter 5
A Course View of Antisocial Behavior and Crime

1 Introduction

The theoretical position that was promoted during the MTSFGCLS was that the results of the quantitative and qualitative developmental changes (Chap. 3) and the system functioning of antisocial behavior and crime (Chap. 4) are synthetized into trajectories, courses of ABC that persons adopt during their life span. As established in Chap. 2, there is a generalized meta-trajectory that is recognized by criminologists, the universal age–crime curve, and it was hypothesized that it applies to all forms of official and self-reported ABC. In addition, criminology has identified behavioral meso- and micro-trajectories that are replicable for all forms of ABC and that they have also been observed in the case for self-control (Morizot and Le Blanc 2003a, b, 2005). This chapter starts by clarifying the distinction between criminological typologies and behavioral trajectories. Then, official and self-reported crime and self-reported antisocial behavior trajectories are identified with data sets from the MTSFGCLS. As in the previous chapter, the central question of this book question becomes: can the number, the shape, and the nature of the trajectories be replicated by generations, genders, types of samples, and forms of ABC?

2 From Criminological Typologies to Behavioral Trajectories

Today, with the advance of theoretical criminology, a criminological typology should be integrative and developmental. It is ideally a set of types that combines behavioral, biological, psychological, social, and structural characteristics of individuals that evolve during the life course. Some typologies are called developmental because they describe the individual growth with longitudinal data on a few or many of the above dimensions. Fréchette and Le Blanc (1987) reviewed more than 20 criminological taxonomies and concluded that they had one or more deficiencies.

© Springer Nature Switzerland AG 2021   125
M. Le Blanc, *The Development of Antisocial Behavior and Crime*,
https://doi.org/10.1007/978-3-030-68429-7_5

First, they were either theoretical or clinical and never multidisciplinary. Second, they were constructed with only one or a few of the above dimensions of the characteristics of a person. Third, they used only official or self-reported offending. Fourth, their behavioral component, most of the time, was not based on a longitudinal measure of antisocial behavior or crime. The typological studies scene changed around 1990. First, the number of published taxonomies diminished greatly. Now, publications point to four typologies with a behavioral and longitudinal perspective. They are associated with the following theoreticians and researchers: Le Blanc, Loeber, Moffitt, and Patterson. Second, they tend to increase the diversity of explanatory factors from the biological, psychological, and sociological domains.

2.1 The MTSFGCLS Typologies

These taxonomies were created as developmental taxonomies with repeated measures at a 2-year interval of SRABC during adolescence (frequency, variety, and seriousness) with a representative sample (POS70) and a court sample (CS70) of boys from Montréal (the description of the samples is in Appendix A and the scales in Appendix B) (Fréchette and Le Blanc 1987: Le Blanc and Fréchette 1989). Five developmental and population trajectories were identified for RSP70 males: (1) abstainer: 3%, (2) occasional: 13%, antisocial behavior at school, in the family or on peers during early or late adolescence, (3) minor sporadic: 27%, a few minor ABCs at one point in time, (4) major sporadic: 38%, a mix of ABC of average frequency, variety, and seriousness that were in progression, and (5) continuous and serious: 19%, at each point in time there was a high frequency, variety, and seriousness of ABC. The profiles of behavioral types of adolescents were clearly differentiated by discriminant function analysis on social and self-controls variables. The scores of the continuous and serious group of adolescents, 19% of the male population, were very much worse than the scores of the other groups of every social and self-control measure. It was concluded that the other four groups, 81% of the population, represented the normal distribution of trajectories of antisocial behavior in an adolescent population during adolescence.[1]

The G60 boys were classified on repeated measures of 14 SRC (see the list and definitions in Appendix B) from early adolescence to the beginning of youth. Four behavioral trajectories were identified: (1) sporadic, 20%: a few nonserious offenses at one point during adolescence; (2) explosive, 12%: a variety of around ten offenses of low seriousness that were discontinued during adolescence or early youth and in some cases there was a minor crime against a person; (3) intermediate seriousness and continuous, 30%: numerous, varied, and continuous offenses, mainly property offenses of all kinds without violent offenses; and (4) continuous and serious: 38%: a higher level of frequency, variety, and seriousness, including aggravation of

---

[1] In a school sample recruited in 2005–2006, the same types were identified (Le Blanc 2010a, b).

violent offenses. What was interesting is that the discriminant function analysis that distinguished these SRC trajectories was mainly on psychological scales and school-related measures. A last interesting observation was that there was a progressive internal and external order between the trajectories in the RSP70 and the CS70 and between them. First, the scores on the social and self-controls variables worsen from the less to the most delinquent group in the population and court samples. Second, these scores are aggravated from the last group, the continuous and serious delinquents, in the representative sample and the less delinquent group, the sporadic, in the court sample. Third, the most delinquent group in the court sample, the chronic and violent, displayed the most deteriorated scores of all the groups.

2.2 The Loeber Pathways

Loeber and his team identified three developmental pathways: covert, from shoplifting to serious theft; overt, from minor to serious aggression; and authority conflict from in the home to at school (Loeber et al. 2006, 2008). These behavioral trajectories were replicated in other longitudinal data sets (Loeber 2019). However, two important questions remain. First, theatrically, the pathways are drawn as if the authority conflict is the foundation of the other two pathways, covert and overt; they seem to be later attached to it in a parallel development. In the analysis of the developmental sequence of ABC mixes, in Chap. 3, it became clear that they exist as pathways, but that they are intrinsically inserted between behaviors of each of them. As a consequence, analyzing each pathway individually does not represent the reality of the development of ABC. Second, empirical knowledge on social and self-control characteristics are missing on the individuals who adopt one or another or a mix of pathways.

2.3 The Cambridge Classification

Many papers were published with the longitudinal data from the Cambridge Study in Delinquent Development. The convicted offenders originated from the population of boys in a South London working class community. Let us bring to our attention two more recent papers: Farrington et al. (2013b) and Basto-Peireira and Farrington (2018).

The first paper proposes a set of five trajectories for successive age ranges. The longest age span is from age 10 to 56. The trajectories were: non-offenders, low adolescence peak, very low rate chronic, high adolescence peak, and high rate chronic. The last two groups were distinguished on a whole range of childhood risk factors from the first three groups.

Recently, Basto-Peireira and Farrington (2018) investigated developmental pathways during the official offending career, from age 8 to 48, of the population of boys from a South London working class community. They identified four sequences of convictions. (1) The dominant pathway was the "versatile serious recidivist" (45%); they were convicted of an average of ten crimes and mostly violent offenses; it is a mix of the overt and covert pathways of Loeber et al. (1993). (2) The second pathway in importance was the "minor recidivists", 30% that added an average of four convicted thefts to a first one: it is a covert pathway in the Loeber et al. model. The versatile serious and minor recidivists are very similar to the two most serious trajectories of Fréchette and Le Blanc (1987): intermediate with property offenses and serious with property and violent offenses. These two trajectories accounted for 69% of the Montréal CS70 compared with 75% of the offenders in the Cambridge Study of Delinquent Development. These figures were calculated on offenders that went through their criminal career during the same historical period. Basto-Peireira and Farrington (2018) identified two other pathways, (3) few violent crimes and (4) few crimes against property.

2.4   The Moffitt Developmental Taxonomy

The Moffitt developmental taxonomy is a theoretical and empirical typology with two main categories of longitudinal antisocial behaviors. They are the adolescence-limited and the life-course persistent. It is very well known in criminology (Moffitt 1994, 1997, 2006; Moffitt et al. 2001) and the last update was recently published (McGee and Moffitt 2019). Skardhamar (2009) published the most extensive critical review of the literature that was published on the Moffitt typology. He argues that the types should not be interpreted literally and that "... *the theoretical arguments are surprisingly unclear on key issues and that the empirical evidence is highly problematic.*" (p. 1). Morizot (2019) concentrated on criminal behavior and reports that Moffitt and other scholars have argued that there are other behavioral types, for example, adulthood-limited offenders, abstainers, and a diversity of life-course persistent offenders.

In our view, the life-course persistent group is appropriately defined in terms of continuous and serious ABC even if the diversity of these behaviors is limited at each age: "...for example, hitting and biting at age four, shoplifting and truancy at ten, to selling drugs and stealing cars at 16, robbery and rape at age 22, and fraud and child abuse at 30" (Moffitt 1994, p. 12). The advantage of that definition is that it is composed of longitudinal markers and its disadvantage is that some other ABC could operationalize this trajectory over time. That argument notwithstanding, Le Blanc and Fréchette (1989) above and Skardhamar's review confirm the existence of this behavioral group regardless of its operational definition and the statistical method of identification. What was most innovative in the Moffitt taxonomy was the discovery of the importance of neuropsychological deficits that are contributing to numerous developmental problems and poor self-control. Piquero (2010) confirm the presence of the life-course persistent in many of the 80 studies that he reviewed. The Moffitt life-course persistent are an ABC trajectory very similar to the Fréchette and Le Blanc (1987) major sporadic and continuous and serious offenders and the Basto-Peireira and Farrington (2018) chronic groups. It also integrates the three pathways of Loeber et al. (1993) and Patterson and Yoerger (1993, 1997, 2002) early onset type.

Moffitt (1993) proposed a second group in the population of offender, the adolescence limited. They are defined as "... *never been antisocial during childhood and being unlikely to remain antisocial into their adulthood.*" (Moffitt 1993, p. 685). These individuals were normal adolescents with a prosocial personality during childhood who experienced personal difficulties during adolescence that are manifested by temporary antisocial behavior. Later (Moffitt 1997) recognized the existence of abstainers and some other groups: childhood-limited aggression, low-level chronic, and adult-onset offenders. Moffitt (1997) claims that the main groups, adolescence-limited and life-course persistent, are found in all studies. Skardhamar (2009) analyzed a dozen studies and concluded: " *The number of groups varies a great deal across studies.*" (p. 12). This conclusion is valid independently of the kind of data, the measures of crime, and the lengths of follow-up. Piquero (2010) confirms the presence of the life-course persistent in many of the 80 studies that he reviewed. The Moffitt life-course persistent is an ABC trajectory very similar to that of Fréchette and Le Blanc (1987) and the Basto-Peireira and Farrington (2018).

2.5   The Patterson Onset Trajectories

Patterson and Yoerger (1993, 1997, 2002) early and late onset trajectories of ABC were proposed at the same time as the previous ones. These groups distinguish themselves by the age at onset of the first arrest, before or after age 14. While Moffitt points out neuropsychological explanatory factors, Patterson selects social learning factors in the home, at school, with peers, and in other interactional situations. These authors would agree that the early onset group of offenders is composed of life-course persistent and that among late starters there are adolescence-limited offenders.

In summary, the last decade of the 1990s has produced five developmental typologies based on the course of ABC. The Patterson classification is the most limited, with one marker, age at onset, and a specific form of antisocial behavior, an arrest for a criminal offense. The Moffitt taxonomy has more scope on the nature and duration of ABC.

The MTSFGCLS trajectories are more representative of the whole reality with self-reported and official data and longitudinal measures for a population and a court sample. From an explanatory point of view, the extreme types, abstainers and life-course persistent, oppose the normal to the extreme abnormal development on neuropsychological, social-self controls, and poor social learning. For example, Fréchette and Le Blanc's data (Fréchette and Le Blanc 1987) showed, for example, that the abstainers have a score of 4.9 on the Eysenck psychoticism scale and the serious and persistent ones 8.9, 95 on parental supervision versus 37, and 8% were member of a gang versus 67%.

In conclusion, these five developmental typologies were great steps in the identification of ABC behavioral development. The Fréchette and Le Blanc (1987) empirical typologies from their representative sample and their court sample seem to represent the whole spectrum of the behavioral component of most recent classifications of antisocial adolescents and offenders. Let us investigate the field of trajectories and individual courses.

3   A Multilayered Trajectories Model of Antisocial Behavior and Crime

Developmental theory states that the global trajectory of ABC is a generalized and universal cycle whatever the descriptive measures, ages, historical periods, genders, forms of ABC, and social groups. It takes the form of a reverse U shape with a rapid upslope and an extended right downslope. This trajectory is the age–crime curve that was first identified by Quételet in the first half of the nineteenth century. In Chap. 2, the MTSFGCLS age–crime curves were drawn for official crime and problem behavior measured by types of offending and antisocial behavior (total, covert, overt, and life-style), generations (G60 and G80), genders, and representative samples of adolescent populations and court samples. In Chap. 3, tables exposed the male age–antisocial behavior development by forms of ABC.

In the MTSFGCLS, the position was that, from a system point of view, ABC is fractal, as confirmed in Chap. 4 with the path analyses. Then, the universal age–crime curve and the age–antisocial behavior curve are a universal *meta-trajectory*. The quantitative and qualitative changes described in Chap. 3 form particular individual courses of ABC. On these trajectories, the stream, the behavioral flow as in a river, vary in prevalence (participation), timing (onset and offset), degree (frequency, variety, and seriousness), and nature (total ABC and covert, overt, lifestyle, conflict, etc.). As a consequence, each individual displays a particular reverse U-shaped trajectory. In between the ABC general or meta-trajectory and all the individual trajectories there are two layers that are called the meso- and micro-trajectories.

Fréchette and Le Blanc's (1987) empirical results were the point of departure of the MTSFGCLS theoretical proposition that states that there are three longitudinal *meso-trajectories* in the population. (1) First, there is the **abstainer** meso-trajectory. Table 5.1 reports the percentage of self-reported delinquency and problem behavior (the scales in Table 1.1 and Appendix B) for abstainers by genders and historical decades for adolescents ages 12–17 (see Appendix A for the description of the representative samples of the population). First, as expected from criminological knowledge, girls abstain more than boys from delinquency; most of the time it is over 20% for girls in comparison of less then 10% for boys. Second, both genders abstain from problem behavior at about at the same degree, below 10% during three of the four decades. Third, the sampling variations between the decades notwithstanding, there seems to be an increase in abstainers in the 2000s for delinquency

Table 5.1 The abstainers in the MTSFGCLS, self-reported delinquency, and problem behavior for representative samples of the 1970s, 1980s, 1990s, and 2000s

Antisocial behavior	Delinquency		Problem behavior	
Gender	Boys (%)	Girls (%)	Boys (%)	Girls (%)
1970s	7	15	6	7
1980s	6	19	7	9
1990s	9	11	13	11
2000s	13	20	8	7

and in the 1990s for problem behavior. The level of abstainers in the 1980s was very similar to comparable data in a USA national sample (Elliott et al. 1987). For younger samples, the level was much higher, at least 10% more (Huizinga et al. 1991; Ayers et al. 1999; Le Blanc and McDuff 1991; Loeber et al. 1991). Moffitt developmental typology now recognizes the importance of this meso-trajectory in the antisocial behavior career picture of trajectories (McGee and Moffitt 2019).

(2) The next meso-trajectory among the population was called *common antisocial behavior and crime* (Fréchette and Le Blanc 1987; Le Blanc and Fréchette 1989; Le Blanc 2015). ABC is temporary in an otherwise law-abiding existence for around 45% of the population samples of the MTSFGCLS. Their ABC behaviors occur around the middle of adolescence. They manifest in a variety of delinquent acts such as vandalism, shoplifting, minor theft, or public mischief. In the parallel domain of problem behavior, they explore sexuality, use of alcohol and drugs, and enter into minor conflicts with their parents or at school. The frequency of these behaviors is very low. This common course has two longitudinal forms. (a) First, the occasional trajectory, a few of these behaviors are active during a short period of time, generally less than a year. It represents 16% of arrests according to Wolfgang et al.'s (1972) data, it accounted for 9% of the reported delinquent acts from a representative sample of the population of USA adolescents (Elliott et al. 1989), and 13% of the 1970s Montréal representative sample of the population (Fréchette and Le Blanc 1987). (b) Second, this common ABC trajectory also has an intermittent path; some of these minor behaviors are repeated at two points in time during adolescence (27%). Le Blanc 1983b argued that these common ABC meso-courses are an epiphenomenon of adolescence, an expression of difficulties with the normative biological, psychological, and social developmental tasks of adolescence. Moffitt (1993) proposes a similar type of explanation concerning her adolescence-limited offender. Whether or not this common trajectory is identifiable for adult-onset ABC needs to be tested.

(3) The last meso-trajectory is called *persistent* (Le Blanc and Fréchette 1989) or life-course offenders (Moffitt 1993) and versatile serious recidivists (Basto-Peireira and Farrington 2018), and most often chronic offenders. This trajectory is the most well-known course in criminology according to the landmark review of more than 80 studies between 1993 and 2005 by Piquero (2010) (see the update by Piquero et al. 2015, and other reviews: Van Dulmen et al. 2009; Jennings and Reingle 2012; Morizot 2019; McGee et al. 2020).

The data of the MTSFGCLS show that the individuals that follow this trajectory represent a very small fraction of the population and many convicted offenders. The number of these offenders changes along the decision points in the criminal justice system. In Montréal, the prevalence varies from 5% of the population and 68% of the wards of the juvenile court that were placed on probation or in correctional institutions during adolescence. Overall, the figures change by type of ABC, nature of the sample, measure (self-reported or official), and decision point in the justice system. They commit a large fraction of all crimes, for example, 50% of the self-reported behaviors (Elliott et al. 1989). These chronic delinquents commit two-fifths of the crimes known to police and two-thirds of the violent crimes according to Wolfgang et al. (1972). The data of the MTSFGCLS show that they start offending during late childhood, between ages 8 and 11; the growth is rapid and significant during adolescence; they maintain a high level of offending during youth; their criminal activity declines thereafter with episodes in the 40s and 50s. This course is characterized by high versatility, frequency, and seriousness (see Chaps. 2 and 3). The growth rate and velocity are rapid during early adolescence and this development is characterized by acceleration, diversification, and stabilization. During that growth, their offending escalates from the less to the more serious crimes on the developmental sequence of crimes and it displays a high level of innovation, retention, and simultaneity. Finally, the persistent offender tends to adopt a similar course for many other forms of antisocial behavior, either simultaneously or before or after their criminal course. In the MTSFGCLS, it is expected that the same developmental characteristics will be identified for all forms of ABC. White (2015) indicates that there are many similarities between the development of crime and drug use and their trajectories and Le Blanc (2009) shows that their progression is interrelated between onset and age 40.

In summary, Piquero (2010) concludes that

> ... consistent with taxonomic theories of crime over the life-course, trajectory-based empirical research does show an adolescence-peaked pattern and a chronic offender pattern, the latter of which evidences declines in most studies. (p. 49).

In addition, Piquero reports that 80 studies identified between three and six trajectories regardless of the research design. In their update with 163 samples and 105 studies, Jennings and Reingle (2012) calculated that 83% of the 72 studies on self-reported violence, aggression, and delinquency declared three, four, or five trajectories (Mode 4) and, of the 52 studies with official records 81% obtained three, four, or five trajectories (Mode 4). As a consequence, there is a third layer of courses, *micro-trajectories*. In the sample of the population of the MTSFGCLS, there are three trajectories between the abstinent and the persistent and in the court sample three delinquent trajectories aside from the persistent one.

In the empirical literature, micro-trajectories are often merged into meso-trajectories because of a deficient strategy of data analysis, as it will be demonstrated later on. Criminologists have addressed the empirical question of identifying behavioral and developmental trajectories with different methodologies according to the review of Le Blanc (2002). In sequence, they started by the use of transition matrices. In the 1980s, they employed ad hoc dynamic classification, that is, the cross tabulation of measures of self-reported offending or antisocial behaviors at two or three points in time, mainly during adolescence. In the 1990s, criminologists started to experiment with group detection methods (statistical models such as group-based modeling, growth curve modeling, latent trajectory modeling, etc.). The frequency of the use of these techniques can be assessed with the list of statistical techniques in the papers by Piquero (2010) and Jennings and Reingle (2012). There are now so many studies that it is difficult to keep track of all of them. However, their focus was predominantly on the number of trajectories and their shape.

More recently, Piquero et al. (2015) and Morizot (2019)) proposed critical reviews of the trajectory studies from the point of view of theory, methodology, statistics, policy, and the future of these researches. These authors agree to suggest that researchers should move out of the mere description of the trajectories and guide their study with theories, use longer prospective studies, analyze diversified types of ABC, give more attention to risk and protective predictors and social and self-controls correlates, and consider policy implications.

The next sections of this chapter comply with some of these recommendations by using longer data sets, i.e., from age 8 to 60, and compare genders and measures of types of ABC, covert, overt, lifestyle, conflict, from three points of views, official data, SRDs, and SRAB. In addition, replications are conducted with two generations. The main hypothesis of the developmental theory is that three layers of trajectories can be documented: a meta-trajectory, two meso-paths, and up to half a dozen micro-courses.

4 The MTSFGCLS Trajectories of Antisocial Behavior and Crime

In Chap. 2, Sect. 2.2.1.2, the theme was the age–crime curve drawn with measures of prevalence and velocity. Numerous researchers concluded that the observed trajectory can be considered *universal*. (1) Its shape was very similar in Montréal for the generations of 1960 and 1980, the genders, a representative sample of the adolescent population, two court samples, and types of offenses. (2) These conviction curves compared very well with the ones published by long-term prospective longitudinal studies with data from childhood to at least around age 60 in various countries (Boston USA: Laub and Samson 2003; London UK: Farrington et al. 2013a; and the Netherlands: Blokland et al. 2005). (3) It has to be remembered that numerous curves with a similar shape have been published with other descriptors of the criminal career from various decision points in the criminal justice system (from arrests to prison) and numerous countries, cities, and samples according to the most recent reviews by Loeber (2012), DeLisi (2015), and Britt (2019). (4) It was also demonstrated that the same shape described very well the curves for covert offense or against property, overt, violent, or offenses against persons, and lifestyle-market crimes.

In addition, it was demonstrated, in Chap. 4, that the official criminal career functions as a developmental system in which the variety of offenses is the spinal column. After the launching of the criminal career at an earlier onset, its continuity depends predominantly on the maintenance of a higher versatility than on the levels of frequency and participation, and it ceases when the frequency decreases. As a consequence, the variety parameter, the number of types of offenses for which a subject was convicted yearly (see Appendix B) is used in all the official trajectory analysis reported in this chapter.

4.1   The Official Crime Trajectories

In the narrative review of 80 studies by Piquero (2010) and 105 publications by Jennings and Reingle (2012), the descriptive parameter used in each study is not specified but it may be presumed that it is the frequency from our reading of many of the 12 papers out of the 80 using convictions (15% of the total). Piquero reports that 59 out of 80 studies (74%) and Jennings and Riengle report that 69 out of 105 (66%) employed self-reports and many teacher observations. A last observation from these reviews is that the longest life span for the trajectory analysis with convictions is from age 10 to 32 and most of these studies were conducted with the South London data gathered by David Farrington cited above. From the Piquero and Jennings and Reingle narrative reviews, it can be concluded that the statistical technique applied was the latent class growth analysis via the zero-inflated Poisson model in the majority of the studies. It would have been preferable, from the results of the system view in Chap. 4, to analyze more descriptors of the career together. However, from our tryouts no model could be fitted with two criminal career parameters, variety with frequency or participation, onset, and offset.

Four questions are investigated in this section. Can the number and shape of micro-trajectories be reproduced with convicted males of the 1960 and 1980 generations? Are the MTSFGCLS conviction micro-trajectories comparable with courses in other long-term criminal career data sets? What are the developmental micro-trajectories for covert or property crimes (PO), overt or violent offenses (VO), and lifestyle-market crimes (LS)? Is there a developmental road from the meta-crime trajectory to the micro-courses?

4.1.1   The Number of Court Males and Shape of Micro-Trajectories

Figures 5.1 and 5.2, and Table 5.2 are used to answer the main question addressed in this book about the replication of results by generations. Figure 5.1 displays six micro-trajectories that represent the diversity of the developmental trajectories characterizing the criminal career. Table 5.2 reports, in the first line of the last column

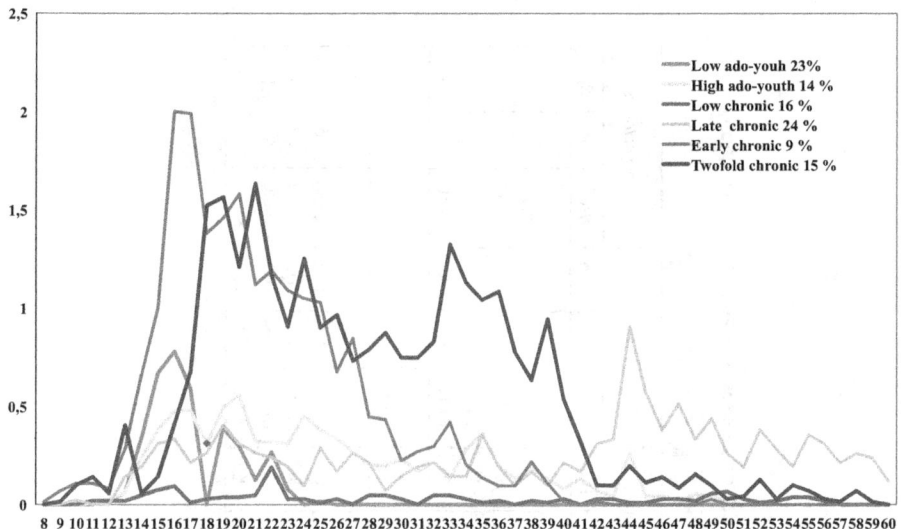

Fig. 5.1 Six micro-trajectories of official criminal variety for the court males of the 1960 generation

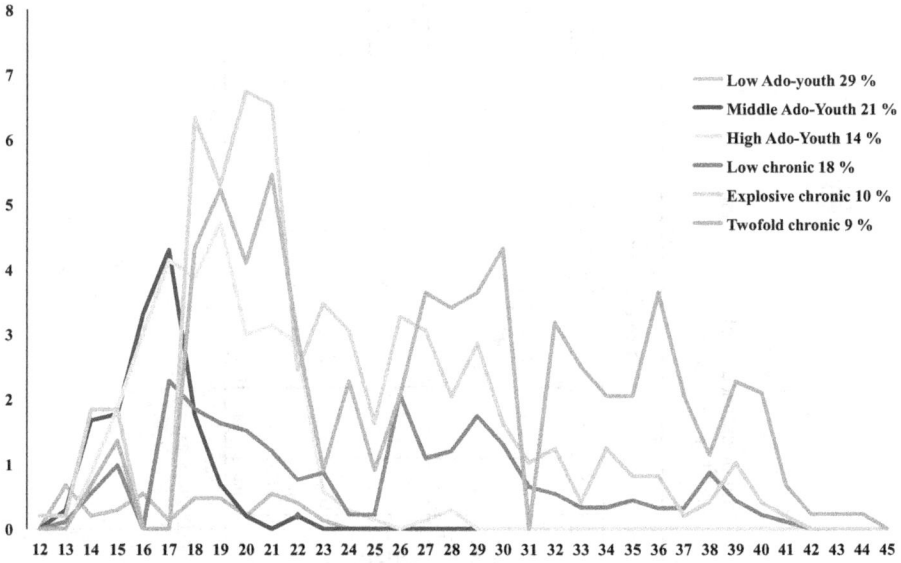

Fig. 5.2 The micro-trajectories of official crime variety for the court males of the 1980 generation

on the right of the table, the three consensual fit statistics: the Bayesian information criterion (BIC), entropy, and posterior probability (bootstrap 1). The lowest BIC is the consensual criteria in choosing the most parsimonious model and it is the most consistent statistic according to Nylund-Gibson et al. (2007). The entropy reflects a

Table 5.2 The comparison of the models of official crime trajectories by generations and types of offenses; statistics of the latent growth class analysis via the zero-inflated Poisson model

Trajectories / Samples	One trajectory			Two trajectories			Three trajectories			Four trajectories			Five trajectories			Six trajectories		
	BIC	Ent	Boo	BIC	En[1]	Bo[2]	BIC	Ent	Boo	BIC	Ent	Boo	BIC	Ent	Boo	BIC	Ent	Boo
J60 8-61																		
Total	29293	na	na	**26481**	**,93**	**,000**	25736	,91	,77	25188	,93	,01	24943	,90	,29	24766	,87	,02
Covert	16336	na	na	**15006**	**,95**	**,000,**	14347	,89	,000	14139	,86	,005	14019	,80	,05	13937	,81	,009
Overt	10398	na	aa	**10398**	**,82**	**000**	9649	,74	,003	9493	,74	,11	9462	,74	,01	9450	,73	,05
Life-style	9193	na	na	**8804**	**,70**	**,000**	8730	,67	,24	8709	,63	,08	8705	,67	,42	8701	,68	,50
J60 12-45																		
Total	29293	na	na	**26481**	**,93**	**,000**	25736	,91	,77	25188	,93	,01	24943	,90	,28	24766	,87	,03
J80 12 45																		
Total	23838	na	na	**20448**	**,96**	**,000**	19880	,93	,07	19540	,90	,04	19330	,87	,084	19166	,86	,02
Covert	13141	na	na	**1608**	**,92**	**,000**	11338	,85	,000	11169	,84	,002	11084	,79	,0,0.	11019	,79	,02
Overt	12044	na	na	**10782**	**,94**	**,000**	10637	,83	,000	10539	,77	,004	10509	,76	,005	10500	,68	,14
Life-style	8126	na	na	**8335**	**,91**	**,000**	8216	,67	,000	8134	,77	,001	8126	,70	,002	8141	,61	,31

1. En: Entropy: level of separation between groups or posterior probability.
2. Boo: Bootstrap (vs n-1 classes).

good classification model of trajectories; the minimum criterion is 0.80 and it should not be lower than 0.70 (Celeux and Soromenho 1996). The bootstrap figure is the statistical significance of the probability of accepting six trajectories given that there were five before. These fit indicators are very satisfactory for the three tests reported in the lines called total (the whole criminal career of convictions for the males of G60 aged 8–61 and aged 12–45, and for G80 males aged 12–45.

Piquero's (2010) narrative synthesis on developmental trajectories of criminal activity concludes that "*… trajectory based empirical research does show an adolescent-peaked pattern and a chronic offender pattern.*" (p. 49). For their part, Jennings and Reingle (2012) conclude: "*… most studies identify what Moffitt refers to as an adolescent-limited type and a life-course persistent offender type …*" (p. 486). A visual analysis of Fig. 5.1 for G60 and Fig. 5.2 for G60 convicted males indicate that there are no adolescent-limited trajectories. The micro-courses peak during adolescence and none can be called a "*adolescent-limited*" trajectory because no path finishes at the end of adolescence. This was also a conclusion of Laub and Samson (2003) with Glueck's sample: "*… the data firmly reject the typology of two offender groups.*" (p. 104). However, in the MTSFGCLS trajectories there are two adolescent and youth trajectories that show a summit during late adolescence and a downlift throughout youth, a decline that finishes during early (ages 18–21), middle (ages 22–25), or late youth (ages 26–29). In Fig. 5.1 there are four chronic courses. This label is given when convictions are observed during at least three periods of the life cycle that were defined previously: childhood: ages 8–11, adolescence: ages 12–17, youth: ages 18–29, and early, the 30s, middle, the 40s, and late maturity, the 50s. This definition of chronicity is totally in agreement with McGee et al. (2020) "*We believe that prospective longitudinal studies starting in childhood or adolescence and following into late adulthood are the only way to investigate persistent offending.*" (p. 6). Figure 5.2 draws the trajectories for G80 males; there are also six paths, three adolescence and youth and three chronic.

Four phenomena emerge from the comparison of Figs. 5.1 and 5.2. (1) The number of micro-trajectories, six, is similar for G60 and G80 offenders (even with G60 ages 12–45 data set, see results of the fit test in Table 5.2).[2] (2) The chronic offenders micro-courses dominate for G60 (four out of six). They are equal in number for G80, three chronic and nonchronic paths. (3) The quantity of convicted G60 offenders in the chronic micro-trajectories is 64% for a potential career span of 54 years compared with 37% for G80 chronic with a career span of 34 years. The lower number of G80 chronic courses probably reflects the lower crime rate for this generation, as argued in Chap. 2. In addition, this quantitative disparity surely reflects the age lag in the follow-ups as recognized in Piquero (2010). In addition, it also represents changes in criminal justice practices and sociological advances, as noted in Chap. 2. (4) Table 5.3 proposes an in-depth description of the trajectories with the parameters of the criminal career: participation (prevalence), onset, frequency, variety, offset, and duration (career span). This type of internal validity is rarely

---

[2] The figure and table on G60 ages 12–45 with these data can be obtained from the author.

Table 5.3 Micro-courses of the males by generation: onset, participation, variety, frequency, offset, and career span

Parameters	Name	G60 Ages 8 to 61						G80 Ages 12 to 45					
		Low Ado-Adu	High Ado-Adu	Low chronic	Episodic chronic	Early chronic	High chronic	Low Ado adu	Middle ado adu	High Ado adu	Low chronic	Ado explosive chronic	High chronic
	Nb. %	106 23	64 14	113 24	42 9	74 16	71 15	149 29	102 21	70 14	92 18	49 10	44 9
Particip.	Min.	1	1	2	1	4	5	1	1	2	1	5	1
	Mean	1	2	5	7	10	13	1	3	5	5	10	6
	Med.	1	2	5	7	10	12	1	3	5	5	9	6
	Max	9	7	11	13	18	22	4	6	8	11	16	14
Onset	Min.	1	12	11	10	8	9	12	13	12	12	12	14
	Mean	26	16	18	20	15	16	17	15	16	17	15	12
	Med.	20	15	17	17	15	16	16	15	15	16	15	16
	Max.	55	20	37	43	20	23	22	18	18	40	18	15
Variety	Min.	1	1	1	2	4	6	1	2	3	1	6	1
	Mean	1	3	5	7	9	10	1	5	7	6	10	7
	Med.	1	3	5	6	9	10	1	4	7	6	10	7
	Max	3	9	11	12	14	15	4	9	12	11	14	13
Freque.	Min.	1	1	3	4	10	20	1	2	5	1	18	1
	Mean	2	7	13	18	37	44	2	8	13	14	39	17
	Med.	1	5	11	14	32	38	1	7	15	13	33	15
	Max	9	43	78	59	104	217	20	24	33	37	150	56
Offset	Min.	13	14	18	42	23	34	13	14	19	26	25	16
	Mean	33	19	37	53	34	43	19	18	22	33	34	30
	Med.	32	18	37	53	34	40	18	18	22	33	34	29
	Max	56	25	57	42	49	60	24	22	28	43	41	42
Duration	Min.	1	1	1	1	9	15	1	1	2	1	9	1
	Mean	8	3	19	32	19	28	2	2	7	17	19	14
	Med.		2	20	34	20	25	1	2	6	17	20	14
	Max	40	10	43	47	40	44	8	8	14	27	27	27

available in publications on trajectories. Often, there are external validity data with individual social and self-control characteristics and risk factors, for example, in the publications by Laub and Samson (2003) and Farrington et al. (2013a). Reading Table 5.3, it is confirmed that the six micro-trajectories of G60 and G80 are graded from the lowest degree of participation, variety, frequency, and duration, and the latest onset and earliest offset, that is, from the low adolescence and youth trajectory to the twofold chronic course.

There are three comparable chronic micro-trajectories that peaked during adolescence and youth and they are characterized by significant criminal activities during the 30s or later for G60 (see Fig. 5.1 and Table 5.2). (1) The low chronic offenders show comparable data for G60 and G80. They are distinguished by an episodic low variety during around 5 years, the lowest frequency and duration, and the latest onset compared with the other chronic. (2) The early chronic attains the highest level of variety during adolescence and youth and they display the lowest onset and highest offset, and a very high frequency. (3) The twofold chronic shows two peaks, one during adolescence and early youth and one later during the 30s and early 40s. They are called twofold because their first peak of variety is below the early chronic offenders and their second sequence of crimes with high variety is well above the other chronic courses during the 30s and later. These two high variety sequences may reflect an imprisonment pause in their career. It should be verified. (4) The G60 convicted males, contrary to the G80 ones, present a late chronic course. Piquero (2010) states that this course is reported in a number of studies and he qualifies this group as unanticipated by theorists. These offenders are convicted the latest for the first time among the chronic and their variety is the lowest until the end of youth. However, their variety is the highest of all the chronic courses from age 40 on, whereas their frequency is relatively low compared with other chronic, but their career span is the longest. This micro-trajectory may be a consequence of the longer follow-up for G60, from ages 8 to 61.

As for adolescence and youth, two micro-trajectories for G60 and three for G80 can be distinguished in degrees in Table 5.3. (1) The G80 three micro-courses are graded on every parameter. However, the only significant gap between these courses and the low chronic is on age at offset and career span. It is earlier and longer for this last group. (2) Reading the statistics in Table 5.3, one gets the impression that none of the G60 adolescence and youth trajectories is replicated by G80 courses. They have similarities on some descriptive parameters but not on others. First, the offenders that have a pettier career are the G60 and G80 low adolescence and youth trajectories with equal participation, variety, frequency, and career span. Second, The G60 high adolescence and youth offenders have very similar statistics to the G80 middle adolescence and youth group. The G60 trajectory with the higher level of variety ends at the end of youth. The middle course disappears during early youth. Finally, the offenders with the lower level of variety terminate their career during the middle of youth. Third, the G80 high adolescence and youth offenders are the most active of all the males of the two generations with a career limited to adolescence and youth. The hypothesis to be tested is that this path, with a longer follow-up, would disappear and the G80 would display four chronic courses instead of three. In fact, the generational trajectories could be inserted between each other.

In summary, the number and shapes of the six micro-trajectories are generally replicated with G60 and G80 Montréal convicted males. The discrepancy between the generational results is the existence of a late chronic course for G60 offenders and three adolescence and youth trajectories instead of two for G80 subjects. In addition, the six courses, regardless of the generation, are ordered by degree on participation, onset, variety, frequency, offset, and career span. The observed disparities in the shapes may be the consequence of characteristics of the data sets, such as changes in the quality of court files 20 years apart, the length of the career under study as mentioned by Piquero (2010), the parameter used, etc. Three main meta-factors have been mentioned in Chap. 2 as particularly important to explain the discrepancies between the generational age–crime curves. First, the age of legal responsibility was changed from 8 for G60 to 12 for G80. It was considered that this decision had the effect of compacting the G80 criminal career by removing the childhood period when many G80 offenders start their career. Second, criminal justice became less punitive, that is, more diversified decisions with diversion from court and the addition of new types of sentences and new science-based treatment programs. These changes may have compacted the G80 curve and reduced recidivism for these male offenders. Third, improvements in the educational, health, and welfare systems and better socioeconomic life conditions may also explain the variations between the G60 and G80 micro-trajectories.

4.1.2   The Comparison of the G60 Trajectories with Other Long-Term Studies

The generational replication is only one of the potential procedures available to prove the generalization of a theoretical proposition. Another one was conducted in Chap. 2 when the MTSFGCLS age–crime meta-curves were compared with other long-term curves from longitudinal studies with data from childhood to late adulthood: the Boston Glueck's court sample ages 7–70 (Laub and Samson 2003); the South London cohort ages 10–56; and the sample from the Netherlands of Dutch offenders (Blokland et al. 2005). All these investigations of trajectories had a similar measure: court convictions. The comparison of the micro-trajectories from these studies is difficult. First, these authors display their courses with smoothed curves and on small-dimension graphs that diminish the distinctiveness of the curves and render their interpretation fuzzy. Second, these authors do not add a table like Table 5.3 above that describes each trajectory with other descriptive parameters of the criminal career except frequency. Third, these authors refer to low, moderate, and high rates to indicate the quantity of convictions without specifying the ranges in numbers that distinguish these categories. In addition, as a second qualifier, Laub and Samson and Blokland use demisters, Farrington peak, and Le Blanc life cycle periods, which were defined at the beginning of this book. These deficiencies in the comparative data notwithstanding, Table 5.4, proposes an interpretation of the

Table 5.4 The comparison of official crime micro-trajectories in studies with convictions and data from childhood to late maturity (around 60 years old or more)

In order of chronicity and peak life periods	Laub and Sampson (2003) Boston Court sample Convictions 7-70	Farrington et al. (2013) London Population Convictions 10-56	Blokland et al. (2005) Nederlands Convictions sample 12-72	Le Blanc 1960 Montréal sample of population convictions 8-61	Le Blanc 1960 Montréal Court sample Convictions 8-61	Le Blanc 1980 Montréal Court sample Convictions 12-45
Non-offenders		Non-offenders 58%		Non-offenders 85%		
Low-rate adolescence and youth	Classic desisters (20%)	Low adolescence peak 23%	Sporadic 71%	One timer adolescence & youth 8% (80%)	Low adolescence & youth 23%	Low adolescence & youth 29%
Middle-rate adolescence and youth						Middle adolescence & youth 21%
High-rate Adolescence and youth	Moderate-rate desisters 26%	High adolescence peak 4%	Low-rate desisters 7%		High adolescence and youth 14%	High adolescence & youth 14%
Low-rate chronic	Low chronic I 24%	Very low rate chronic 10%	Moderate-rate deisters 6%	Low chronic 4% (10%)	Low chronic 24%	Low chronic 19%
	Low chronic II 8%				Late chronic 9%	
Moderate rate chronic	Moderate-rate chronic 18%				Early chronic 16%	Early chronic 10%
High-rate chronic	High-rate chronic 3%	High-rate chronic 5%	High-rate persiters 2%	High chronic 3% (9%)	Twofold chronic 15%	Twofold chronic 9%

similarities and contrasts between the shape and the characteristics of six sets of micro-trajectories.

All the offenders from the court samples were recruited in juvenile court and six trajectories were identified: Boston 1940s court delinquents followed from ages 7 to 70 (Laub and Samson 2003), and Montréal 1960s court juvenile offenders traced from ages 8 to 61 and 1980s court juvenile offenders from ages 12 to 45. One set of data is a representative sample of the 1977 cohort of cases convicted in the Netherlands followed from ages 12 to 72 and four trajectories were identified (Blokland et al. 2005). There are two population samples. First, the total population of 8 and 9 years old in a South London community traced from ages 10 to 56 (Farrington et al. 2013b). Second, a G60 random representative school sample of adolescents aged 12–16 recruited in Montréal and measured from ages 8 to 61. The reader will note that the paths into offending are organized into the above periods of the life cycle, the central zone being adolescence and youth, and the levels of offending, an by evaluation as of low, moderate, and high, as used by the authors.

Let us start with the two population samples. In Table 5.4, the non-offenders represent 58% of the boys living in a London working class inner city community. In Montréal, they account for 85% of the boys that were recruited from the whole range of socioeconomic statuses.

The 25% difference may be explained by the wider range of social statuses in Montréal. In addition, at that time, the rates of official and self-reported juvenile delinquency were significantly lower in higher socioeconomic districts (Le Blanc 1969). It should be noted that in the Montréal population 80% of the offenders are the classic official one-timers identified by Wolfgang et al. (1972) and in the Netherlands there is a group of sporadic delinquents or one-timers (71% of the offenders). This type of career is surely present in the low-rate adolescence and youth paths of Farrington and the Montréal G60 and G80 delinquents. This is a micro-trajectory that certainly represents a good number of the offenders in the five of the six data sets; it does not stand out when there are two paths, adolescence- and youth dominated versus chronic courses that spead through three life periods, childhood, adolescence, and youth and, more generally, one or more of the three maturity periods. The adolescence and youth paths are proposed in all the conviction samples: London (low and high), Boston (moderate and high), Netherlands (low, and moderate), and Montréal (low, moderate, and high). The peak of these adolescence and youth courses seems to be during late adolescence (the exact figure cannot be identified in the published smoothed curves). However, it is obvious that the downslope decreases more slowly than the upslope and it ends during, early, middle, or late youth. It is interesting to note that around 40% of the males adopt this path, more when the career span is longer, G80 for example, and less in a population sample.

The next and most important group of trajectories is the chronic paths. They represent more than 60% of the micro-courses in Boston and Montréal G60. This proportion diminishes in the other samples. First, the low-rate chronic offenders are identified in five samples. Second, what is particularly interesting is that the Boston and Montréal G60 male results agree on the presence of a late-chronic path with the lower rate of offending during adolescence and youth and the highest during the three maturity periods with just less than 10% of offenders. Third, they identify an early-chronic path with very high offending during adolescence and youth and continuity thereafter. Fourth, they also present a trajectory that was called twofold chronic because there is a peak during adolescence and youth, a pause at the intersection at late youth and early maturity, and an increase in the criminal activity level during middle and late maturity.

In summary, the contemporary data sets confirm the existence of many similar paths identified in the G60 data set. In addition, the Boston juvenile court sample recruited during the 1940s is reproduced with the G60 micro-trajectories. Let us now verify if the micro-trajectories for the whole criminal career are similar by types of offenses.

4.1.3   The G60 Offending Trajectories by Types of Offenses

In Chap. 2, Fig. 2.5 displayed the age–crime curves for covert (POs), overt (VOs), and lifestyle-market crimes (LSOs). The shapes of the meta-trajectories of these types of offenses were very similar to the overall age–crime curve. However, the peak was earlier, during middle adolescence for POs, at the end of the same period for VOs, and in early youth for LSOs. These meta-paths and the descriptive data in Table 2.6 confirmed a changing offenses mix along the life course. Four results attracted our attention. (1) POs were the spine of the offending career of the G60 and G80 males; they dominated prevalence and velocity data. (2) VOs adopted a secondary role during adolescence and after they were often and gradually replaced by LSOs. (3) During maturity POs progressively lost their dominance, but they were characterized by the highest participation rates with a fading difference to VOs and LSOs. (4) LSOs became more prevalent than VOs during maturity, after the 30s. In addition, in Chap. 4 it was concluded that these three types of offenses function as autonomous and interconnected systems. Let us see if the development of the types of offenses can be represented by a comparable set of micro-trajectories.

Table 5.2 lists LCGA results by types of offenses in the lines called covert, overt, and lifestyle for G60 and G80 convicted males. The three fit indicators were satisfactory, particularly when the BIC was at its highest value. The number of micro-trajectories diminishes from six for POs to five for VOs, and four for LSOs. These numbers of paths are similar for G60 and G80 males and the set of micro-trajectories is similar for the total and the covert careers. Table 5.5 lists the micro-paths by generation, types of offenses, and the proportion of offenders in each course. These percentages vary more or less for each micro-trajectory.

Five courses are common between generations and types of offenses: two adolescence and youth limited paths and three out of four chronic courses. First, among the micro-paths of the four chronic offenders, three are represented in each generation and type of offender. Only the late chronic are not identified in the G80 data set, probably because it is truncated at age 45 compared with age 61 for G60. The low, early, and twofold chronic offenders account for around 40% of the category of

Table 5.5 The comparison of G60 and G80 micro-trajectories by types of crimes: percentages for covert, overt, and lifestyle-market offenses

Trajectories	Montréal G60				Montréal G80			
	Total	Covert	Overt	Lifestyle	Total	Covert	Overt	Lifestyle
Low-rate adolescence and youth	23[a]	27	38	29	29	35	42	59
Middle-rate adolescence and youth					21	18		
Height-rate adolescence and youth	14	26		17	14	18	22	
Low chronic	24	20	33		19	18	17	19
Late chronic	9	7	10					
Early chronic	16	11	8	27	10	6	10	9
Twofold chronic	15	11	11	27	9	5	10	13

[a]Percentage

persistent convicted offenders, whereas the low chronic amount to 20%. This is the second most important course of all the micro-courses; the low chronic maintains a low but continuous diversity of crimes. The early and twofold offenders represent around 10% of the convicted males. The early chronic show the highest variety during childhood, adolescence, and early youth, whereas the twofold offenders show the second highest versatility scores for these periods and, during the three maturity periods, they exceed the early chronic offenders.

Second, the adolescence and youth limited category of offender gather around 60% of the offenders of the two samples. It is to be noted that there is no adolescence-limited trajectory, as suggested by Moffitt. The low-rate adolescence and youth trajectory is adopted by the higher percentage of offenders; they attain the variety peak during the second part of adolescence and cease during youth.

Third, some paths show dissimilarities between generations and types of crimes. (1) the late chronic, the offenders that show the highest versatility from age 40 to 60 after displaying the lowest versatility from onset, are only observable for G60 and covert and overt crimes. An explanation, indicated earlier, may be the short career length for G80, from age 12 to 45, in comparison with age 8 to 60 for G60. The same explanation could apply to the middle-rate adolescence and youth total and overt careers. (2) It is also interesting to note that the early and twofold chronic, particularly for G60, rally nearly 30% of the LSO offenders in comparison with around 10% for chronic POs and VOs. The features of LSOs may explain this disparity between micro-trajectories of the predatory crimes, property and personal,. It was established in Chap. 2 that the lifestyle (driving under the influence of alcohol, etc.) and the market crimes (buying and selling stolen goods, drug and sex trafficking, etc.) are initiated, more prevalent, and complementary to other sorts of crimes during the maturity periods. In addition, Kazemian and Le Blanc (2004) showed that the mode of perpetration developed from a more impulsive to a professional modus operandi throughout the career. LSOs need more organization as a business.

In summary, the number, shape, and features of the micro-trajectories of covert and overt crimes are very similar and they replicate the six micro-paths of the whole criminal career. However, the micro-trajectories of the four lifestyle-market crimes are principally concentrated around the chronic courses. Laub and Samson's (2003) six micro-trajectories for property, violent, and alcohol/drug crimes are reproduced in our five paths that are very similar across types of crimes in the MTSFGCLS. The variation between G60 and G80 males, as noted before, seems to reflect changes in design over time and as a consequence in macro-sociological changes (see Chap. 2 and Appendix C).

4.1.4   From a Meta-Trajectory to Micro-Courses Through Meso-Paths

A last question emerged from a detailed reading of Table 5.2. Is there a developmental road from a meta-crime trajectory to a micro-course? The three fit indicators for the whole career (Table 5.2 total lines) indicate that the models with two, four meso-paths, and six micro-trajectories emerge because of small improvements on their previous models. For example, concerning the G60 total career, they are 2812 BIC points between the meta-path and the two meso-trajectories (10% increase), 745 points between two and three meso-courses, 548 points between three and four trajectories (15% from the meta-trajectory), 245 points from four and five paths, and only 177 points from five and six courses (16% from the meta-path; these discrepancies are similar for G80 and the covert offenses). These numbers are very low considering that the BIC of the meta-trajectory is 29,293. From a strict number point of view, an analyst could choose any set of trajectories and accept them as the optimal BIC, the lowest one; choosing the six trajectories solution is not entirely convincing in the points difference (or percentage between solutions). As a consequence, analysts should also look at the building of the set of micro-trajectories.

Figure 5.3 displays the curves of the two models, two and four meso-trajectories, and Table 5.6 presents the statistics for the two models. The general shape of the two sets of curves is similar: a rapid uplift with a peak toward the end of adolescence than a slower downlift. It is basically the shape of the age–crime curve studied in Chap. 2. The first graph seems to display two continuous or chronic trajectories: a low adolescence and youth peak and an early and high versatility path. From the statistics in Table 5.6, the first group of offenders displays a later onset, very much less variety and frequency, an earlier offset, and a shorter career span. This meso-path is composed of 56% of the G60 convicted offenders.

In the four meso-trajectories set, the above low adolescence and youth peak path clearly becomes an adolescence and youth pattern (in blue) that is initiated around age 12 and ceased toward the end of youth; they represent 27% of the G60 court males. What is more interesting is that the early and high rate offenders are subdivided into three paths in the four trajectories set. First, there is a low chronic trajectory above the previous one (32% of offenders). Second, there is the usual early chronic course (23%) that starts fast during childhood, attains the highest peak during adolescence, and becomes very low during the 40s and 50s. The third path of

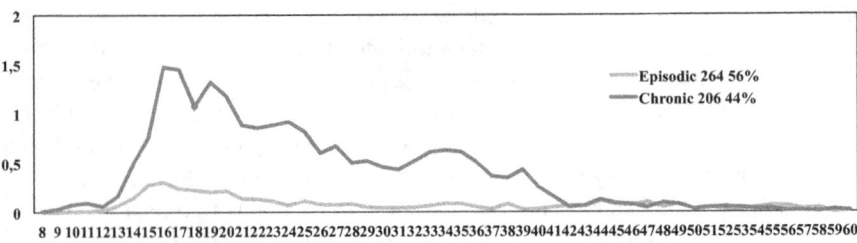

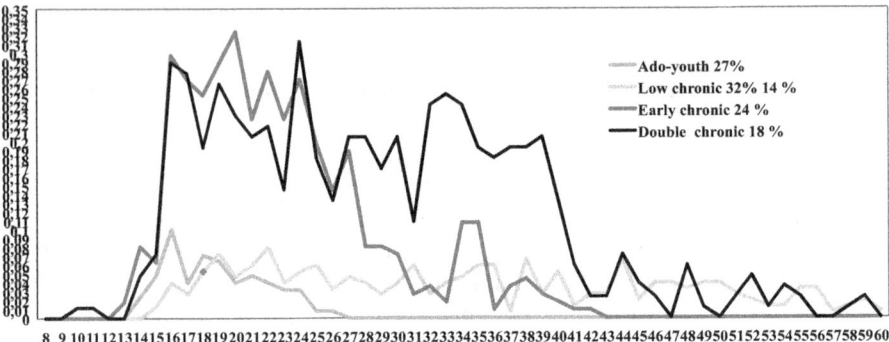

Fig. 5.3 The generation of 1960 total criminal career: two and four variety meso-trajectories

18% of offenders has a twofold shape; to our knowledge, it was never identified in other studies. It starts during childhood, battles with the previous group for dominance during adolescence and youth, and, surprisingly, increases its criminal activity during early and middle maturity to the highest level of all groups. This trajectory is also present in the G80 sample and for covert crimes.

In summary, among the two trajectories model, the one with the highest level of criminal activity explodes into three meso serious career paths and a clearer adolescence and youth trajectory when the analysis moves from four meso-paths to six micro-courses. First, as illustrated before, there are two adolescence and youth trajectories, a lower and a higher one. Second, a fourth chronic path emerged, the late chronic trajectory; these offenders had a very low level of criminal activity until the end of youth and the highest level of variety during the maturity years, higher than the three other chronic groups.

The fractal nature of crime that was postulated and demonstrated in Chap. 4 is also an important feature of trajectories. There is a meta-trajectory, the age–crime curve; various sets of meso-paths, which can be subdivided from the meta-course, and the optimal result for official crime is six micro-trajectories. This fractal nature of criminal courses is valid for generation, G60 and G80, and forms of offending, covert, overt, and lifestyle crimes. All these data are not reported here because of the numerous figures and tables, which would take up too much space (they are available from the author).

Table 5.6 Meso-courses of the G60 males: participation, onset, variety, frequency, offset, and duration

Parameters		Two trajectories		Four trajectories			
Name	Total	Low adolescence-youth peak	High-early offenders	Adolescence-youth peak	Low chronic	Early chronic	Twofold chronic
Number %	470	264	206	126	150	111	83
		56%	44%	27%	32%	23%	18%
Participation							
Minimum	1	1	4	1	1	3	5
Mean	6	3	10	1	4	9	12
Median	6	3	10	1	4	8	12
Maximum	22	12	22	5	12	18	22
Onset							
Minimum	8	10	8	11	10	8	9
Mean	18	20	15	16	22	15	16
Median	16	17	15	16	19	15	16
Maximum	55	55	29	8	55	24	23
Variety							
Minimum	1	1	3	1	1	3	6
Mean	6	3	9	2	4	8	10
Median	6	3	8	2	4	8	10
Maximum	15	12	15	8	12	14	15
Frequency							
Minimum	1	1	6	1	1	8	14
Mean	20	7	34	4	10	10	41
Median	13	5	29	2	6	24	35
Maximum	217	78	217	78	59	104	217
Offset							
Minimum	13	13	19	13	15	21	34
Mean	36	33	39	19	42	34	44
Median	37	31	39	18	41	34	41
Maximum	60	60	60	27	60	49	60
Career span							
Minimum	1	1	4	1	1	3	15
Mean	18	13	23	2	2	19	28
Median	19	7	23	1	20	20	26
Maximum	47	47	44	10	47	40	44

4.2   The Self-Reported Official Crime Trajectories[3]

The seriousness of offenses, one of the descriptors of the criminal career proposed by Sellin and Wolfgang (1964) and recognized by Blumstein et al. (1986) is absent from the trajectory narrative reviews (Piquero 2010; Jennings and Reingle 2012). It is also interesting to note that the word seriousness is not listed in the index of the last two textbooks on the development of antisocial behavior and crime (Morizot and Kazemian 2015; Farrington et al. 2019). Le Blanc and Fréchette (1989) analyzed the aggravation of the criminal activity with Sellin and Wolfgang's (1964) measure of crime seriousness and showed that there were stages of seriousness during escalation and desistance. In Chap. 3, the analysis of the development of the crime mix showed that there was a phenomenon of aggravation and deaggravation in terms of seriousness of the crime mix. In Chap. 4, the central launching role of onset was established in the study of crime as a system. In addition, the trajectory literature was disappointing, because in more than 100 studies, only two parameters of criminal activity, most often frequency and sometimes variety, are used, and never together.

Le Blanc and Fréchette (1989) identified trajectories using ad hoc cross tabulations with the parameters of the criminal career estimates from interviews at ages, 15, 17, and 30 with onset, variety, frequency, and seriousness. At around age 40, new self-reported interviews were conducted with a representative sample of 12 crimes from the least to the most serious ones (see the description of the sample in Appendix A, the 1970 court sample composed of 470 males born around 1960 and five birth cohorts or generation 1960, and Appendix B for the definitions of the self-reported crime measures). The 12 categories of crime were regrouped into two scales, minor and major crimes. The trivial offenses were vandalism, shoplifting, minor theft, and disorderly conduct (average Sellin and Wolfgang score of 2). The serious crimes were theft by breaking and entering, motor vehicle and aggravated theft, armed robbery, aggravated assault, sex offenses, and drug trafficking (average Sellin and Wolfgang score of 14). As the group base trajectory modeling technology appeared inapplicable because it could handle only one descriptor of the career, the K-means clustering technology was used with Gordon's (1999) procedure composed of seven criteria to estimate the internal and external validity of the obtained set of micro-trajectories (Le Blanc and Morizot 2003). The sample size was 470 convicted males (the number recommended by Piquero 2010 is 500); in addition, Gordon (1999) suggested that a trajectory should be retained only if its size is at least 5% of the total sample. The parameters onset and variety are employed (using frequency produced the same results).

The different analyses conducted suggested that a five micro-trajectories solution was the most appropriate. The hierarchical and optimization methods both

---

[3] The statistical analyses were conducted by Julien Morizot and it became an oral presentation by the author at the American Society of Criminology 2003 Annual Meeting, 13–16 November in Chicago.

suggested that this solution was optimal as additional courses did not provide new meaningful significant paths, both conceptually and statistically. Gordon (1999) suggested the use of the following criteria to select the optimal solution. (1) The percentage of the total variance that can be accounted for by a cluster solution was calculated for solutions from 2 to 10 clusters and then plotted. A key point emerged for solutions 5 and 6. The five clusters solution was chosen because in the six clusters solution there were groups that had less than 10% of the offenders. The final five micro-paths solution explained 45% of the total variance. (2) The coefficients of homogeneity obtained for the five micro-trajectories solution were all adequate in the order: $H = 0.86$, $H = 0.84$, $H = 0.72$, $H = 0.70$, and $H = 0.50$. (3) The cluster separation with 2 (dependent variables) × 2 (measurement points) repeated measures multiple analysis of variance (MANOVA) was undertaken on the petty and serious crimes scales. The between-subjects ($\Lambda = 0.23$; $F(8, 240) = 32.42$; $p < 0.0001$), within-subjects ($\Lambda = 0.25$; $F(6, 116) = 56.88$; $p < 0.0001$), and interaction ($\Lambda = 0.17$; $F(24, 405) = 11.33$; $p < 0.0001$) multivariate omnibus tests were all significant. Results of the univariate tests of the MANOVA, of the within-subjects contrasts, and of the post hoc comparisons are available from the author. In general, these tests confirmed clearly that the five offending trajectories were significantly different across time. (4) Finally, Gordon (1999) recommends conducting an external validation of the set of trajectories. Le Blanc and Morizot (2003) report such a test with scales of self-control constructed by Morizot and Le Blanc (2003a, b, 2005). A 3 × 4 repeated measures MANOVA was undertaken with these scales and the multivariate tests were all significant. All the developmental trends in self-control were coherently linked to the offending micro-trajectories.

Figure 5.4 displays the five micro-trajectories in order of seriousness, from left to right, with the mean T-scores and the description of the micro-paths is in raw scores in Table 5.7. (1) Late low minor adolescence and youth crime (10%): this first path starts the latest, at the end of adolescence, and is characterized by a low level of variety, frequency, and seriousness during adolescence and youth with a rare major crime during maturity. (2) Minor and aggravated adolescence and youth crime (36%): this second micro-course starts earlier, during early adolescence, the level of crime during adolescence and youth is much higher, particularly for major crimes, and very few offenders are active at the age 40 interview. (3) Serious low chronic (27%): this third group of offenders maintains a low level of major criminality during adolescence and youth and many report a few major crimes during their 30s; they start the latest of the chronic and their levels of variety, frequency, and seriousness are higher than those of the first two groups. (4) Serious explosive chronic (11%): this group of males displays a rapid start with the highest level of major and minor criminality at the age 15 interview and they maintain the second highest level of minor and major crimes during youth and later. (5) Serious early chronic (16%): these males start minor crimes during childhood and rapidly escalate to major offenses; they show the highest level of variety, frequency, and seriousness during youth, at the age 30 and 40 interviews. In addition, to our knowledge, the results of self-reported and official micro-trajectories were only compared on the frequency and variety parameters of the criminal career (see Piquero 2010 for

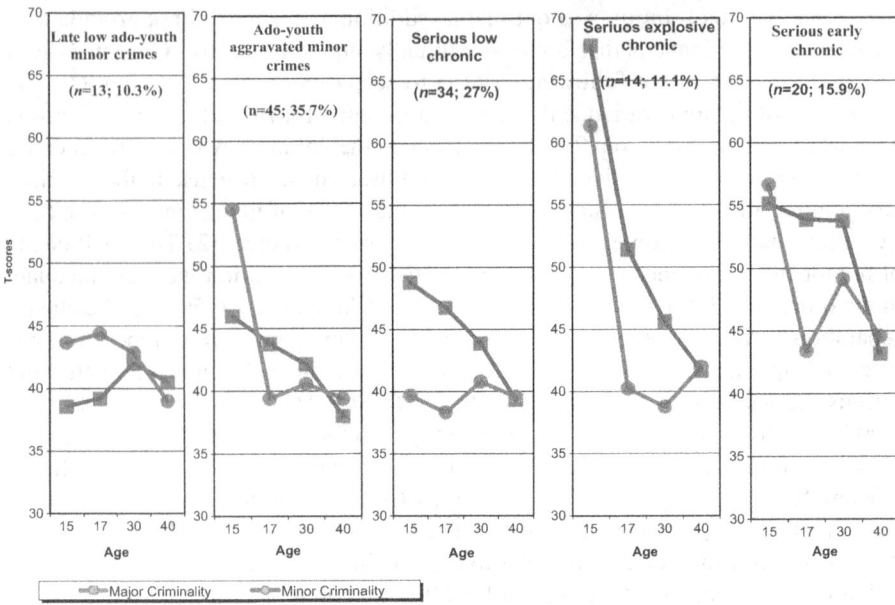

Fig. 5.4 The self-reported crime micro-trajectories of the generation of 1960

comments), never between these parameters and the seriousness of crimes. With the MTSFGCLS, this comparison is available on the same life-course span. The G60 male self-reported interviews on crimes graded by seriousness at ages 15, 17, 30, and 40 can be compared with their official crime data from age 12 to 45. A parallel can be drawn between the five micro-trajectories described in the previous paragraph and the five micro-paths obtained with LCGA and reported in Table 5.2 line G60 12–45. The self-reported and official results indicate two categories of paths. First, two adolescence and youth courses, one minor and one aggravated, and three chronic courses that show crimes during early maturity, the 30s. The percentages of offenders in these two groups is very similar; around 40% for adolescence and youth courses and 60% for the chronic paths. In sum, the two methods for the description of the criminal career, self-reports and official, and the two parameters, incidence (frequency and variety) and seriousness, produce very similar results.

Tzoumakis et al. (2012) identified the micro-trajectories for the frequency of violent offending (aggravated theft, personal attack, and sex offenses) of the G60 males from age 15 to 30 interviews with group-based modeling. Five violent paths were obtained. Of the convicted subjects, 45% reported one of these violent crimes. Among them nearly two-thirds were classified in the youth onset very low frequency path (64%); 14% had a late adolescence onset with a stable low frequency course; 9% adopted a middle adolescence onset with a progression of frequency thereafter; 4% embraced the middle adolescence onset with an average decreasing frequency; the final course was the late adolescence onset high frequency on a downslope (10%).

Table 5.7 The Self-reported Offending Trajectories: Descriptive Data for Onset, Offset, Variety, and Frequency

	Offending trajectories				
	Late low ado-youth 10%	Minor aggravated ado-youth 36%	Serious low chronic 27%	Serious explosive chronic 11%	Serious early chronic 16%
Minor crimes					
Onset	18.1	12.2	23.8	14.4	11.1
Offset$_a$					
Age 15 onward	4 (30.8%)	26 (57.8%)	20 (58.8%)	9 (64.3%)	1 (5.0%)
Age 17 onward	4 (30.8%)	4 (8.9%)	2 (5.9%)	2 (14.3%)	2 (10.0%)
Age 30 onward	4 (30.8%)	10 (22.2%)	8 (23.5%)	0 (0.0%)	8 (40.0%)
Active at age 40	1 (7.6%)	5 (11.1%)	4 (11.8%)	3 (21.4%)	9 (45.0%)
Variety (maximum 5)					
15 years	0.58	1.72	0.16	2.15	1.68
17 years	0.62	0.15	0.03	0.21	0.37
30 years	0.46	0.24	0.26	0.11	1.50
40 years	0.15	0.13	0.15	0.50	0.72
Frequency (maximum 20)					
15 years	1.01	3.01	0.36	4.93	3.82
17 years	0.78	0.24	0.04	0.52	0.81
30 years	1.46	0.52	0.62	0.09	4.25
40 years	0.31	0.23	0.43	1.35	1.88
Major crimes					
Onset	23.4	14.6	13.7	12.7	12.6
Offset^a					
Age 15 onward	8 (61.5%)	15 (33.3%)	8 (23.5%)	1 (7.1%)	0 (0.0%)
Age 17 onward	0 (0.0%)	10 (22.3%)	7 (20.6%)	1 (7.1%)	0 (0.0%)
Age 30 onward	3 (23.1%)	18 (40.0%)	16 (47.1%)	8 (57.2%)	14 (70.0%)
Active at age 40	2 (15.4%)	2 (4.4%)	3 (8.8%)	4 (28.6%)	6 (30.0%)
Variety (maximum 7)					
15 years	0.01	0.83	1.14	3.38	1.73
17 years	0.02	0.58	0.91	1.43	1.67
30 years	0.38	0.41	0.59	0.80	1.85
40 years	0.21	0.04	0.08	0.64	0.43
Frequency (maximum 28)					
15 years	0.01	1.38	1.91	6.38	3.58
17 years	0.07	1.02	1.56	3.15	3.65
30 years	0.92	0.91	1.50	2.14	3.52
40 years	0.48	0.12	0.36	1.55	1.29

^{a}Offset = cumulative proportion of individuals who have desisted

In Table 5.8, a few disparities are notable between the three sets of data, official and self-reported crimes and violent offenses. First, most of the violent offenders (64%) had a youth start and an occasional violent crime, whereas it is only 10% for the violent offenders lowest course for all the self-reported crimes. Second, the reverse is also evident. The chronic violent offenders amount to 23% compared with 54% for all the self-reported crimes. In summary, as in the previous chapter, there is a gap between self-reported crimes in general and violent offending.

Finally, it is interesting to note that the six-site cross-national study of the development of physical aggression from early childhood through middle adolescence identities in all four samples trajectories: abstainers, a decreasing very low rate of teacher reports, childhood peak middle rate, and continuous high rate (Broidy et al. 2003). The last path looks like the chronic trajectory in all the previous analyses of official and self-reported crimes and overt behaviors.

4.3 The Self-Reported Antisocial Behavior Trajectories

In this last section, antisocial behavior trajectories are identified for the males and females of the court sample of the 1990s. They are also compared with the above official and self-reported crime courses.

4.3.1 The Self-Reported Antisocial Behavior Trajectories of the Court Males

In Chap. 3, the developmental process of ABC, its escalation–de-escalation and aggravation–deaggravation, was replicated with three independent measurement procedures; official register of crimes, self-reported data from interviews on the perpetration of crimes, and self-reported data on a vast diversity of antisocial behaviors. In Chap. 4, it was established that ABC and its components were systems, particularly SRAB and all its particular forms.

The group-based trajectory modeling technology was also used for the following analyses for a comparison with official courses. Table 5.9 displays these results.

The comparison of the results of group-based trajectory modeling (GBTM) in Table 5.9 with Table 5.2 is stunning, as in five of the six analyses of antisocial

Table 5.8 G90 Males: Comparison of Official and Self-reported Offending Micro Trajectories

Official micro-trajectories: ages 12–45 (%)		Self-reported trajectories: ages 12–40 (%)	
Low variety adolescence and youth	32	Late low minor adolescence and youth	10
High variety adolescence and youth	11	Minor aggravated adolescence and youth	36
Low chronic	21	Serious low chronic	27
Twofold chronic	15	Serious explosive chronic	11
Early chronic	19	Serious early chronic	16

Table 5.9 The Comparison of the Models of Self-reported Antisocial Behavior Trajectories by Types of Behaviors: Statistics of the Latent Growth Class Analysis Via the Zero-inflated Poisson Model

Trajectories		One			Two			Three			Four		
		BIC[1]	Entro[2]	Boos[3]	BIC[1]	Entro[2]	Boos[3]	BIC[1]	Entro[2]	Boos[3]	BIC[1]	Entro[2]	Boos[3]
Delinquency		6046	na	na	**5654**	**0,63**	**0,000**	5618	0,55	0,55			
	Covert	7174	na	na	6524	0,76	0,000	**6316**	**0,76**	**0,000**	6252	0,75	0,004
	Overt	5822	na	na	**5191**	**0,71**	**0,000**	5121	0,63	0,21			
Problem behavior		5975	na	na	**5844**	**0,61**	**0,000**	5848	0,64	0,37			
	Conflict	5145	na	na	**5009**	**0,53**	**0,000**	5024	0,48	0,08			
	Lifestyle	6663	na	na	**6330**	**0,72**	**0,000**	6331	0,58	0,01			

behavior there are only two courses for which the BIC is optimal, like other statistical indicators. Table 5.9 shows that only covert antisocial behavior is represented by the three categories of trajectories that were identified with official and self-reported crime: a meta-path, two meso-courses, and four micro-trajectories. For all other forms of AB, delinquency and problem behavior and their components, covert, overt, conflict, and lifestyle, there are only two solid trajectories. In all the trajectories, according to Table 5.10, the levels of variety and participation diminish with age, from early adolescence, before age 16, to late adolescence, between ages 16 and 18, and thereafter. It is the same general tendency that was observed for the age–crime curve and the meta-, meso-, and micro-trajectories, regardless of the generation, the sample, and the measure, official and self-reported.

In the six analyses there are two common results. First, a minor course that starts later even if it is during childhood and displays a lower participation and less versatility at every follow-up interview between middle adolescence and middle maturity, the late 30s. Second, a major path starts earlier during childhood and manifests much higher levels of participation and variety at all interview ages. It is interesting to note that the two paths of delinquency, as for covert and overt AB, tends to group around half of the court males. Conversely, the major trajectory clearly dominates the minor path with 65–75% of the court males in the two paths of problem behavior, and also for the conflict and lifestyle courses.

An unexpected result is the presence of an adolescence-limited covert delinquency with 8% of the court males in the four trajectories model. It is the first case of the identification of this course among all the results in this chapter; it manifests by an average beginning at 11½ and an explosion of versatility and activity during the second half of adolescence followed by the absence of SRAB during adulthood.

In addition, in all the previous trajectory analyses in this chapter there was a distinction between low and high versatility paths, which were called meso-courses: (1) adolescence and youth and (2) chronic. They seem to be reflected in the SRAB results with the minor (1) later onset and lower variety and participation and major (2) earlier onset and higher variety and more continuous participation trajectories. As for the covert four micro-trajectories, they reproduce this distinction with two minor courses (1) the low minor or negligible path with the latest onset and the lowest intensity and (2) the adolescence-limited course and two major paths (1) a low chronic trajectory with low continuity over time and (2) the major chronic with the earliest onset, the highest versatility and continuity. Comparing the data from Table 5.10 with those of Tables 5.6 and 5.7, the four SRAB covert courses look very much like official and self-reported crime courses. The differences may be reflected by the number of points in time, four, compared with yearly official data.

In summary, the existence of two SRAB meso-trajectories, the adolescence and youth limited and the chronic courses corroborates previous results with official and self-reported crime. Let us see if it is the same conclusion for the convicted females of the court sample of the 1980 generation.

Table 5.10 Court Males of 1990: Trajectories of Types of Self-reported Antisocial Behavior: Means of Onset, Variety, and Participation

Types of SRAB	Delinquency		Overt		Covert						Problem behavior		Conflict		Lifestyle	
					2				4							
Subjects	251	248	288	213	282	217	106	39	120	234	132	374	180 36	326	129	362
%	50	50	58	42	57	43	21	8	24	47	26	74		64	29	71
	Min[a]	Maj[b]	Min	Maj	Maj	Min	Neg[c]	Ali[d]	Mch[e]	Mch[f]	Min	Maj	Min	Maj	Min	Maj
Onset age	9.52	9	10.9	9.5	10.1	12.1	12.9	11.5	11	9.9	8.7	7.6	9	7.7	12.2	10.4
Variety ages																
16	3.74	3.82	1.7	5.1	6.4	2.09	0.43	2.26	4.97	6.53	1.59	3.73	0.91	4.2	1.13	4.18
18	2.91	3.04	0.85	4.1	5.5	1.23	1.35	6.81	0.72	5.71	0.99	4.29	1.14	2.98	1.34	5.10
24	1.71	1.82	0.37	2.4	3.23	1.13	1.65	0	0.97	3.77	1.48	2.82	1.11	1.61	2.18	4.05
30	1.10	1.67	0.14	1.9	2.53	0.89	1.13	0	0.83	2.75	1.23	2.30	0.73	1.23	1.98	3.51
Active ages																
16	0.94	0.93	0.79	0.98	0.97	0.68	0.39	0.77	1	0.99	0.91	1.00	0.68	0.99	0.66	0.99
18	0.87	0.88	0.58	0.97	0.96	0.51	0.55	1	0.43	0.99	0.71	0.99	0.74	0.95	0.69	0.99
24	0.80	0.89	0.51	0.81	0.86	0.58	0.72	0	0.55	0.98	0.70	0.89	0.78	0.89	0.71	0.74
30	0.64	0.69	0.14	0.74	0.69	0.43	0.52	0	0.45	0.79	0.61	0.82	0.67	0.79	0.63	0.80

[a]Minor
[b]Major
[c]Negligible
[d]Adolescence-limited
[e]Low chronic
[f]Major chronic

4.3.2 The Females Self-Reported Antisocial Behavior Trajectories

The 1990s court sample was composed of 150 adolescent females. Only 20% (30) were convicted of a crime but none between ages 24 and 60. Their age–crime curve adopted the universal shape (Chap. 2, Sect. 2.2.1.2.3). This meta-trajectory is very similar to the low adolescence and youth limited path of the G60 and G80 males. No females could be classified as chronic offenders according to our definition, because none had a conviction during maturity, after age 30. It has been well known for a long time that a minimal proportion of females are considered recidivists by the justice system (Glueck and Glueck 1934 and more recently Tracy and Kempf-Leonard 1996). Concerning the prevalence of official problem behavior adjudicated in the Montréal juvenile court, they were more prevalent for females than for males (63% compared with 47%).

Piquero's (2010) narrative review of 80 studies lists less than ten independent studies (some with more than one paper) that analyzed female trajectories and most of them focused on alcohol, drugs, or smoking. In 2015, Cauffman, Monahan, and Thomas published a study with a court sample of 172 seriously offending females and analyzed their antisocial behavior trajectories with GBTM using six biannual interviews from ages 14 to 25. They report five micro-trajectories: low variety (40%), early desisters (21%), moderate desisters (22%), late desisters (10%), and persisters (7%).

In this analysis, the measures were the onset and variety of self-reported problem behavior, delinquency, sexual activity, relational violence, and drug use. Let us remember that 80% of the females were adjudicated in the Montréal juvenile court for these reasons. Their definitions are described in Table 1.1 in Chap. 1 and Appendix B. The analytical procedure was the same as for the self-reported crime trajectories in Sect. 5.4.2. Cluster analysis was conducted with the ages at onset, and the delinquency and drug-use scale. Lanctôt and Le Blanc (2003)[4] report four within-individual courses of females' participation in delinquency and drug use during adolescence and youth. They explained that variance was 51% and the homogeneity coefficients of each path were 0.69, 0.80, 0.61, and 0.64 respectively, which is considered to be very good.

The first micro-trajectory, delinquent explorers without drug use, includes females ($n = 15$, 16%) who experienced drug use for the first time later than all other females; they waited until adulthood. Moreover, even if their involvements in conduct problems and delinquency started at a young age, their delinquency was only exploratory. In fact, a few delinquent acts were committed up to age 15. After that age, their delinquent behaviors vanished.

The second micro-path, low adolescence and youth delinquent and drug users ($n = 31$, 33%), is composed of females who display benign delinquency and drug use;

---

[4]These statistical analyzes were conducted by Julien Morizot and it became an oral presentation with the author at the American Society of Criminology 2003 Annual Meeting, 13–16 November in Chicago.

they are the ones who initiated them the latest. They also distinguish themselves by having the weakest versatility during adolescence and youth.

The third course, explosive adolescents ($n = 21$; 22%), denotes a high involvement in drug use and in delinquency until mid-adolescence. Then, this involvement significantly declined, especially regarding delinquency. These females are those who started experiencing drug use and delinquency at the youngest ages.

The fourth trajectory is composed of continuous drug users and delinquents ($n = 27$, 28%). These convicted females had a high and persistent involvement in drug use throughout adolescence and youth. Their participation in delinquency declined from late adolescence on but remained at a higher level in comparison with the females of the other micro-trajectories.

In addition, the females' profile for risky sexual activities for each path is very similar to the profile of their drug use. In addition, the pattern of relational violence is similar to that of delinquent acts for each of the four groups. These findings give credence to the external validity of the identified four micro-trajectories.

In the paper by Lanctôt et al. (2004), using the same court females sample, time span, and clustering procedure as above, the authors looked at the trajectories of self-reported overt behaviors (physical and psychological violence as defined in Table 1.1 and Appendix B). Three paths were identified for the adjudicated females: (1) no overt behavior (44%); (2) explorers, (42%); and (3) childhood onset, high adolescence diversity, and rare youth decliners (13%).

In summary, persistence in SRAB is rare among females convicted in the Montréal juvenile court under the Young Offender Act of Canada or the Youth Protection Act of Quebec for delinquency or severe problem behavior. According to Cauffman et al. (2015), offending for the same age period from the middle of adolescence to the middle of youth was also rare. Earlier studies had the same conclusion. In addition, there are similarities between the SRAB trajectories of females and males on its total score. For each gender, two meso-courses are very clear: they are composed of an adolescence and youth limited path and a chronic course.

5 Conclusion

The MTSFGCLS theoretical position was, first, that trajectories are the convergence of the developmental mechanisms and the system functioning of ABC and, second, that they are multilayered or fractal; the meta-trajectory, the age–crime curve, subdivides itself into meso- and micro-courses. Five multidisciplinary and developmental taxonomies were described in Sect. 5.1. Regardless of the self and social control variables, the nature of the sample, and the length of the follow-up, the population samples recognized three principal major trajectories: abstainers, limited time offenders, and persistent or chronic offenders. The last two groups were much better represented in criminal justice samples.

The analyses of the data sets of the MTSFGCLS confirmed that criminology could start with two solid sets of trajectories for theoretical and applied purposes, regardless of the measures of antisocial behavior and crime (onset, participation, variety, frequency, or seriousness), the generation of the samples (G60 and G80), the gender (convicted females and males), the source of the data (official or self-reported), the types of offenses (covert, overt, lifestyle, or conflict behavior), and the statistical method used (cluster analysis and group base trajectory modeling). It was established that the ABC meta-trajectory or the age–crime curve displays a similar shape in all the analyses, a very rapid uplift until a peak during late adolescence followed by a much slower downlift. This meta-path is split into two principal meso-paths in all statistical analyses.

The first meso-path, *adolescence and youth limited*, is identified in all statistical analyses. ABC starting during late childhood or early adolescence reaches a peak during late adolescence and this course ends during early, middle, or late youth. It is interesting to note that in all analyses, except one, it was impossible to distinguish the Moffitt adolescence limited trajectory (Moffitt 1993). In the domain of trajectory research it is certainly the theme that was the object of most theoretical comments and empirical analysis (Skardhamar 2009; Piquero 2010). It is probably the length of the follow-up on the ABC career that explains this conclusion, most of the trajectory publications truncate their data set at the latest during youth, before age 30.

The second meso-path always observed is what has been called life-course persistent by Moffitt (1993), chronic by Farrington (Farrington et al. 2013a), or continuous and serious by Le Blanc and Fréchette (1989). It is to be remembered that this continuity in ABC takes the form of intermittency (Farrington et al. 2020). In Table 2.2, it was confirmed that the duration of the career is much shorter than the number of years an offender is active. For the G60 population sample it was an average of 2 years on a career span of 4.8 years. For the convicted males, it was 6.5 compared with 20.5.

This multilayer composition of the ABC set of trajectories was confirmed by distinguishing micro-courses between the above two meso-paths. First, the adolescence and youth path subdivided into two or three courses depending on the age at termination or the career during youth (early, middle, or late) or the incidence of offending (variety, frequency, or seriousness). Second, similarly, the chronic meso-course subdivides into three or four called low, early, late, and twofold chronic. These results compared very well with other sets of trajectories in our other longitudinal data sets.

In summary, all the above results confirm Nagin and Tremblay's (2005) point of view that the number of trajectories in a sample is not immutable, unchanging through time, and, we could add truncating of the data on onset and the length of follow-up. However, the similarity of the meso-trajectories is outstanding in all the analyses in this chapter and the resemblance of the micro-paths is exceptional.

Chapter 6
Conclusion: A Journey from Exploration to Generalization and Formalization

1 How Should We Know About the Development of Antisocial Behavior?

The course of a research career is often a set of successive answers to opportunities rather than a result of precise long-term planning, as exposed in our criminological autobiography on fundamental and applied research (Le Blanc 2017). This book is based on the Montréal Two Samples Four Generations Cross-sectional and Longitudinal Studies (MTSFGCLS), which was an improvised journey. This conclusion is composed of two parts. The first section is organized around propositions for the future of longitudinal research in developmental criminology. The second section states a formalized theory of the development of antisocial behavior and crime.

This book is about within-individual behavioral changes, the spinal canal of which is called developmental criminology. During our journey with the MTSFGCLS, five antisocial behavior and crime landscapes were viewed: the measurement, epidemiology, process, system, and course perspectives on antisocial behavior. The consequences of our empirical results in these domains are drawn for the future of longitudinal research. This part starts from past appraisals of the developmental criminology (Le Blanc 2012, 2015; Le Blanc and Fréchette 1989) and paradigmatic papers (Le Blanc and Loeber 1998; Loeber and Le Blanc 1990). The themes are research design, measurement, and replication.

© Springer Nature Switzerland AG 2021
M. Le Blanc, *The Development of Antisocial Behavior and Crime*,
https://doi.org/10.1007/978-3-030-68429-7_6

1.1   *The Future Research Design*

The study of the development of antisocial behavior activities evolved slowly after its birth with the description of the age–crime curve by Quételet 200 years ago. Le Blanc (2015), in a retrospective review of the longitudinal research designs, identified three phases of improvement of the research projects.

The first phase took place between 1930 and 1950, characterized by two types of data gathering. The first procedure was retrospective natural histories. These pioneering studies employed various types of data, interviews, and official records from different sources. Sheldon and Eleanor Glueck conceived the second design; it was a mix of official and self-reported crime, social, and psychological data gathered through a small number of waves with differing interval lengths between them. Participants and informants reported these data on white delinquents and nondelinquents from Massachusetts.

The second phase took place around 1970. Two innovative sets of longitudinal studies were introduced. (1) Wolfgang et al.'s (1972) landmark inquiry made efficient use of official arrest records and investigated the dynamics of offending. Their results contributed to advancing new substantive questions, such as specialization, offense switching and diversity in offenses, and trajectories. (2) Five longitudinal studies were under way during the 1970s, three international and two American: the Cambridge Study in Delinquent Development (CSDD) (West 1969; West and Farrington 1973); the Montreal Two Samples Four Generations Cross-sectional and Longitudinal Studies (Le Blanc and Fréchette 1989); the Dunedin Multidisciplinary Health and Development Study, which recruited a cohort of all children born in Dunedin (New Zeeland) (Moffitt et al. 2001); the five-wave Houston Long-Term Multi-Generation Study (Kaplan 1975, 1980, 1984, 1986); and the nine-wave National Youth Study directed by Elliott (Elliott 1994; Elliott et al. 1985, 1989). What distinguished these studies from the works of the previous generations was that they increased the number of panels and the life-course span covered. They paid more attention to the metric qualities of their measures. They gathered a good representation of the questions, measures, and tests from existing criminological knowledge and numerous cross-sectional studies that were reported in the criminology, psychology, and sociology literature. For their part, the Le Blanc, Kaplan, and Elliott studies were distinguished because they were theory-driven rather than multifactorial.

Finally, Le Blanc (2015) noted that the decade of the 1980s saw the launch of a cohort of North American longitudinal studies that were improvements over the studies of the previous periods in many ways as they adopted many propositions of the blueprint for a New Research Strategy for Understanding and Controlling Crime (Farrington et al. 1986). We call them the 1985 generation projects. They offered major contributions to developmental criminology, and their description and results are synthesized in the book by Thornberry and Krohn (2003). Five projects began during the same historical period in four American cities of different sizes, but without a major metropolitan area: the Rochester Youth Development Study (Thornberry), the Pittsburg Youth Study (Loeber), the Denver Youth Survey (Huizinga), the Seattle Social Development Project (Hawkins), and the Montréal Longitudinal and Experimental Study (Tremblay). The first three projects were sponsored by the Office of Juvenile Justice and Delinquency Prevention, which favored the use of similar measures of delinquency and antisocial behavior and some common risk and protective factors from the domains of neighborhood, family, school, peer, routine activities, and psychology. The last two programs involved an experimental preventive intervention.

All these longitudinal designs had major impacts on the development of knowledge in developmental criminology. However, some priorities emerged. First, an important task for the progression of knowledge, that is not habitual from behavioral science researchers, is to reanalyze existing data sets with theoretical and empirical questions that were not on the table when the initial data were gathered. It is a low-cost task that has proven fruitful in the work of Laub and Samson (2003) with Glueck's' court sample. In this book, the process view was reanalyzed with a measure of the crime mix and extended to other antisocial forms of behaviors and many earlier conclusions were confirmed with a longer career span, age 61 instead of age 30. Some studies tried to avoid the social status gap in offending (more lower social status individuals display more offending, such as the CSDD and the 1985 generation projects, by selecting a working-class community or over-sampling subjects from such milieus.

A second imperative for the study of the antisocial behavior and crime career is the recruitment of a large criminal justice sample, either of arrested or convicted delinquents, from their initial contact with this system, as in the Philadelphia study (Wolfgang et al. 1987), and the MTSFGCLS. Arrestees would be preferable, to eliminate the impact of plea-bargaining that leaves aside many committed crimes, and reduce the seriousness of a large number of others. From our experience, samples of around 500 individuals are insufficient when advanced multivariate statistical techniques, such as path and trajectories analysis, are employed with more than a few variables and many points over time. In addition, the sample should contain around five birth cohorts to protect the data set from an unusual cohort (see also Farrington et al. 1986). A criminal justice sample produces, like an electronic microscope, a clearer vision of the development mechanism of antisocial behavior crime as shown by the publications from many longitudinal studies.

A third crucial element is the length of the age span under study. It should start during childhood, around age 8, because many antisocial behaviors, even crimes, are initiated between ages 8 and 12. Many longitudinal follow-ups stop at the end of youth, age 30. The time span from childhood through adolescence and youth is insufficient even if, as our results showed, most of the mechanisms have been operated by that age. However, changes in the course of the career still happened during the 40s and 50s and later, particularly with regard to the number and nature of the trajectories. A related design parameter is the spacing of the data. For official crime, the natural time interval is age or yearly data. The Rochester, Pittsburg, and Denver studies introduced yearly interviews on antisocial behavior until the end of adolescence, and then with longer intervals of time during youth. We would recommend yearly or biyearly data on antisocial behavior, at least until the end of youth and even during maturity.

Fourth, two lessons were offered by Glueck's studies. (1) Multiple informants can provide significant data; it is particularly the case for official and SRAB and crime. (2) The data should be multidisciplinary, as practiced by Glueck; they were from the domain of biology, psychology, and sociology. It is now much easier to do so because in these three domains there are reliable and valid measures that can be imported into longitudinal studies. The Rochester, Pittsburg, and Denver studies collected a large array of sociological variables, but lack common biological and psychological variables. This was contrary to the Dunedin study.

Finally, Stouthamer-Loeber and van Kammen (1995) and Stouthamer-Loeber 2012), from their rich experience in the management of the Pittsburg Youth Study, propose some important technical guidelines for future longitudinal data collection, storage, consent, confidentiality, and research conditions.

1.2   Down the Road with Conceptualizations and Measurements

Our evaluation of the knowledge acquired on the dynamics of offending is that it does not lack appropriate conceptualization. Certain contributions have been extremely important, such as those of Wolfgang et al. (1972), which introduced, implicitly or explicitly, most of the concepts that have been used in the study of the development of crime, as well as those of Blumstein et al. (1986) and Loeber (1982, 1987) with their masterly effort to update all the concepts of the dynamic of offending. The five chapters of this book confirm our hypothesis that the dynamic of offending also applies to all forms of antisocial behavior regardless of whether they are offenses or problem behaviors. The principal weakness is not in the definition of the parameters of all types of antisocial activity, nor is it in the method used to examine the mechanisms and processes of their development. Developmental criminologists have to pay much more attention to the conceptualization of some forms of antisocial behavior and crime that were introduced during the beginning of the second millennium in all societies.

The first key change is the advent of the numeric world. The introduction and dissemination of all types of electronic devices and the availability of new means of communication has increased the prevalence and incidence of fraudulent, aggressive, and intimidating behaviors for which there were no clear ethical, legal, and social definitions of their level of antisociality and no limits and sanctions were consensual for these new behaviors. It is a swamp in which researchers must select behaviors that are antisocial, choose the more significant, formulate them into precise questions, test if the content is understood by potential respondents, verify if they allow a diversity of responses, compile scales, and check their reliability and validity. In this book, the numeric antisociality was not totally absent; it was insufficiently covered, but it is absolutely necessary to introduce this phenomenon for future longitudinal and cross-sectional research.

A second key measurement problem is the heteromorphy of the antisocial behaviors. It refers to acts that have different forms at different stages of the life cycle. For example, a fraud may have various forms and seriousness: examples of heteromorphic fraud could be for an adolescent getting onto a public bus without paying and an adult of older age not declaring all their income. Another example of a conflict with a person could be measured with parents during childhood, teachers during school, and the spouse during maturity. There is a need for more research on the question of heteromorphy. In Chap. 1, some encouraging results were obtained, but there is still much to be done conceptually and empirically.

A third problem is the conceptualization of two forms of crime, what we called lifestyle-market offending. Regardless of whether the measure of offending is official or self-reported, most researchers analyzed two types of offenses, against property and against persons or violent crimes and other crimes. Laub and Samson (2003) proposed a third category called drug and alcohol offenses for the Glueck's data set. In our G60 and G80 data sets, most of the official offenses were part of the property and violent categories. There was a minority of offenses that researchers usually classify into the category other crimes and forget them in their analyses thereafter. Among these crimes, we identified two categories: offenses relative to the use and traffic of alcohol, drugs, and cigarettes; and offenses relative to the participation in illegal markets such as buying and selling stolen goods, offenses relative to the support of prostitution (not as a client), shylocking, etc.

In Chap. 2, what was most interesting about the age–crime curves was that property crimes dominated throughout the whole career but much more during adolescence and youth; violent crimes had the second place during that period, and lifestyle-market offenses were more numerous than violent offenses after the period of youth. This result has never been reported as far as we know. Our interpretation is that there was a growth in the prevalence of illegal markets over the years and many predatory criminals becomes the working class (blue collars) in these markets after incarceration and because legal jobs are not easily available to them. This interpretation has to be tested with interviews with older criminals who were convicted for lifestyle-market offenses after a predatory criminal career to identify all the roles then can be played in these markets and how to interpret the relationship between their predatory offenses and their lifestyle-market offenses.

A fourth and last problem requires empirical investigations by researchers; it is the organization of all the forms of antisocial behavior and crime. The dominant theoretical and empirical position is that they are organized into a hierarchical structure (Fig. 1.1). This sort of interconnectedness between the types antisocial behavior and crime was tested by a good number of researchers and described in Chap. 1. Our results were not totally convincing as confirmatory factor analysis could not handle a structure with five levels: individual behaviors, scales, types, categories, and total antisocial behavior and crime. Some exploratory works with a factor analysis procedure from top-down instead the usual reverse hierarchical procedure lead us to formulate and explore the hypothesis that all forms of antisocial behavior and crime are interconnected in a network (Fig. 1.2). This hypothesis was explored in Chap. 1 in an unsatisfactory manner as we did not know of any appropriate statistical procedure to analyze such a network.

1.3   Future Replications

Thirty years ago, Le Blanc and Fréchette (1989) argued that replication should be considered an integral component of the research process. In the introduction to this book, we traced the formulation of this fundamental principle of science into the seventeenth century. Later, Selvin (1965) stated that definitive empirical results include either a replication of a researcher's own work or a reproduction by other researchers. We followed that recommendation with Hirschi's social control theory (Hirschi 1969) in Le Blanc and Caplan (1985), with our self-reported measures of delinquency between the 1970s and the 1980s in Le Blanc and Tremblay (1988), and with our social and self-controls theory for the same periods (Le Blanc et al. 1988).

In criminology, McNeeley and Warner (2015) reported data for the period 2006 to 2010. Out of 691 publications in criminology, only 6 (0.9%) were direct replications, 10 (1.4%) were empirical generalizations or conceptual replications, and 98% were original research. A direct replication requires a comparable sample in every respect, the same procedures for data gathering, common instruments and methods for the construction of identical variables, and the use of the same methods of data analysis. In this context, only half (3) reported the same results with a direct replication. Virtually all the conceptual reproductions confirm the initial results of these studies (90%). What distinguished them were most often the characteristics of the sample and the historical moment, not the measurement or the methods.

In summary, it is extremely rare that a true replication is published in the criminological journals. The above figures clearly tell us that publishing such papers does not increase the prestige of a researcher; it is not worth his time. What we find are different researchers who address the same question under a common concept with an assortment of different samples, methods, and increasingly sophisticated statistical analysis. Consequently, it is essential that criminologists seriously set about performing this scientifically fundamental task. A group of seven renowned criminologists signed a recent paper on the importance and necessity of replication in criminology (Farrington et al. (2018). It was one of the main goals of this book to add the reproductions of our empirical results by gender, types of samples, historical periods, and sociocultural contexts. Let us display the balance sheet of this undertaking chapter by chapter.

The measurement chapter offered a magnificent view because of the wide spectrum of behaviors considered and the very high metric properties of the scales regardless of the gender, the samples (representative and court), the historical periods (1970s, 1980s, 1990s, and 2000s), the ages, and the sociocultural context. In this case, we report validations of the self-reported measures in Québec, Spain,

France, Brazil, Algeria, and Senegal. A standing question in developmental crimi-nology was investigated, the heteromorphy across periods of the life cycle. The results were interesting; however, this question needs more conceptualization and empirical research with new advanced statistical techniques. The last picture was about the structural content of SRAB. The theoretical position was that the structure displays a hierarchy of five levels: particular behaviors (63 in our questionnaire), scales (12), forms (covert, overt, conflict, lifestyle), categories (delinquency and problem behaviors), and total antisocial behavior. Many publications tackled the question of structure during the last 20 years with only a few of these levels. We concluded that the confirmatory factor analysis method was unable to handle such a complex model without a very large sample: around 500 subjects is insufficient.

Chapter 2 added video camera to self-reported data, official crime, and problem behavior. Most of the epidemiological view was devoted to the age–crime curve. The general shape of the curve was replicated by gender, types of samples, histori-cal periods, and types of crimes. These conclusions add four confirmations to all the results published since Quételet; it is a generalization in criminology. This general shape is similar to the curve of many pandemics, as we saw with COVID-19. However, there were gender, normative, historical, and type of crime gaps.

1. The gender gap manifested in the following results. Females, compared with males, had much lower statistics on the career parameters (onset, participation, variety, frequency, offset, and duration) and a much lower prevalence and inci-dence as well as a shorter career: the curve ends at age 25. Their self-reported antisocial behavior was lower on covert and overt acts, equal on conflict behav-iors, and higher on lifestyle activities.
2. The normative gap that was expected was that the members of a representative sample would show lower statistics on criminal career parameters than the mem-bers of a court sample. This was clearly confirmed. The court males of G60 and G80 were really a special group in the population of Montréal adolescents because their curve was very much lower.
3. The generation gap between G60 and G80 was not evident on the general shape of their age–crime curves. However, when the curves, were enlarged some phe-nomena were observable: the peak was higher during adolescence for G80 and for G60 the curve was spread over a longer period, until age 61. In addition, the criminal career statistics were higher for G60, even if the career span was restricted to ages 12 to 45 instead of 8 to 61. These variations were explained by legal changes (the age of criminal responsibility was moved from age 8 to 12 for G80), criminal justice changes (more diversion and less correctional placements, particularly in secure milieus), and the advent of a significantly more generous welfare state for G80 (see Appendix C).
4. The last gap concerns the changes in the crime mix during the life cycle. Usually, researchers analyze two forms of offenses, property and violent, and they forget about victimless crimes. In addition, the question of the crime mix is not inves-tigated. We conceptualized what we called lifestyle crime; this concept and its operationalization needs much more work to be satisfactory. It was noted, as

everybody does, that property offenses always dominated violent offenses along the life course, from onset to late maturity. However, it does so less during adolescence and part of youth compared with violent offenses and, after these phases of life, it was less the case to the benefit of lifestyle crimes. Future research must pursue and replicate these results.

After all these descriptive data, it was time to expand and replicate Le Blanc and Fréchette's (1989) results, 30 years later, on the developmental mechanisms of growth and decline of antisocial behavior and crime. In our revised conception, there are quantitative changes or gears of activation–deactivation and qualitative changes or the gears of aggravation–deaggravation. The results in Chap. 3 confirmed our previous one. The quantitative gears of activation are the launching, diversification, explosion, and stabilization, and the mechanisms of deactivation are the slackening, declivity, specialization, and vanishing. The results were similar for the males of G60 and G80. What needs to be done is to test these generalizations in other communities and countries and with criminal justice females with large samples. The qualitative developmental changes of aggravation and deaggravation were tested for official and self-reported offending and self-reported antisocial behavior. Age-specific offenses and mixes were observed at each period of the life based on the ages at onset and offset. The content of these sequences of mixes were very similar during the uplift but in reverse order for the downlift. The offenses and antisocial behaviors that appeared earlier during the life of the convicted males were also those that disappeared earlier. In addition, there were indications that the sequences were graded in terms of seriousness. These conclusions apply to the G60 and G80 convicted males. However, the sequence for these latter offenders was more compacted, the offenses and self-reported antisocial behavior mixes were composed of a greater diversity of behaviors when they were launched and terminated. Versatility was the norm in all cases. Most of the aggravation and deaggravation switching was to the adjacent stage, rarely jumping over the next stage, and even less often reversing to an earlier stage. The most impressive result was the sudden and massive collapsing of 10 out of the 15 forms of SRAB during a short period, from age 21 to 25. The aggravation–deaggravation mechanisms still have to be tested with an improved measure of seriousness in other communities and countries and with females.

Since our 1989 book, we have arrived at the point of view that these developmental mechanisms are internal interacting elements of a developmental system (Fig. 4.2). As a consequence, Chap. 4 tested a system functioning for antisocial behavior and crime and their particular forms. The first part of the chapter showed that antisocial behavior and crime display all the characteristics of a system. Using the convicted G60 and G80 males, the overall parameters of the criminal career, and path analysis for the first time in criminology, we tested and confirmed the hypothesis that a comprehensible diversity of SRAB might function as a developmental system. This system is fractal and multilayered. It is structured in multiple strata as expected in Fig. 1.1: first, delinquency and problem behavior; second, covert and overt, lifestyle, and conflict behaviors respectively; third, a diversity of lifestyle and conflict categories of behaviors. As for the previous chapters, there is a need to test these results with data from females and from other communities and countries. At the end of this system scenery, criminologists must not forget that systems of anti-social behavior and crime are extremely complex and the analyses in this chapter are only a first exploration of this view.

The last view of our antisocial behavior and crime journey came from the scenery on its courses. Our theoretical position was, first, that trajectories are the conver-gence of the developmental mechanisms and the system functioning of antisocial behavior and crime and, second, that they are multilayered or fractal. The meta-trajectory is the age–crime curve, and it is subdivided into meso-paths and then into micro-courses. It is our position that the vast body of empirical literature on trajec-tories presents common results, usually between four and six courses, that we called micro-trajectories, whereas the theoretical publications propose a consensus on the existence of two main trajectories, chronic and limited, which we called meso-trajectories.

The analyses of the data sets of the MTSFGCLS confirmed that developmental criminology could start with two solid sets of trajectories for theoretical and applied purposes regardless of the measures of antisocial behavior and crime (onset, partici-pation, variety, frequency, or seriousness), the generation of the samples (G60 and G80), the gender (convicted females and males), the source of the data (official or self-reported), the types of offenses (covert, overt, lifestyle, or conflict behaviors), and the statistical method used (cluster analysis and group base trajectory modeling).

Two meso-paths were observed. The *adolescence and youth limited* is identified in all statistical analyses. Antisocial behavior and crime start during late childhood or early adolescence and reaches a peak during late adolescence, and this course end during early, middle, or late youth. It is interesting to note that in all the analyses, except one, it was impossible to distinguish the Moffitt adolescence limited trajec-tory (Moffitt 1993). The second meso-path always observed is what has been called *life-course persistent* by Moffitt, *chronic* by Farrington, or *continuous and serious* by Le Blanc and Fréchette (1989). This multilayer composition of the antisocial behavior and crime set of trajectories was confirmed by distinguishing micro-courses between the above two meso-paths. First, the adolescence and youth path was subdivided into two or three courses depending on the age at termination of the career during youth (early, middle, or late) and the prevalence (participation) and incidence of offending (variety, frequency, or seriousness). Second, similarly, the chronic meso-course is subdivided into three or four paths with the basic course of the age–crime curve that were called *low* (prevalence and incidence in comparison with the next three), *early* (highest during childhood and adolescence), *late* (highest during maturity and low before), and *twofold* chronic. In summary, the similarity of the meso-trajectories is outstanding in all the analyses in this chapter and the resem-blance of the micro-paths is exceptional. We have to repeat reproductions by com-munities, countries, and for females.

One of the goals of this book was replication. We are very proud of our results within the limits of the MTSFGCLS. They are certainly valid for the period from the 1970s to the 2000s. Are they valid for the time before or after that period? There are two ways of answering this question: reanalyzing the data of previous longitudinal studies or repeating a study with the above design of the future. Our results are North American and a good way of getting beyond this ethnocentrism is to produce replications in diverse cultural milieus on other continents.

2   A Discursive and Axiomatic Theory of the Development of Antisocial Behavior

Criminology rarely produced replications of research results and formalizations of theories, two signs of maturity in hard science. To our knowledge, only three publications formalized narrative explanatory theories: DeFleur and Quinney used set theory over Sutherland's differential association theory (1947), Empey and Lubec (1971) relied on logical rules to formulate their axiomatic theory of lower class delinquency, and Le Blanc and Caplan (1993) employed Gibbs' method (Gibbs 1972) to formalize Hirschi's social control theory (Hirschi 1969). In addition, Le Blanc and Fréchette (1989) translated their results on the development of male criminal activity into mathematical equations. In this last section of this book, we go one step further. This journey is the formalization of a general theory of the development of antisocial behavior. This is done using a rigorous method.

Gibbs (1972) stated that "… there is no effective consensus in the field as to the appropriate mode of theory construction and no trend in that direction…" (p. 4), but he added 13 years later (Gibbs 1985) "… any formal mode is superior to the discursive mode" (p. 24). His method was designed for the formulation and analysis of explanatory theories (for a detailed definition application to Hirschi's social control theory see Le Blanc and Caplan 1993). We adapt Gibbs' method to a descriptive theory of the development of antisocial behavior instead of an explanatory theory. According to his method, a theory has two parts. The first section is called the extrinsic part or the dictionary of the theory. The second section is called the intrinsic part; it consists of statements in the form of empirical assertions or hypotheses that can be empirically tested with replications.

2.1   The Extrinsic Part of the Developmental Theory of Antisocial Behavior

The extrinsic part is composed of a unit term and three sets of elements: constructs, concepts, and measures. The **unit term** refers to the class of persons the theory fits; this theory applies to the development of male and female antisocial behavior during their life cycle. The other components are the constructs (in bold), concepts (in gray), and the measures (italic). A **construct** is a definition of terms that are neither complete nor empirically measurable. They are specified by concepts or terms that are complete, but not empirically applicable. These terms have to be specified by a *measure*.

2.1.1   Antisocial Behavior: Acts that Violate Social Norms and that Are Harmful to Others

Official antisocial behavior: these acts are listed in a country's criminal code and they are defined by governmental agencies responsible for youth protection, schooling, driving of motor vehicles, use of alcohol, etc.; these data are obtained from a criminal justice or other agency. In the MTSFGCLS, the measures are listed in Appendix B.

Self-reported antisocial behavior: this concept refers to behaviors that are reported by the   research subjects during one or many interviews or through questionnaires or by other persons in their environment (parents, school teacher, friend, etc.). There is a social or a scientific consensus on the spectrum of such behaviors. In the MTSFGCLS, they are regrouped into valid and reliable scales that are replicated by genders, cultural communities, types of samples, and historical periods.

2.1.2   The Antisocial Behaviors Manifest in Three Categories

Covert behaviors: these behaviors concern the furtive appropriation of goods. They are measured as official crimes against propriety and self-reported acts of theft and fraud. *Appendix B lists the measures of this concept.*

Overt behaviors: these behaviors are attacks or harmful actions against persons or their goods. They are measured as official crimes against persons or vandalism and as interpersonal conflict and aggression by self-reported instruments. *Appendix B lists the indicators and scales used.*

Lifestyle behaviors: these behaviors are characterized by behavioral habits that are not normative, that are associated with social marginality. They are measured as official crimes if they concern the use of drugs, dangerous driving, and the participation in illegal markets (drugs, alcohol, stolen goods, prostitution, etc.). Their self-reported measures focus on sexual promiscuity and the use of alcohol and drugs. *Appendix B lists these measures.*

2.1.3   The Career Developmental Parameters Are the Same for Official Crime and Self-Reported Antisocial Behavior (See Also Table 2.1)

Onset: the age at the first antisocial act.

Participation: the presence of an antisocial behavior at a particular age or period of life.

Frequency: the number of a particular acts at a specific age or period of life.

Variety: the number of different acts at a specific age or period of life.

Offset: the age at which the last act was committed.

Duration: the length of the antisocial behavior career. *There are two measures: (1) the career span: the age at offset minus the age at onset; (2) the number of active years or the sum of the years a subject was convicted or reported antisocial behaviors.*

Seriousness of behaviors: a legal classification, an evaluation of the harmfulness of acts, or a rating of the severity of a behavior by experts or the population. *The measures are reviewed in Chap. 3.*

Behavioral mix: a combination of forms of antisocial behavior at a particular point in time. *Ladders of behavioral mixes with upward and downward courses are described in Chap. 3.*

2.2 The Intrinsic Content of the Developmental Theory of Female and Male Antisocial Behavior

Gibbs (1985) defines a theory as being a set of propositions that can be tested empirically. They are derived successively from basic premises on relationships from constructs, to concepts, and to measures. Then, the propositions are formulated from the connections between the developmental parameters of the antisocial career. For example, at the level of constructs, it could be stated: the incidence of antisocial behavior is related to its age at onset; at the level of the constructs, it would be: the age at the onset of antisocial behavior is associated with the level of frequency; at the level of measures, a sign of direction is always added, it will be: the age at onset correlates negatively with the frequency of antisocial behavior, or the earlier the onset, the higher its frequency. Le Blanc and Caplan (1993) used this procedure to analyze Hirschi's social control theory. Duncan (1984) confirmed, that, at the level of measures, a variable is a combination of basic elements, in our case, the career parameters. In our 1989 book, we applied this empirical procedure and it was formulated with mathematical equations. The formulation of our theory of the development of antisocial behavior draws from the Gibbs and Duncan procedures.

The basement of our theory is a solid set of official and self-reported measures of antisocial behavior that was replicated for genders, types of sample (population and court), historical periods (1970s, 1980s, 1990s, and 2000s), and forms of antisocial behaviors (covert, overt, conflict, lifestyle). The scientific value of these measures in the MTSFGCLS was also confirmed by empirical reproductions in Spain, Brazil, Algeria, France, and Senegal. In addition, numerous conceptual replications of similar measures were cited throughout our journey in the measurement country. With these solid measures, the MTSFGCLS was able to confirm some generalizations in criminology.

2.2.1 A Gender Gap

Females show a prevalence and incidence of official crimes of all categories that is very much lower than those of males. Females display a higher prevalence and incidence of official problem behavior. Males report a much higher prevalence and incidence of self-reported delinquency than females. Females declare more lifestyle SRAB than males. The two genders show similar levels of prevalence and incidence of interpersonal conflict behavior.

2.2.2   A Normative Gap

Any criminal justice sample of males displays a very much higher level of prevalence and incidence of official and SRAB than a sample representing the population, regardless of the generation.

2.2.3   A Generation Conundrum

Self-reported antisocial behavior, including self-reported delinquency, problem behaviors, covert, overt, and lifestyle acts, are quite stable over time in representative school samples and for both genders. This relative stability will be observed for the other parameters of the antisocial behavior career. On the contrary, OO decreases over time in official statistics and court samples. Covert behaviors will diminish significantly, whereas overt, lifestyle, and numeric crimes will increase. Research must be undertaken to disentangle factors that may explain that decreases such as the length of the longitudinal follow-up, changes in the criminal code, a later age of legal responsibility, more diversion and less punitive practices in the criminal justice system, more treatment-oriented programs in correctional institutions, and, overall, at least in Québec, the general improvement of society, and a stronger welfare state.

2.2.4   An Age–Antisocial Behavior Puzzle

The shape of the official and self-reported age–antisocial behavior curve is a generalized phenomenon for their forms, delinquency and problem behavior, and overt, covert, and lifestyle acts. It is also reproduced for genders, population, and criminal justice samples, and historical periods. It manifests a rapid growth, a peak toward the end of adolescence, and a slower and extended decline until old age, regardless of the parameter of the career. The variations between the curves are in height and velocity, not in shape.

2.2.5   The Developmental Mechanisms of Antisocial Behavior

The combinatory measures of quantitative changes are defined in Table 3.1. Quantitative changes, escalation and de-escalation during a criminal career, assessed by official and self-reported crimes, is observed for court males. Childhood is particularly activating (the parameters are the highest: launching, diversification, explosion, and stabilization), the early and late adolescence and early and middle youth are periods of continuity (the parameters are quite stable), and late youth and the maturity phases are moments of deactivation (the parameters are the lowest: slackening, declivity, specialization, and vanishing). The generic mechanism of quantitative development is in operation for all forms of SRAB.

Qualitative changes in age-specific behavioral mixes during the life course manifest in a particular sequential order for onsets (aggravation) and offsets (deaggravation) of acts of OO and SRAB. They show concomitance with the well-known stages of human development that we recognized (childhood, adolescence [early and late], youth [early, middle, and late], and maturity [early, middle, and late]). The onset mixes of antisocial behavior are spread over a longer period of time and they are more numerous than their offset mixes; they are more concentrated for OO than for SRAB. The behavioral mixes launched earlier during childhood and adolescence disappeared faster during youth and early maturity. Males are generally switching to an adjacent stage of more serious behaviors. There is a sudden and massive collapsing of many mixes of official and SRAB during a short period of time, from ages 21 to 25.

Replications of these two developmental processes have still to be conducted with females and in other communities. The escalation–de-escalation and aggravation–deaggravation results were very solid as they apply to the data from three independent measurement procedures: official register of crimes, self-reported data from interviews on the perpetration of crimes, and self-reported data on a vast spectrum of antisocial behavior.

We will move to a third level of complexity of our developmental theory of antisocial behavior. At the first level, we were manipulating individual measures; at the second level, we were working with two measures; and, at the next level, many parameters of the career were combined to synthetize the convergence of the developmental mechanisms and the system functioning of antisocial behavior.

2.2.6   Antisocial Behavior Is a Developmental System

Developmental criminology has to adopt the perspective that antisocial behavior and all its forms function as autodynamic systems. The parameters of the career are in coevolution, interaction at each point in time, and causal continuity during the life cycle. These phenomena are sensitive to the initial condition, onset, and probabilistic. The launching and continuity mechanisms are the result of contemporary and causal interactions between participation, variety, and frequency; the dominant role is played by variety. The decrease in participation and frequency during maturity quickens the outcome of the career. The antisocial behavior system is fractal; the system functioning is similar for types of antisocial behavior, such as covert, overt, and lifestyle or delinquency and problem behavior. The individuality of these subsystems manifests as particular statistical figures in the path analysis statistics; this is the contextuality of the overall antisocial behavior system. In a nutshell, to attain a larger generalizability of these conclusions about system autodynamic, the results of the system view must be replicated with females, other generations, and diverse communities.

2.2.7   The Life Course Trajectories of Antisocial Behavior

Regardless of the nature of the sample and the length of the follow-up, the results from SRAB trajectory analysis with population samples display three major trajectories: abstaining from antisocial behavior and crime, limited-time, and persistent or chronic antisocial behavior and crime. The last two groups were much more prevalent in criminal justice samples.

In criminal justice samples, official and self-reported offending is represented by a multilayered set of paths. The higher layer is the meta-trajectory, which was called the age–crime curve. There were also two generalized meso-paths for OO and SRAB: (1) the adolescence and youth limited trajectory that starts during late childhood and ends during youth; and (2) the chronic path that shows antisocial activities during maturity and a much higher yearly prevalence and incidence. The last layer is composed of five or six courses regardless of gender, the data (OO or SRAB), and the historical period. Two or three of them were adolescence and youth paths with varying degrees of prevalence and incidence and termination during early, middle, or late youth. Three or four courses were chronic paths depending on the length of the follow-up (to age 61 four paths, to age 45 three courses): the low chronic, early chronic (the highest level during childhood and adolescence), twofold chronic (two peaks: one during adolescence and the other during early maturity), and late chronic (the highest level between the ages of 30 and 60) offenders. In all these types of courses, there was offending during three periods of life.

All these theoretical and replicated propositions emerged and then received solid support from the MTSFGCLS data sets. However, they still have to be tested again and again in other countries, cities, and communities, with particular attention to females, a variety of minority groups, and particularly across historical periods. Beyond these tests, it is time to move from this descriptive developmental theory to an explanatory developmental theory, the above-mentioned theoretical propositions becoming dependent variables in a theoretical model composed of an interconnected development of structural and social–self-control measures (Le Blanc 2006, 2019). We have undertaken this task with the MTSFGCLS data sets.

Appendix A: The Baseline and Replication Samples of the Montréal Two Samples Four Generations Cross-Sectional and Longitudinal Studies

The course of a research career often consists of successive responses to opportunities rather than precise long-term planning. This was the case for mine (Le Blanc 2017). This appendix starts with the step-by-step building of the MTSTGCLS over a period of 50 years.

The Origins of the MTSFGCLS

Travis Hirschi (1969) published the most important book in criminology of the twentieth century "Causes of Delinquency." My career was launched, after reading his book at the end of my Ph.D. studies, with the idea of replicating his landmark book. A RSP70 sample (representative sample of the population and for the five birth cohorts recruited during the early 1970s and born around 1960, or the generation of 1960) to test his theory by replicating his empirical results in a distinct cultural context, the French-speaking population of Montréal, Québec. The initial design was a two-wave panel study with a stratified random sample of adolescents aged 12–17 living on the Island of Montréal enrolled in private and public Catholic high schools and a proportional group of adolescents who were not in school, either placed in institutions for delinquents, at work, and school dropouts. Compared with Hirschi's sample, we had adolescents of only one religion, Catholic, one race, white, and one ethnic group, the historically dominant population in Québec of French-speaking ancestry. This sample had three roles in the MTSFGCLS. First, it served as the historical baseline followed by three successive cross-sectional studies during the 1980s, 1990s, and 2000s. Second, it was the first data gathering of what became a longitudinal study of a sample of representative adolescents reinterviewed intermittently up to age 50. Third, it took place as a base for comparisons with an adjudicated sample.

At the same time, the early 1970s, my colleague and office neighbor Marcel Fréchette was starting a two-wave panel study of the psychological development of

© Springer Nature Switzerland AG 2021
M. Le Blanc, *The Development of Antisocial Behavior and Crime*,
https://doi.org/10.1007/978-3-030-68429-7

delinquents. He was recruiting the whole French-speaking population of adolescents adjudicated at the Montréal juvenile court under the Juvenile Delinquents Act. It is called the court sample of the 1970s (CS70) and is composed of five birth cohorts born around 1960. He was collecting ten objective and projective psychological tests, self-reported interviews on the perpetration of 14 criminal offenses graded by seriousness, and data on all aspects of their life, particularly family, school, and peer. This adjudicated sample offers a microscopic and in-depth view of delinquency because of the high participation rate for all forms of official offending (OO) and self-reported antisocial behavior and crime (SRABC). This sample, like the RSP70 one, was reinterviewed intermittently until their early 50s. Twenty years later, during the early 1990s, a similar court sample was recruited, CS90. It became a replication sample that was reinterviewed until the end of youth.

The Social Sciences and Humanities Research Council of Canada created a new 5-year funding program and we applied. It was proposed to merge the RSP70 and CS70 samples for the data gathering of their respective planned second waves. This move had three consequences for the second and following waves of data gathering. First, some personality measures were integrated into the self-administered questionnaire of the RSP70 subjects. Second, social control variables were introduced into the CS70 interview of delinquents. Third, the same self-reported delinquency questionnaire was administered to the subjects of the two samples. It is the instrument developed for the RSO70 that is described in Chap. 1 and Appendix B.

The next step in the building of the MTSTGCLS was completed during the second half of the 1980s. I participated in two longitudinal studies that recruited their subjects when they were in first grade in school from a low socioeconomic school district in Montréal (Tremblay et al. 1986: Le Blanc and McDuff 1991). They were reinterviewed during adolescence with the RSO70 multidisciplinary questionnaire. This was also used for RSP90 and RSP00 (for the 2000s) school adolescents. These data sets were introduced to look at the impact of social changes over time and to develop a clinical instrument to evaluate delinquents and adolescents with problem behaviors of all kinds, the MASPAQ (Measures of Social and Psychological Adaptation of Adolescents of Quebec, 1996, 2010).

The last step in the development of the MTSTGCLS consisted of adding new waves of data around ages 30, 40, and 50 for RSP70 and CS70, and age 30 for CS90. This decision was not initially planned; it was a response to the question, why not? They were not initially planned as part of a long-term longitudinal program, but became such after a visit by David Farrington to my research center in early 1980 during his sabbatical, and the availability of special research funding in Canada and Québec. All the RSP and CS samples were recruited to be employed to attain my initial goal of replicating social control theory, which we did with the RSP70 sample (Caplan & Le Blanc 1985), and, later, an integrative multilayered social and self-control theory of antisocial behavior was formulated (Le Blanc 1983, 1997, 2006, 2019).

In summary, The MTSTGCLS is composed of four representative samples of the Montréal school population recruited in the 1970s (RSP70), 1980s, (RSP80), 1990s (RSP90), and 2000s (RSP00) and two samples of adjudicated adolescents interviewed initially during the 1970s (CS70) and 1990s (CS90). All these samples are used in one or more chapters of this book.

The Baseline Samples of the 1970s

The first generation of the MTSTGCLS included two samples of white French-speaking males recruited before the middle of the 1970s. The RSP70 sample is composed of 1611 males recruited in 1974. This representative sample of the general population of adolescents of the Island of Montréal was proportionally stratified according to the size, the levels, the tracks, the socioeconomic status, and the type of school (public or private). In addition, some males who were not in school were added to the sample according to their respective proportion in the general population (full-time employed, school dropouts, and delinquents). In 1976, for the second wave, a random subsample of 458 males was selected from the 1611 participants and personality questionnaires were administered for the first time. Analyses on many sociodemographics, social, and behavioral variables showed that the participants constituting this subsample did not differ from those of the original sample (Fréchette and Le Blanc 1987; Le Blanc and Fréchette 1989). Thus, although this subsample may not be ideal, the 458 males can be considered representative of the 1611 subjects. It is worth noting that adolescents who were of a different ethnic and racial origin were extremely rare in the French-speaking school system at that time (Appendix C). These males were aged 12–16 years at the first assessment. Table A.1 presents the age range at each data gathering as well as attrition data. They represent late baby-boomers, who were born around 1960, and they were part of five birth cohorts: 1956–1957 age 11–12 (13.5%), 1958 age 13 (13.3%), 1959 age 14 (34.5%), 1960 age 15 (23.8%), and 1961 age 16 (14.9%).

The CS70 was composed of almost all the adolescent males adjudicated under the Canadian Juvenile Delinquents Act or under the Québec Youth Protection Act by the Montréal area Juvenile Court in 1973–1974. These adolescents were sentenced to probation or, in most cases, to a residential placement of various security levels. At the beginning of the study, the size of this sample was 470 males aged 13–17. Table A.1 presents the mean, the age range at each data gathering, and attrition data. They were part of five birth cohorts like the RSP70 subjects: 1956 age 12–13 (7%), 1957 age 14 (32%), 1958 age 15 (34%), 1959 age 16 (24%), and 1960 age 17 (3%). As the two samples were not assessed at exactly the same mean age, the RSP70 subjects were generally 1 year younger than the adjudicated males at each data gathering. In spite of that, for the ease of presentation, we will use the mean ages of 15, 17, 30, 40, and 50 instead of the exact mean age for each sample.

At the first wave of data collection, in the spring of 1974, the participants in the representative sample completed self-administered questionnaires at school or at home. Two years later, in the spring of 1976, they completed the same questionnaires. During adulthood, trained interviewers tracked the entire group of initial participants and met those who were found. The males from the adjudicated sample were first recruited during a 2-year period, starting in the spring of 1973. Trained interviewers, at all measurement waves, tracked and met these males. As time passed, waves were added at around 23, 30, 40, and 50 years old and the two initial panel studies became long-term longitudinal studies. As a consequence, at all the

Table A.1 The 1970s males court and representative samples, size and attrition

Interviews at	T1 15 years	T2 17 years	T3 23 years	T4 30 years	T5 40 years
		Adjudicated males			
Not found	—	63		78	37
Deaths	—	6		27	13
Refused	—	5		45	51
Completed Interviews	470	396 (85%)[1]	219 (random)	246 (55%)	160 (69%)
Ages range	13-18	15-20	20-25	28-34	39-43
Mean age	15	17	23	32	41
		Representative males			
Not found	—	—	—	87	6
Deaths	—	—	—	9	1
Refused	—	—	—	53	25
Completed Interviews[1]	1611	458 (random)	—	309 (69%)	276 (90%)
Ages range	12-16	14-18	—	27-33	37-42
Mean age	14	16	—	30	39

1. Percentage of completed interviews from the previous data gathering less the deaths.

new waves of data gathering, we kept the initial measures and added measures appropriate to the age group of the wave, principally concerning work, marriage, and children, but also antisocial behavior.

Of the initial 470 adjudicated adolescents, 38% were interviewed four times (Table A.1). These males were more difficult to keep involved in the study because they were harder to find for four reasons: there was no contact with them for an average of 10 years between the waves of data gathering, adjudicated males moved more frequently, they are rarely listed in conventional agencies and phone books, and they more often refused to participate. It is worth noting that there were many more deaths in this sample than in the representative one, 46 vs. 10. These reasons for attrition were less frequent in the representative sample, 62% of the males were interviewed at all measurement waves. Our levels of respondent retention during the life course are not as impressive as in the more recent longitudinal studies that began in the 1980s; it was between 80% and 90% for samples during adolescence (see Thornberry and Krohn 2003). However, these studies were contacting their subjects every year or six months and they had sophisticated mechanisms to help them to do so, whereas our longitudinal follow-up was not planned.

Regardless of conditions of the studies, attrition was always an extremely serious threat to the internal and external validity of the results of a longitudinal data gathering, especially for studies of antisocial behavior characterized by an age curve. This is particularly the case for unplanned studies like ours because of the absence of mechanisms to keep in contact with the subjects and the time length between the waves of data gathering. The most rigorous comparison of completers and noncompleters of the adjudicated and representative samples were performed using personality measures by Morizot and Le Blanc (2003a) (unpublished data for social control scales show the same kind of results). The males for whom self-control data were available at all measurement points were compared with the non-completers with six ANOVAs performed on the personality scales and an independent one for each trait level and for each sample. No statistical difference was observed for any personality trait for the adjudicated male sample from age 15 onward. The same result was obtained for the representative male sample. Thus, the adjudicated and representative males who completed the personality questionnaires for all waves from adolescence to midlife can be assumed to be comparable with the initial males of the two samples. Such a conclusion is not surprising, for example, in the Rochester study of high-risk youths, the researchers did not find any differential attrition in their analysis; the differences were small and not statistically significant on demographic, behavioral, and social variables for up to 12 waves between 13 and 22 years of age. Retention mechanisms were numerous and the waves spans were yearly.

The Replication Samples of the 1980s, 1990s, and 2000s

In 1970s criminology, there were very few comparisons of self-reported delinquency across historical periods. One argument often put forward in behavioral sciences was that social change manifested with such magnitude that many results cannot be reproduced from one generation to the next, in our case, male adolescents born around 1960, to a subsequent one, male adolescents born around 1980 or later. In between the 1970s and the 1990s, two replication samples became available. Our self-reported questionnaire on antisocial behavior and social and self-controls was administered to French-speaking adolescents from lower socioeconomic milieus to two childhood samples: (1) 873 first-graders reinterviewed at an average age of 15 from 1104 initial subjects: 47% boys, 53% girls (Tremblay, Le Blanc, and Schwartzman, 1986) and (2) 998 nursery school male children reinterviewed yearly between age 10 and 12 from a group of 1121 boys; Le Blanc and McDuff 1991). The data gathered with these samples were to be used for two purposes: first to document the continuity between antisocial behavior during childhood and adolescence and, second, to validate our instruments on antisocial behavior and social and self-controls. From these samples, it was possible to form a sample called RSP80 that had the same distribution of genders, ages, and socioeconomic statuses as the RSP70 sample. It was concluded that there were more similarities than dissimilarities across generations on antisocial behavior and social and self-controls (Le Blanc and Tremblay 1988).

These results and our work on the developmental mechanisms of offending (Le Blanc and Fréchette 1989; Loeber and Le Blanc 1990) triggered a similar question. Could the results on this development with late baby-boomers be replicable, 20 years later, with a sample of the Y generation? To answer that question, we recruited a new sample of adjudicated males and females.

It is composed of 656 adolescents aged 12–18 (Table A.2). They lived in the Montréal area and they were adjudicated equally under the Canadian Young Offenders Act (criminal code and statutory offences) or under the Québec Youth Protection Act of 1979 (particularly for problem behaviors such as drug abuse, truancy, incorrigibility, chronically absconding from school, etc.). The adolescents of this sample were placed in institutions of various security levels or on probation because of a criminal act or placed in residence or supervised in the community by a social worker because of serious problem behavior. They represented virtually the entire population of adolescents who had been adjudicated in 1992–1993 in Montréal. These adjudicated subjects were interviewed twice during the first and second halves of adolescence, at an interval of approximately 2 years, and for two more waves later. The sample was composed of 506 males and 150 females and was called CS90.

The average age of the males was 16 years. In comparison with the CS70 males, more of them were born from parents who had recently emigrated to Québec. Of the 150 females, 17% were adjudicated for a criminal offence under the Young Offenders Act and all the others were wards of the court for severe problem behaviors under the Youth Protection Act. Their average age was 15. Let us note that in the 1990s adjudicated sample 84% of the adolescents were born in Québec and 30% of females and males had parents who had immigrated to Québec. The vast majority of immigrant parents originated from Haiti and, in order, from the Caribbean, South America, and South East Asia. Appendix C describes these changes from the 1960s to the 2000s.

The 2000 representative sample is composed of 4023 adolescents, females (49%) and males (51%). It is a stratified random sample of schools according to the socioeconomic status of their community in the Montréal metropolitan area. The age distribution is the following: 12 (10%), 13 (19%), 14 (21%), 15 (21%), 16 (19%), and 17 (11%). In addition, it is interesting to note that 81% of these adolescents

Table A.2 The 1990s adjudicated females and males: sample size, age range, and attrition at each data gathering

Interviews at	T1 15 years		T2 17 years		T3 23 years		T4 30 years	
	F	M	F	M	F	M	F	M
Not found			25	106	24	140	65	284
Deaths			0	1	2	10	4	15
Refused			2	12	11	64	17	37
Completed Interviews	150	506	123 83%	393 78%	113 76%	292 59%	64 45%	170 35%
Ages range	13-18	12-18	15-21	15-22	20-26	19-27	27-33	28-34
Mean age	15	15.8	17.4	18.3	23.1	23.9	29.7	30.6

were born in Québec whereas 33% of at least one of their parents emigrated to Québec.

There is an important distinction between the composition of the 1970s and the 1990s adjudicated males' samples and the 1970s and the 2000s representative samples. Social change in the composition of the samples is observable as the proportion of parents who emigrated to Québec increased drastically. In the 1970s, they were so few immigrant parents that we did not ask the question, there were only a few males with parents who had emigrated to Québec and they were English speaking and outside of the sampling design. In the second case of the 1990s, parents had emigrated from all over the world. It will be interesting to see if this major social change had any effect on the development of antisocial behavior and social and self-controls along the life course between the representative and the adjudicated males.

Later on, in the middle of the 2000s, we recruited a representative school sample of females and males to test our conclusions with previous 1970s, 1980s, and 1990s samples. We expected that most of the knowledge we produced with the 1970s males would stand for the next three generations, that most of our results would become pervasive generalizations.

Appendix B: The Measurement of Official and Self-Reported Antisocial Behavior and Crime

Official Offenses and Problem Behaviors

In Canada, the Royal Canadian Mounted Police operates a register of criminals based on police and court registers. Québec has its own police services, Sureté du Québec, and municipal services in the largest cities like Montréal. Juvenile and adult courts are of provincial jurisdiction, whereas the correctional services are provincial for a prison sentence of less than 2 years, and federal for a penitentiary sentence of more than 2 years. The MTSFGCLS had access to the data at all these levels of the system of justice. The court files are used because they are the most reliable, particularly about convictions. For juveniles, the same information was available from the files of the Juvenile Courts, not only official offenses (criminal, provincial, and municipal), but also all cases of a decision under the Youth Protection Act. The analysis of the development of official offenses and problem behaviors relies on all these registers. The period covered with these data was from age 8 to age 61 for offenses and age from birth to age 17 for problem behaviors. The crimes are listed by categories and with their criminal code number (Table B.1).

Self-Reported Crimes

A semi-structured interview (SSI) was used with the subjects of the two court samples. They were asked to recall the offenses that they had committed. The longitudinal analyses of self-reported offenses are based on the data from these interviews. The advantages of an SSI over a questionnaire have been discussed at length by many authors without any clear recommendations (Belson and Beeson 1969; Gold 1966; Hardt and Bodine 1965; Nettler 1974). However, Hindelang et al. (1981) showed that there is no major difference between these two methods. The SSI was chosen, at the beginning of the MTSFGCLS, because there was little knowledge on

© Springer Nature Switzerland AG 2021
M. Le Blanc, *The Development of Antisocial Behavior and Crime*,
https://doi.org/10.1007/978-3-030-68429-7

Table B.1 The list of crimes by research categories and criminal code numbers

Breaking and entering

Breaking and entering with intent, committing offence or breaking out: 348

Being unlawfully in dwelling house: 349

Theft from mail; 356

Motor vehicle theft

Motor vehicle theft: 333.1

Taking motor vehicle or vessel or found therein without consent: 335

Theft: 322

Fraud

Forgery: 366

Use, trafficking or possession of forged document: 368

Making, Possession, etc., of counterfeit money, Uttering, etc., counterfeit money: 449,450,452

Theft, forgery, etc., of credit card: 342

False pretense or false statement: 362

Fraudulently obtaining food, beverage or accommodation: 364

Identity fraud: 403

Exchequer bill paper, public seals, etc.: 369

Stolen good

Possession of property obtained by crime: 354(1)

Trafficking in property obtained by crime: 355.2, 355.4

Obliterated vehicle identification number: 354(2)

Mischief

Simple: 430

Public mischief: 140

Arson and Other Fires: 433, 434, 435,436

Conspiracy: 465

Crime against persons (violence)

Aggression

Assault: 265

Assault with a weapon or causing bodily harm: 267, 268

Using firearm in commission of offence: 85

Pointing a firearm: 87

Kidnapping: 279(1)

Forcible confinement: 279(2)

Hostage taking: 279.1

Murder-homicide

Planned and deliberate murder: 229, 231(2)

Second degree murder: 229, 231(7)

Culpable homicide: 222(4)(5)

Manslaughter: 234

Causing death by criminal negligence: 220

Sex crimes

Rape

Sexual assault: 271

Obscene materials: 163

Immoral theatrical performance: 167

Bestiality: 160

Corrupting of children: 172

Sexual interference: 151

Prostitution

Procuring sexual services: 286.3

Keeping common bawdyhouse: 210

Obtaining sexual services for consideration: 286.1

Arms, tools, disguise

Possession of weapon for dangerous purpose: 88

Unauthorized possession in motor vehicle: 94

Possession of prohibited or restricted firearm with ammunition: 95

Possession of break-in instrument: 351(1)

Disguise with intent: 351(2)

Personating peace officer: 130

Threads

Uttering threats: 264.1

Theft with violence

Robbery: 343

Stopping mail with intent: 345

Other crimes

Road code

Operation while impaired: 320.14(1)

Failure to stop after accident: 320.16(1)

Operation while prohibited: 320.18(1)

Public disorder

Vagrancy: 179

Causing disturbance, indecent exhibition, loitering, etc.: 175(1)

Failure or refusal to comply with demand: 320.15(1)

False alarm of fire: 437

Keeping gaming or betting house: 201

(continued)

Table B.1 (continued)

Drugs

Possession for purpose of trafficking; 5(2), L.C. (1996, ch.19)

Trafficking in substance: 5(1), L.C. (1996, ch.19)

Production of substance: 7(1), L.C. (1996, ch.19)

Possession of substance; 4(1), L.C. (1996, ch.19)

Alcohol permit act-9.1

Justice

Failure to comply with condition of undertaking or recognizance: 145(3)

Failure to attend court: 145(2)

Failure to appear: 487.0551(1)

Failure to comply with probation order: 733.1

Obstructing justice: 139(1)

Offences relating to public or peace officer: 129

Prison breach, Escape and being at large without excuse: 144, 145(1

Lifestyle and market crimes

Stolen goods

Possession of property obtained by crime: 354(1)

Trafficking in property obtained by crime: 355.2, 355.4

Obliterated vehicle identification number: 354(2)

Drugs

Possession for purpose of trafficking; 5(2), L.C. (1996, ch.19)

Trafficking in substance: 5(1), L.C. (1996, ch.19)

Production of substance: 7(1), L.C. (1996, ch.19)

Possession of substance; 4(1), L.C. (1996, ch.19)

Alcohol permit P-9.

Prostitution

Procuring sexual services: 286.3

Keeping common bawdyhouse: 210

Obtaining sexual services for consideration: 286.1

Road code

Operation while impaired: 320.14(1)

Failure to stop after accident: 320.16(1)

Operation while prohibited: 320.18(1)

Arms, tools, disguise

Possession of weapon for dangerous purpose: 88

Unauthorized possession in motor vehicle: 94

Possession of prohibited or restricted firearm with ammunition: 95

Possession of break-in instrument: 351(1)

Disguise with intent: 351(2)

Personating peace officer: 13

the modus operandi for specific criminal offenses. It was felt that using a standard questionnaire was too restrictive and that the questionnaire would be too complex.

A non-exhaustive list of some interesting features of that method would be the following. The direct personal contact with the subjects may help to eliminate general or specific resistance to reporting offenses and it may produce conditions that can encourage communication. It was expected to control for cognitive bias, for example, the capacity in reading or the capacity of concentrating, or motivational errors, for example, interest or fatigue. The interviewer can also prevent insufficient validity and reliability because he is able to probe, for example, a frequency that seems surprising, or, for something that may have been forgotten, or check on comprehension, for example, when the respondent hesitates or shows signs of difficulties.

Some features of the SSI that are more important for our studies. One is the possibility it offers with regard to precision and in sequencing events. With the interview it is possible to explore, in detail, many aspects concerning the exact nature of the offense. But, other information is also available, such as the presence of a series of crimes, the number and characteristics of accomplices, the presence of planning and instruments, the nature of intimidation and intoxication. In fact, it is possible to construct a time chart of the offending of an individual. This is related to the most interesting feature of an SSI, the ordering of crime events. The interviewer can locate more precisely the transition events in the life of the individual – when he left school, when his father left home and so on – and to inquire about psychosocial factors – what was the supervision or the sanctions at certain ages, what was his occupational aspiration, and so on. These types of information may be of much more importance when the knowledge base is lacking as in the case of the development of offending.

The SSI raises the question of the importance of the characteristics of the interviewers. Even if interviewer characteristics, such as age, sex, or race, do not seem to play an important role in distorting answers to survey questions about crimes (Hindelang et al. 1981), it is important to note that this is true for adolescents but it may not be the case for children or adults. It is our experience, which has been shared by others, that with a child, mother-type interviewers have a better rapport with young subjects, and that with young adults an older adult seems to elicit more valid and reliable information. Not only should we control the importance of these structural characteristics, but interpersonal skills should also be questioned. In particular, with an SSI, it is our experience that more skilled persons produce more detailed data. We have tried to control these impacts by selecting highly skilled persons at the interpersonal level, by training them adequately, and by reviewing each of their interviews and giving them feedback on problems.

The interviewer starts the part of the interview on offending with the first crime and he/she has a set of a 14 precisely defined categories of offenses to cover and types of conduct disorders were added (use of drugs, fights, etc.). For each offense, the interviewer has a list of questions to cover: when the offense was first and last performed, the period during which there was any series of this type of offense, the frequencies obtained, how was the offense was completed (planning, instrument, violence, accomplices, etc.).

Table B.2 The list and definition of the self-reported crimes

Petty larceny: acts of minor gravity such as theft of sweets, cigarettes, toys, small amounts of money, school supplies or shoplifting at the corner store, for example.
Shoplifting: ore serious offences than the preceding one with a coefficient of greater risk (in department stores, for instance) or carried out in a well-planned and organized way.
Vandalism: destruction or deterioration of private or public property, such as misdemeanors, damage to property, fires, breakages, and so on.
Common theft: precise group of thefts excluding those involving breaking and entering or personal robbery; ranges from the theft of various objects, including bicycles and sums of money to receiving stolen merchandise.
Burglary: all kinds of illegal entry, breaking and entering for purposes of theft, whether successful or not; includes intention and attempt, theft inside a motor vehicle and possession of tools for purposes of burglary.
Personal larceny: crime depriving the victim of a possession by means of physical attack; principal offenses are theft with violence, aggravated theft, theft from a delivery person, purse snatching, pickpocketing, etc. Implies the use of force

in any form, but on condition that it is against one or several private individuals.
Theft of motor vehicles: theft of any motorized vehicle, from motorcycles to cars, heavy trucks, trains, airplanes, boats, and so on.
Aggravated theft: thefts of a more criminal nature: business or bank hold-ups, the theft of arms, mail, and so on.
Personal attack: physical attack against a person without any element of theft: assault, assault and battery, grievous bodily harm, murder and attempts; by extension, this category can also include threats, suicide attempts as well as possession of arms (with intent to threaten or attack someone).
Public mischief: disturbing the peace, illicit presence, vagrancy, running away (if officially charged), possession of forbidden objects, sounding a false alarm, etc.
Drugs: possession of drugs and trafficking.
Sexual offenses: indecency, indecent exposure, soliciting, rape and attempted rape, and so on.
Fraud: appropriation by means of trickery, such as the fabrication of false documents or forged money, the use of forged check or stolen credit cards, false representation, bank or business frauds, and so on.

Concerning the nature of the selected offenses, an inventory of the delinquent acts perpetrated by youngsters who appear before the Juvenile Court gave us a list of 14 categories for measurement purposes. Each category, which included different acts under a general heading, was given a precise definition. An effort was made to obtain the greatest homogeneity possible within the categories while maximizing the differences between the acts. The definitions of the 14 types of criminal offense are shown in Table B.2.

Self-Reported Antisocial Behaviors

The starting point of the MTSFGCLS was Nye and Short's (1957) 21behaviors questionnaire. After reading Hirschi's (1969), his list of behaviors was integrated with Nye and Short's list. In addition, a panel, composed of the author and two Ph.D. students, selected the most often used, simple, and clear questions in previous studies and they added some serious antisocial behaviors that had been rare at the time of previous questionnaires. In addition, we wanted to represent all the principal categories of criminal behavior and problem behavior that are formally sanctioned by the State. To do this, we created questions that represented some categories of delinquent acts, sufficient in number, that are reported in the juvenile delinquent statistics of Canada. For problem behaviors, we constructed questions that referred to motives that social workers state in their report when they to refer an adolescent to juvenile court under the Youth Protection Act (Messier 1989). As a result of this process, we added 18 behaviors.

Later, in the late 1980s and early 1990s, 24 behaviors were included in our questionnaire to cover all the categories of antisocial behavior that are now part of the list of 76 behaviors below. After multiple item analysis and factorial analysis our five data sets from these decades, we wanted to better operationalize the hierarchical structure of antisocial behavior (Fig. 1.1) and take into account social changes since the 1970s. As a consequence, for example, we subdivided the drug behavior question into four behaviors: soft, chemical, hard, and selling drugs. We also introduced workplace deviance, sexual aggression, prostitution, psychological, and family violence, and other questions, particularly in the 2000s, concerning the numeric experience.

The Format of the Questions for Each Behavior

Two strategies were used to ask the questions. With the population samples, a self-administered questionnaire was used. With the court samples, it was an interview during which each behavior was written on a card and the respondents made two piles, those that they had never done and those that they had enacted. For each behavior, three questions were asked. The form of each question was the following:

Note: questions with a "S" are part of the school scales, whereas questions with a "W" constitute the work scales.

Have you purposely disturbed your teacher and other pupils in class?

(a) Have you ever done this? (Beginning at the second interview "ever" was replaced by "since the last interview").

    1- yes   2- no

(b) If so, how old were you the first time you did this?

    -------------- Age

(c) During *the present school year*, have you purposely disturbed your teacher and the pupils in your class? (beginning at the second interview "present school year" was replaced by "in the last year")

    1. Never
    2. Once or twice
    3. Several times
    4. Very often

We used these four frequency categories after a comparison of results with a free response in numbers and asking about the meaning of "several times" and "very often" (Le Blanc et al. 1977). The results suggested a limited range for "several times," between 3 and 5, and an much wider range for "very often," between 10 and a few hundred. We also tested for the selection of a response window, "last year" versus "last 3 years," and we observed that the memory was more precise and reliable in the first case. This conclusion was confirmed by the reviews of Le Blanc (1989) and Menard and Bowman-Bowen (2015).

The monetary value of the description of stolen items, in a longitudinal and a comparison over time study as in the MTSFGLS, is a very difficult question. Should the script of the behaviors be adjusted for inflation, without monetary values, or with specific objects such as a car, a bicycle (the International Self-Reported Delinquency Study by Junger-Tas et al. 2012)? To our knowledge there is no discussion of these questions and no comparative studies in the self-reported delinquency literature. For example, Hindelang et al. (1981), in their landmark study in the late 1970s, used less than $2, between $2 and $50, and more then $50; Elliott et al. (1985), a few years later, used $5, between $5 and $50, and more than $50. After exploratory interviews with adolescents in the 1970s, our chosen initial values were $10, between $10 and $100, and more than $100. If we had taken inflation into account, the monetary values, according to the Government of Canada's method of calculation, would be 25$ and 250$ in the 1980s, 30$ and 380$ in the 1990s, and 45$ and 450$ in the 2000s. We did not make such estimations and we kept our initial values, which became ordinal categories rather than interval measures. We had three reasons for this choice. First, we thought that these estimations were not sufficiently precise and clear for the subjects and that they were not easily interpreted while they were reporting their behaviors. Second, as we were comparing four generations, we thought that using the same ordinal categories would avoid the problem of monetary heterotopy. Third, this problem is amplified by objects, for example, for bicycle: they cannot be the same for children, adolescents, and adults, whereas ordinal monetary values may not have the same significance for these categories of subjects.

Criminologists used descriptive and boundary parameters for many years; with self-reported antisocial behavior scales they take the following form.

There are four descriptive parameters. (1) Participation: an individual takes part in at least one behavior composing a scale: current, during the last year, responses (c) recoded 1 = 0, 2, 3, 4 = 1, or cumulative, for a specific previous time period, responses (a) above. (2) Variety: the number of different behaviors constituting a scale reported by an individual: current, during the last year, responses (c) recoded 1 = 0, 2, 3, 4 = 1, or cumulative, for a specific previous time period, responses a above. (3) Frequency: the sum of number of times that each behavior constituting a scale was carried out last year, responses (c) above. (4) Seriousness: the median score for the behaviors constituting a scale based on a legal classification or the harmfulness of an act, or by ratings of severity by experts or the population.

There are three boundary parameters. (1) Onset: the individual youngest age at onset of the behaviors constituting a scale. (2) Offset: the individual oldest age at termination of the behaviors constituting a scale. (3) Duration: the age interval between the youngest age at onset and the oldest age at termination of the behaviors constituting a scale.

The List of Antisocial Behaviors

The following list of behaviors is the result of the adaptation of the initial 21 in Nye and Short's questionnaire of 1957 to a larger spectrum of antisocial acts, social changes, and the necessity of a heteromorphic measure. Table B.3 presents our list of antisocial behaviors.

Table B.3 The list of antisocial behaviors

1S. Having purposely disturbed your teacher and other pupils in class?

1W. Having purposely disturbed your colleagues at work?

2. Having drank a bottle of beer, a glass of wine, a glass of hard alcohol?

3. Having told your parents that you refused to do what they ordered you to do?

4. Having taken something from a store without paying for it, and then kept it?

5 Having threatened to beat up somebody in order to force him to do things he didn't want to do?

6. Having sniffed glue to the point where you didn't feel quite like your ordinary self?

7S. Having purposely damaged or destroyed musical instruments, sporting goods or other equipment in school?

7W. Having purposely damaged or destroyed machines or other equipment at work?

8. Having run away from home for more than 24 hours, more than a day?

9S. Having been kicked out of school?

9W. Having been fired from work?

10 Having been involved in a fistfight with someone?

11. Having sold drugs (any kind)?

12. Having purposely damaged or destroyed things that didn't belong to you?

13. Having hung around outside, loafing around at night when you were supposed to be home?

14. Having broken in a door or a window in order to enter a place and take something?

15. Having set off a false alarm?

16. Having threatened or abused others to get what you wanted?

17S. Having talked back impolitely to one of your teachers?

17W. Having talked back impolitely to one of your boss?

18. Having had sexual relations (other than kissing) with a person of the opposite sex?

20S. Having been thrown out of a classroom by a teacher?

20W. Having been thrown out of a room by a boss?

21. Having used a weapon (stick, knife, gun, rock, ...) while fighting with someone?

22. Having purposely damaged or destroyed something that belonged to your parents or another member of your family?

23. Having driven a motor vehicle (car, motor bike) without a license?

24. Having taken money from home without permission and kept it without any intention of giving it back?

25. Having bought, used or sold something you knew was stolen?

26.Having gotten angry easily and hit someone because you were being teased or threatened?

27. Having gotten angry and wanted to fight after someone accidentally knocked into you because you thought he had done it on purpose?

28. Having had sexual relations with a person of the opposite sex for money, drugs or other things?

29S. Having taken and kept objects worth 10$ and more that belonged to school?

29W. Having taken and kept objects worth 10$ and more that belonged to your employer?

30. Having bet or gambled money with peoples other than your family?

31. Having beaten hit or harshly pushed one of your parents?

32S. Having used a cheat sheet or other forbidden methods to cheat on an exam?

32W. Having cheated at work?

33. Having entered a place without paying the obligatory cover charge?

34.Having made a crank phone call?

35S. Having skipped school without a legitimate excuse?

35W. Having missed a day of work without a legitimate excuse?

36. Having taken and kept something worth 100$ and more that didn't belong to you?

37. Having purposely set a store or another place on fire?

(continued)

Table B.3 (continued)

38. Having beaten up someone who did nothing to you?

39. Having had sexual relations with a person of the same sex for money, drugs or other things?

40 Having used fake ID cards to get in somewhere?

41S. Having purposely damaged a school (breaking windows, dirtying walls...)?

41W. Having purposely damaged your place of work (breaking windows, dirtying walls...)?

42S. Having skipped a class while you were at school?

42W. Having skipped work while you were at work?

43. Having participated in a fight between gangs?

44. Having carried a weapon (a chain, a knife, a gun, etc.)?

45. Having taken and kept something worth between 10$ and 100$ that didn't belong to you?

46. Having taken and kept a bicycle that didn't belong to you?

47. Having had sexual relations (other than kissing) with a person of the same sex?

48. Having taken hard drugs (heroine, morphine, opium, crack...)?

49. Having encouraged other teenagers to hassle someone you didn't like?

50. Having taken someone else's motorcycle to go for a ride without asking permission?

51 Having taken and kept something worth less than 10$ that didn't belong to you?

52. Having gotten drunk on beer, wine or other hard alcohols?

53. Having beaten hit or harshly pushed your b other or sister while fighting with him or her?

54.Having purposely damaged an antenna, tires or other parts of an automobile?

55. Having used stimulants (''speed'', ''pep pills'', etc.) or hallucinogenic drugs (LSD, STP, PCP, mescaline, THC, etc.)?

56. Having entered a place where you had no right to be (for instance: empty inhabited house, shed, train tracks, house under construction,)?

57. Having thrown rocks, bottles or other objects at people?

58. Having taken someone else's automobile to go for a ride without asking permission?

59. Having used marijuana or hashish (joint, pot)?

60. Having taken an automobile to sell it?

61. Having used physical force (or threatened to do so) in order to dominate other teenagers?

62. Having accused others of starting a fight and pretended that it was their fault?

63. Having sexual contact (getting undressed, touching, intercourse...) with a person that was five years younger then you?

65.Having forced someone to do sexual things that he (or she) didn't agree to do (getting undressed, touching, intercourse, ...)?

66. Having used prescribed medecines?

67. Having used non-prescribed medicines?

68. Having tried or used a credit card or a bankcard that was not yours?

69. Having forged a check, change a check that you knew had no funds or used forged currency?

70. Having been drunk in a public place?

71. Having produce a false income tax report?

aut5 Having driven a motor vehicule (car, motor bike) that was not insured?

aut8 .Having driven a motor vehicule (car, motor byke) at least 20km/h faster then the speed limit?

aut9 Having lost my driving permit (the right to drive)?

aut10 Having driven (car, motor bike) after drinking too much, more then the legal limit?

Act25 How many hours a week do you habitually gamble (with monbey like poker, casino, et.)?

The Antisocial Behavior Scales

Numerous item and factor analyses were conducted with the MTSFGCLS representative and adjudicated samples recruited in the 1970s, 1980s, 1990s, and 2000s samples (see Appendix A). In fact, 11,770 females and males representing the population of adolescents ages 12–17 in the Montréal metropolitan area and 1237 adolescent drop-outs, adjudicated or in a drug treatment program, responded to the questionnaires. All of them were French-speaking adolescents from all the levels of socioeconomic status, initially interviewed in public and private schools, residential correctional facilities, at home, or in our offices.

Table 1.1 reports the behaviors that constitute each scale and Table 1.2 lists their reliability coefficients. Le Blanc (1996, 2010a, b) reports for the representative samples, that the alphas by samples, genders, and ages are over 0.80 for all the delinquency scales and over 0.75 for all the problem behavior scales. Similar results are reported for the two samples of adolescents adjudicated in the Montréal juvenile court.

In Chaps. 3, 4, and 5, we had to be more parsimonious because of the analytical strategy, for example, for the development of the antisocial behavior and crime mix, and the statistical techniques used (for example, paths and trajectory analysis). After the statistical analyses on the heteromorphy and the structure of ABC in Chap. 1 (Table 1.1), the following second, third, and fourth level scales were created. Figure 1.2 illustrates the broader theoretical model with these level scales. The scales at each successive level are the summations of the previous level scales.

The second level scales were: (1) factor 1 was composed of motor vehicle theft and risky driving and is called "exciting behavior"; factor 2 regrouped "covert behavior" and the most important scales were theft and fraud; (3) factor 3 was called "strolling behavior," i.e., wandering around committing disorderly conduct and vandalism; (4) factor 4 reflected what was named "conflict behavior" or authority conflict and it manifested as authority conflict in the home and at school; (5) factor 5 was about physical and psychological violence; this was called "overt behavior"; factor 6 was about "arousing behavior" and the principal scales were drug use and sexual relations; they evoke a reaction in the forms of a sensation, an immediate response.

There were six scales at the third level and two at the fourth level. First, the delinquency domain, (fourth level scales) was equivalent for antisocial behavior and crime (as a convicted violation of the criminal code); it was divided into three forms of official offenses, covert or property crimes (theft and fraud), overt crimes against persons, and lifestyle crimes. The same antisocial behavior scales were present in this domain. Second, the problem behavior domain (the other fourth level scale) was composed of two conflict scales: conflict with parents and conflict at school and at work.

Appendix C: Legal, Criminal Justice, and Sociological Changes in Québec from 1960 to 2000

Introduction

This sketch of the evolution of Québec society is the background to our results on the development of antisocial behavior and crime over time. It is composed of three parts: first, the changes in the juvenile and adult laws and criminal justice systems; second, the evolution of delinquency and criminality in Québec until 2010; third, a résumé of sociological changes in many domains.

C.2. Changes in the Québec Criminal and Delinquency Laws and Their Criminal Justice Systems

In 1892, the Parliament of Canada adopted the Act Respecting the Criminal Law, which applied to Québec and all provinces (the adoption is a federal responsibility and the application is a provincial function). This code was quite similar to the British law of 1878. It was revised occasionally up to 2017. The revisions of the content were to do with drugs, homosexuality, abortion, terrorism, firearms, sexual offenses, cannabis, and white-collar crimes, but also concerned evidence, procedure, sentencing, and the impacts of technological changes. The bulk of the property and personal crimes were rather similar for all the generations of the MTSFGCLS subjects from the 1970s.

The Canadian juvenile justice system had two primary sources at the end of the nineteenth century. First, it was based on the English doctrine of *parens patriae*; Canada was then part of the British Empire (Farrington 1979). Second, during the second half of that century, social problems became more complex because of large migrations to Québec's cities and the USA. Then, the Québec Parliament adopted two laws, one for industrial schools (child protection) and one for reform schools (delinquents) as had been done earlier by neighbors Massachusetts, New York, and Maine (D'Amours 1982). The next step was the adoption of the Canadian Juvenile Delinquent Act (JDA) in 1908.

© Springer Nature Switzerland AG 2021
M. Le Blanc, *The Development of Antisocial Behavior and Crime*,
https://doi.org/10.1007/978-3-030-68429-7

The JDA instituted a court exclusively for juvenile delinquents, as was done in the USA in 1899 (Platt 1969); it delimited the range of delinquency; it specified the objectives to be achieved; it called for specialists to enlighten and support the court; it determined procedures (referral to the adult court, notification of parents, etc.). This new justice system was based on a totally different philosophy of justice from that of the past and a new view of delinquency, as pledged in its preamble. The delinquent was represented as the product of his environment and as someone in need of help rather than punishment. The State was a good father who must treat the delinquent youngster with justice, not like a criminal, but like a child who, because he is on a downward path, needs counseling, encouragement, help, and support. To accomplish this, the State must give a great deal of discretionary power to the persons in authority. The definition of the delinquent advanced in this act merits a special note. Delinquent meant:

> ... a child (under eighteen years of age in Quebec or sixteen or seventeen in other provinces) who commits an infraction of any of the provisions of the Criminal Code, or of a federal or provincial statute, or a regulation or ordinance of a municipality or who is guilty of sexual immorality or any similar form of vice, or who commits any other infraction...

This definition, however, had the disadvantage of being rather elastic. It covered minor marginal behavior as well as serious criminal acts. The conduct described here ranges from activities that adults consider improper for a minor (sexual promiscuity, use of alcohol, etc.) to the most serious crimes specifically defined by the Criminal Code, from behavior prohibited by various laws and regulations (such as the municipal regulations on curfews) through those especially provided for juveniles (school attendance, etc.) or those passed in provincial legislations (against neglect, abandonment, situations of moral or physical danger, etc.) in which the child is a victim.

In this definition, delinquency emerges as an all-inclusive idea, because, when all was said and done, a delinquent could be any young person who needs protection or who has contravened a law. This Canadian definition of delinquency, by the way, was not very different from those adopted by most US states and western countries during the same period or in the following years (Corrado, Trépanier, and Le Blanc 1983). The JDA was in force when the population and court samples were recruited in the 1970s by the MTSFGCLS.

Toward the end of the life of this law, in 1979, the Parliament of Québec adopted a new Youth Protection Act (YPA). It included a provision for diversion from court and usual judicial measures (fine, probation, institution) for the criminal and other federal offenders. As before, policemen still had the discretionary power to close a file, admonish the adolescent, ask his parents to pick him up at the police station, or return him to home instead of filing a charge to a prosecutor. Instead, the policemen and the prosecutor were obliged to send the adolescent to the local social services. The YPA specified that an adolescent could be send directly to court only if he had committed one of the most serious personal crimes or was a multirecidivist of the most serious property offenses (there was a list agreed upon by social services and the justice) (see Le Blanc and Beaumont 1992).

Contrary to the previous law, the Young Offenders Act (Canada, 1982), which came into effect in 1984, proposed a restricted concept of delinquency. An adolescent could be prosecuted only for an infraction of the Criminal Code or other federal laws and regulations and excluding provincial laws or municipal regulations. This tightening of the definition of delinquency was accompanied by a stricter distinction between childhood and adolescence. The YOA applied only to minors from 12 to 18, the age bracket corresponding to the beginning and end of adolescence. In addition, Canada was implementing a formalized system of justice, more like the adult system, with more care to the due process, legal representation, the decision process, and transfer to adult courts. It was not an orthodox justice model, as in many USA states and some western societies in the 1980s. It was rather a modified justice model as Corrado (1992) called it.[1] This type system is more offender-centered: some are diverted and some are punished, they are represented by layers, a clinical diagnostic is demanded, the diminished responsibility of the offender and the respect of special needs are stated, the sanction of behavior and treatment are sustained. Québec has always been the most progressive province in using these offender-centered provisions: for example, more cases were diverted and there was an important development of new alternative measures by social services, representation in court for all offenders, more open correction centers, more treatment programs (psychoeducational) in correctional institutions, fewer transfers to adult courts, etc. (see Statistics Canada yearly reports on juvenile courts).

The Youth Criminal Justice Act (YCJA) was adopted in 2003 by a Conservative government. As a consequence, the YCJA leaned more toward an orthodox criminal justice model; this is clearly the case in all provinces in Canada, except for Québec. As an expert observer, I can conclude that it had no significant impact on the MTSTGCLS subjects who went through the system during the 1990s.

It is important to remember, reading our results, that the MTSFGCLS subjects of the population and court samples of the 1970s were processed under the JDA during their adolescence. The comparable samples of the 1990s were convicted under the YOA during the same phase of life. On the contrary, the adult criminal career of these two generations of subjects took place in the context of a criminal justice system with a common philosophy and similar mechanisms, some adaptations to the social changes notwithstanding.

A few words on the adult criminal justice system: it is very similar in structure and procedure to the systems in the USA and other countries that based their system on "common law." There are some variations. For example, prosecutors and judges are selected from among public and private lawyers. They were all trained in law schools. The judges had specialized as prosecutor or defense lawyer for criminal cases were experienced lawyers, and selected by nonpolitical committees of peers. Plea bargaining was common in the juvenile and adult systems. At all levels of the system, police, courts, and correction, the Québec criminal justice personnel, according to surveys,

---

[1] For more in-depth papers, see chapters in Corrado et al. (1992); for papers on the Québec system of juvenile justice (see Marceau and Trépanier 1985; Biron and Trépanier 1994; Trépanier 2003).

were more progressive in implementing new strategies, measures, and treatment pro-grams. Overall, it is known that the Canadian justice system is less repressive than the US system (Statistics Canada regularly documents that observation with police, court, and correctional data). It is our opinion that the subjects of the juvenile court samples of the 1970s and 1990s received a quite similar treatment by the criminal justice system during their adult criminal career until their early 60s for the 1970s court sample and the middle of their 40s for the 1990s court sample. The adult crimi-nal justice system changed at three levels for the 1960 generation of delinquents during their adulthood. (1) Public defense lawyers became available for low-income individuals, either from a governmental agency or through mandates to private law-yers. (2) Some new forms of sentence were introduced, for example, community work and restorative arrangements, and the criminal code was adapted to social changes and the alternating Conservative–Liberal political parties in parliament. (3) In the correctional system there was the introduction of a more rational system of decision making, an increase in treatment-oriented programs of all kinds, and there was an increase in the level of education and training of the guards, as well as in the number of psychology, psychiatry, and criminology professionals. The generation of 1980 delinquents had the advantage of improvements in all of these domains.

On the contrary, there were dissimilarities between these two periods for the juvenile justice system. For the cohorts of the generation of 1980, entrance into the system, in most cases, was through social services and in court there was legal rep-resentation. New measures were introduced, for example, community work; there were new nonresidential measures (workshop, group homes, apartments, etc.), a policy of reduction of the length of the sentences, and a reduction of the number of placements in secure units.

In summary, when we compare the epidemiological data of the court samples of the 1970s and the 1990s some aspects will have to be remembered. (1) For the great majority of offenses against person and property, there were no significant changes in their definition. (2) The judicial decisions were more treatment than punishment oriented and few juvenile delinquents were placed in secure juvenile and adult cor-rectional institutions. Some aspects were dissimilar between the 1970s and the 1990s. (1) For the first generation there was no representation by a lawyer during all their appearances in juvenile court compared with the second generation. (2) There was less diversity in the dispositions available (only acquittal, fine, probation, and placement) for the 1970s. As the JDA applied from age 8 to 18 and the YOA from age 12 to 18, we compare the 1970 and the 1990 groups from age 12 on. In addition, we limit our epidemiological comparisons of the criminal career with the time lapse from age 12 to 45 because in the 1970s the follow-up goes up to age 61.

C.3. Evolution of Juvenile and Adult Criminality Since 1960

In Canada, Statistics Canada reports annually uniform and reliable police, court, and correctional juvenile and adult data from the 1960s. In Québec, historians and other social scientists have been interested in crime and criminal justice and some studies start with the arrival of the French in New France in the sixteenth century (Boyer 1966). Ouimet (2005) reports statistical series from the third quarter of the nineteenth century on many crime, justice, and correctional phenomena. Ouimet published the latest analysis for adult criminality, with data from the last 50 years (Ouimet 2005, 2010) and Le Blanc reports on juvenile official and self-reported delinquency (Le Blanc 1999, 2010a, b).

These authors conclude that during the 1970s, the level of criminality exploded in Québec. However, it was much lower than in the USA and within the range of the lowest rates in western countries. During the 1980s, stability in the adult rates of all forms of crime was observed. Contrary to this tendency, it was the period when juvenile delinquency rates were the highest of all previous and subsequent decades. Let us remember that the 1970s is the period when the initial population and court samples were recruited and beginning their criminal career. In the 1990s, juvenile delinquency was diminishing substantially, particularly property crimes. These crimes by adults decreased by 30–50%. This tendency continued in the 2000s and 2010s, whereas violent crimes, particularly sexual aggression and assaults, represented a higher proportion of all crimes during the 2000s. The exception was homicide, which had been on a downward slope since 1975. The court sample of the generation of 1980 was entering into delinquency during the 1990s and in their adult criminal career in the 2000s.

In light of these tendencies, it could be expected that the criminal career of the male generation of the 1980s would be less intensive than that of the generation of the 1960s, that is, a later onset, less frequency, shorter in duration, and with a higher ratio of violent crimes.

C.4. Sociological Changes Over Five Decades in Québec and Montréal

This section outlines a presentation of the evolution of Québec from 1960 to the 2000s, with some specific characteristics for the city of Montréal, which was the site of the MTSFGCLS. Let us remember that the adolescents of the first population and court samples, five birth cohorts in each, were born around 1960 and interviewed for the first time during the first half of the 1970s when they were in high school or entering into the juvenile criminal justice system. Only a rapid overview will be presented because an enormous body of social sciences literature is available on the subject in Québec. This summary is based on the landmark data sets gathered by Langlois, a sociologist (Langlois et al. (1991); Langlois 1999.

The specificity of Québec in North America has some historical roots. (1) When the British colonized New France in late 1750, it occupied most of its territory that had already been explored in North America. It was what is now called the Eastern provinces of Canada (Nova Scotia, New Brunswick, Newfoundland, Prince Edwards Island, Québec, and Ontario) and a large corridor around the Mississippi River between the Adirondacks and the Rockies from the Hudson Bay down to the Gulf of Mexico (Saint-Louis, New Orleans, etc.). (2) When the revolution of the 13 British colonies began, the French Canadians were tempted to join them. However, to prevent this possibility, the British invaders signed an agreement with the French Canadian elites of Québec (religious and civil) according to which they could kept the French language and the Catholic religion forever on what is now Québec territory. (3) As a consequence of this deal, the catholic hierarchy (priests and sisters and brothers of numerous congregations) developed and benevolently operated for 200 years until the 1960s, the systems of institutions for education, health, welfare, and juvenile and adult correction. (4) Following the British invasion, immigrants from Great Britain (principally from Ireland and Scotland) arrived in Montréal and developed trade (fur, wood, etc.), industries (boats, railways, breweries, etc.), and finance (bank, insurance, etc.) and created their own religious, education, health, and welfare institutions, mostly in Montreal. (5) During the second half of the nineteenth century there was a high level of migration to the manufacturers of the Eastern states of the USA, and from rural areas to villages, cities, and Montréal.

As a consequence of this historical context, Québec developed a strong sociocultural identity, obviously in addition to being Canadians and North-Americans. We will outline some of the major changes in Québec and Montréal paying particular attention to what was happening during the life span of each of the samples of the MTSFGCLS, in particular for the five cohorts of males born around 1960 and the males and females of the five cohorts of 1980.

C.4.1 Demography

(1) At the end of the Second World War, there was a massive and sudden urbanization that was followed by a continuous migration to all the cities of Québec, particularly to Montréal. The Greater Montreal population was growing more rapidly than the whole Québec. (2) The population aged 0–14 was more rapidly diminishing during the adolescent years of the 1960 generation or the 1970s, whereas the 1980 birth cohorts were experiencing a slower decrease in this age group to the profit of the age 65 group. This phenomenon was supported by a decrease in births, particularly for the 1960s cohorts, and a multiplication by seven of the voluntary interruption of pregnancy from 1976 onward. (3) The interprovincial and international immigration were relatively stable during the first three decades of the MTSFGCLS. However, it was more significant in the 1990s and the 2000s when the 1980 birth cohorts were going through adolescence and youth. In addition, it was more diversified in terms of continents of origin (Asia, Central and South America, North Africa and Middle East, the Caribbean). The latter four groups of immigrants were more numerous than in the rest of Canada and were concentrated in Montréal.

C.4.2. Language

The 1960 birth cohorts were immersed in a French-speaking milieu, from the 1950s onward; around 82% of the population of Québec declared French as their first language and for a little less than 10% it was English. These proportions are not very different for Montréal, with a little more for English, more immigrants, and more visible minorities, 10% in Montréal compared with 6% for Québec; these proportions are lower than in the rest of Canada. Let us note that the 1960 birth cohorts were almost exclusively in direct contact with only French-speaking adolescents, although the 1980 birth cohorts were in direct relation, in their class in school, with a greater diversity of immigrants.

C.4.3. Government

During the 1970s and the 1980s, there were discussions on the independence of Québec and the political party in power introduced two referenda on the subject, which were lost.

C.4.4. Family

The males of 1960 were raised in a traditional family, that is, with two biological parents married in the Catholic church with the children baptized and a high level of church attendance; very few males had parents who were divorced or lived in another type of household when the MTSFGCLS started. The situation was radically different for the 1980 birth cohorts. In Québec, increasing numbers of children, not only in Montréal, were born outside of marriage, had divorced or separated parents, who did so before they had been married for 5 years, or lived in a single-parent family. These changes were continuous rather than abrupt.

C.4.5. Health

All the birth cohorts of the MTSFGCLS had access to universal, complete, and free health care insurance and free dental care during childhood. This program began during the childhood of the generation of 1960. Life expectancy was lower for the 1960s cohorts, between 70 and 75 years, than for 1980 cohorts, 80+ years.

C.4.6. Education

The system of education, from primary schools to university, became public, nonreligious, and low cost (very low tuition costs in universities) during the 1960s and 1970s (day care for children is now included in this system). As in all North American states, the education level increased in Québec (for example, university diplomas increased from 4% to 20%), but somewhat less than in other provinces of Canada. The dropout rate in high schools was higher for the 1960 cohorts than for the 1980 one. At that time a Québec law had made it compulsory for all new immigrants to attend a French-speaking school. As a consequence, the racial, ethnic, and language diversity grew rapidly in schools, particularly in Montréal.

C.4.7. Economy, Work, and Poverty

The gross interior income began to increase when the 1960 cohorts entered youth and it was multiplied by nine when the 1980 cohorts entered adulthood. Because of all the social programs, the proportion of taxes increased from 17% to 27%. More women were in the labor market for the 1990 cohorts. The level of unemployment fluctuated in a cycle, with peaks during the 1980s and 1990s. Consequently, the 1970 cohorts were young adults during the first peak and the 1980 cohorts entered youth when the second cycle ended. The proportion of families with low incomes was relatively stable when the two generations were children and adolescents. The proportion of persons who receive welfare was higher than before when the 1960 cohorts were under 18 years of age and it increased for the 1980 cohorts. Finally, poverty is a transient situation because half of the poor households move in and out of that condition over a period of a few years.

C.4.8. Consumption

New goods were adopted rapidly by all categories of household. This is the case for long-lasting ones: heating, air conditioning, washing machine, telephone, television, etc. It is also evident for the numeric (computers, cellphones, Internet, etc.) and communication (Twitter, Facebook, etc.) instruments.

C.5. Conclusion

In sum, Québec became a modernized society during the MTSFGCLS. This society took great care of its citizens with universal and free health services and educational system and its generous welfare support compared with other western states. This development was continuous. However, the members of the 1980 birth cohorts had an advantage because these changes were mature when they went through adolescence, youth, and adulthood. It is interesting to note that, in parallel, it was observed that adult and juvenile criminality diminished substantially as imprisonment did and that alternative measures, before and in court, were diversified and that correctional treatment improved. A researcher must merge the data sets of Langlois (1999), Ouimet (2010), and Le Blanc (2010a, b) to test macro social causal hypotheses. Against this background, it was expected that the criminal career of the 1980 birth cohorts will be less aggravated than that of the 1960 cohorts, with a later onset, less frequency, less variety, and of shorter duration.

References

Abraham, F. D. (1995). Introduction to dynamics: A basic language and a basic metamodeling strategy. In F. D. Abraham & A. R. Gilgen (Eds.), *Chaos theory in psychology*. Westport: Greenwood Press.

Achenbach, T. M. (1992). *Manual for child behavior checklist12-3 and profile*. Burlington, VT: University of Vermont.

Achenbach, T. M., McConaughy, S. H., & Howell, C. T. (1987). Child/adolescent behavioral and emotional problems: Implications of cross-informant correlations for situational specificity. *Psychological Bulletin, 101*(2), 213–232.

Akman, D., & Normandeau, A. (1968). The measurement of crime and delinquency in Canada: A replication study. Acta Criminologica, 1, 135–173.

Andriensen, A., Paoli, L., Karstedt, S., Visschers, J., Grenfeld, V. A., & Pleysier, S. (2018). Public perception of the seriousness of crime: Weighing the harm and the wrong. *European Journal of Criminology, 1*, 1–24.

Ayers, C. D., Williams, H., Hawkins, J. D., Peterson, P. L., Catalano, R. F., & Abbott, R. D. (1999). Assessing correlates of onset, escalation, and desistance of delinquent behavior. *Journal of Quantitative Criminology, 15*, 277–305.

Bachman, J. G., O'Malley, P. M., & Johnston, J. (1978). Youth in transition: Adolescence to adulthood. In *Change and stability in the lives of young men*. Ann Arbor: Institute for Social Research.

Bartlett, R., Holditch-Davis, D., & Belyea, M. (2005). Clusters of problem behaviors in adolescents. *Research in Nursing & Health, 28*, 230–239.

Basto-Peireira, M., & Farrington, D. P. (2018). Advancing knowledge about lifelong crime sequences. *British Journal of Criminology, 59*, 354. https://doi.org/10.1093/bjc/azy033.

Bazon, M. R., & Estevâo, R. (2010). Juvenile criminal behavior and peer influences: A comparative study in the Brazilian context. *Universitas Psychologia, 11*, 1157–1166.

Belson, W., & Beeson, M. (1969). *Identifying difficulties and facilitating factors in getting information from boys about their stealing and about associated matters: An exploratory study*. London, UK: The Survey Research Center, London School of Economics.

Benson, M. L. (2002). *Crime and the life course: An introduction* (1st ed.). New York: Routledge.

Benson, M. L. (2013). *Crime and the life course: An introduction* (2nd ed.). New York: Routledge.

Bergheul, S., & Le Blanc, M. (2006). Validation des mesures de l'adaptation sociale et personnelle pour les adolescents algérien. *Revue Européenne de Psychologie Appliquée, 56*, 72–85.

Biron, L., & Trépanier, J. (1994). La justice des mineurs. In D. Szabo & M. Le Blanc (Eds.), *Traité de criminologie empirique. Phénomène criminel, justice pénale et mesures pénales* (pp. 183–220). Montréal: Les Presses de l'Université de Montréal.

Blokland, A. J., Nagin, D. S., & Nieuwbeerta, P. (2005). Life span offending trajectories of a Dutch conviction cohort. *Criminology, 43*, 919–954.

© Springer Nature Switzerland AG 2021
M. Le Blanc, *The Development of Antisocial Behavior and Crime*,
https://doi.org/10.1007/978-3-030-68429-7

Blumstein, A. (1967). Science and technology. The challenge of crime in free society. Washington, DC, U.S Government Printing Office.

Blumstein, A., Cohen, J., Roth, J. A., & Visher, C. A. (1986). *Criminal careers and "career criminals". (Volumes 1 & 2)*. Washington, DC: National Academy Press.

Blumstein, A., Cohen, J., & Farrington, D. P. (1988a). Criminal career research: Its value for criminology. *Criminology, 26*, 1–35.

Blumstein, A., Cohen, J., & Farrington, D. P. (1988b). Longitudinal and criminal career research: Further clarifications. *Criminology, 26*, 57–74.

Bongers, I. L., Koot, H. M., van der Ende, J., & Verhulst, F. C. (2004). Developmental trajectories of externalizing behaviors in childhood and adolescence. *Child Development, 75*, 1523–1537.

Boyer, R. (1966). *Les crimes et chatiments au Canada-français*. Montréal: Cercle du livre de France.

Brandibas, G., & Favard, A.-M. (2003). Le lien social chez les adolescents scolarisés. *Psychologie de l'éducation, 53*, 71–86.

Brewers, R., Cale, J., Goldsmith, A., & Holt, T. (2018). Young people, the Internet, and emerging pathways into criminality: A study of Australian adolescents. *International Journal of Cyber Criminology, 12*, 115–132.

Briggs, J., & Peat, F. D. (1989). *Turbulent mirror*. New York: Harper & Row.

Britt, C. L. (2019). Age and crime. In D. P. Farrington, L. Kazemian, & A. R. Piquero (Eds.), *The Oxford handbook of developmental and life-course criminology* (pp. 13–33). Oxford: Oxford University Press..

Broidy, L. M., Nagin, D. A., Tremblay, R. E., Bates, J. E., Brame, B., Dodge, K. A., Fergusson, D., Horwood, J. L., Loeber, R., Laird, R., Lynam, D. R., Moffitt, T. E., Pettit, G. S., & Vitaro, F. (2003). Developmental trajectories of childhood disruptive behaviors and adolescent delinquency: A six-site, cross-national study. *Developmental Psychology, 39*, 222–245.

Canada. (1892). *Act respecting the criminal law*. Ottawa: Parliament of Canada.

Canada. (1908). *Juvenile delinquent act*. Ottawa: Parliament of Canada.

Canada. (1982). *Young offenders act*. Ottawa: Parliament of Canada.

Canada. (2003). *Youth criminal justice act*. Ottawa: Parliament of Canada.

Caplan, A., & Le Blanc, M. (1985). A cross-cultural verification of Hirschi social control theory. *International Journal of Comparative and Applied Criminal Justice, 9*, 123–138.

Carlson, J. M., & Williams, T. (1993). Perspectives on the seriousness of crimes. *Social Science Research, 22*, 190–207.

Cauffman, E., Monahan, K. C., & Thomas, A. C. (2015). Pathways to persistence: Female offending from 14 to 25. *Journal of Developmental and Life Course Criminology, 1*, 236–268.

Celeux, G., & Soromenho, G. (1996). An entropy criterion for assessing the number of clusters in a mixture model. *Journal of Classification, 13*, 195–212.

Charlebois, P., Le Blanc, M., Tremblay, R. E., Gagnon, C., & Larivée, S. (1995). Teacher, mother, and peer support in the elementary school as protective factors against juvenile delinquency. *International Journal of Behavioral Development, 18*, 1–22.

Chesney-Lind, M., & Shelden, R. G. (1998). *Girls delinquency and juvenile justice*. Pacific Grove, CA: Brooks/Cole Publishing Company.

Childs, K. K., & Sullivan, C. J. (2012). Investigating the underlying structure and stability of problem behavior across adolescence. *Criminal Justice and Behavior, 40*, 57–79.

Clark, W. W. (1922). *The Whittier scale for grading juvenile offenses*. Whittier, CA: California Bureau of Juvenile Research, Whittier State School.

Clark, J. P., & Tiff, L. L. (1966). Polygraph and interview validation of self-reported delinquent behavior. *American Sociological Review, 31*, 516–523.

Cohen, J. (1986). Research on criminal career: Frequency rates and offense seriousness. In A. Blumstein, J. Cohen, J. A. Roth, & C. A. Visher (Eds.), *Criminal careers and "career criminals"* (Vol. 2). Washington, DC: National Academy Press.

Collins English Dictionary. (2005). *Collins English Dictionary*. Toronto: Harper Collins Publishers.

Corneau, M., & Lanctôt, N. (2004). Mental health outcomes of adjudicated males and females: The aftermath of juvenile delinquency and problem behavior. *Criminal Behavior and Mental Health, 14*, 251–262.

Corrado, R. (1992). The evolution and implementation of a new era of juvenile justice in Canada. In R. R. Corrado, N. Bala, R. Linden, & M. Le Blanc (Eds.), *Juvenile Justice in Canada* (pp. 137–228). Toronto: Butterworths.

Corrado, R. R., Trépanier, J., & Le Blanc, M. (1983). *Current issues in juvenile justice*. Toronto: Butterworths.

Corrado, R. R., Bala, N., Linden, R., & Le Blanc, M. (1992). *Juvenile justice in Canada*. Toronto: Butterworths.

Cronbach, L. J. (1951). Coefficient alpha and the internal structure of tests. *Psychometrika, 16*, 297–334.

Cusson, M. (2005). *La délinquance, une vie choisie*. Montréal: HMH.

D'Amours, L. (1982). Survol historique de la protection de l'enfance au Québec de 1608 à 1877. In *Rapport de la Commission parlementaire sur la protection de la jeunesse. Annexe 1: Aspects historiques*. Québec: Assemblée Nationale du Québec.

DeFleur, M. L., & Quinney, R. (1966). A reformulation of Sutherland differential association theory and a strategy for an empirical verification. *Journal of Research in Crime and Delinquency, 3*, 1–22.

DeLisi, M. (2015). Age-crime curve and criminal career patterns. In J. Morizot & L. Kazemian (Eds.), *The development of criminal and antisocial behavior. Theory, research, practical applications* (pp. 51–64). New York: Springer.

Dentler, R. A., & Monroe, J. J. (1961). Social correlates of early adolescent theft. *American Sociological Review, 26*, 733–743.

Doherty, E., & Bacon, S. (2019). Age of onset and offending behavior. In D. P. Farrington, L. Kazemian, & A. R. Piquero (Eds.), *The Oxford handbook of developmental and life-course criminology* (pp. 34–48). New York: Oxford University Press.

Duncan, O. D. (1984). *Notes on social measurement: Historical and critical*. New York: Russell Sage Foundation.

Eisner, V. (1969). *The delinquency label: The epidemiology of juvenile delinquency*. New York: Random House.

Elder, G. H. (1974). *Children of the Great Depression: Social change in life experience*. Chicago: University of Chicago Press.

Elder, G. H. (1998). The life course as developmental theory. *Child Development, 69*, 1–12.

Elliott, D. S. (1983). Social class and delinquent behavior in a national youth panel: 1976–1980.

Elliott, D. S. (1994). Serious violent offenders: Onset, developmental course, and termination. *Criminology, 32*, 1–22.

Elliott, D. S., & Huizinga, D. (1983). Social class and delinquent behavior in a national panel. *Criminology, 21*, 149–177.

Elliott, D. S., & Huizinga, D. (1989). Improving self-reported delinquency. In M. C. Klein (Ed.), *Cross-national research in self-reported crime and delinquency* (NATO ASI Series) (Vol. 50, pp. 155–186). Boston: Kluwer Academic Publishers.

Elliott, D. S., & Menard, S. (1996). Delinquent friends and delinquent behavior: Temporal and developmental patterns. In J. D. Hawkins (Ed.), *Delinquency and crime: Current theories* (pp. 28–67). Cambridge: Cambridge University Press.

Elliott, D. S., Huizinga, S., & Ageton, A. (1985). *Explaining delinquency and drug use*. Beverly Hills, CA: Sage.

Elliott, D. S., Dunford, F. W., & Huizinga, D. (1987). The identification and prediction of career offenders utilizing self-reported delinquency and official data. In J. D. Burchard & S. N. Burchard (Eds.), *Prevention of delinquent behavior primary prevention and psychopathology* (Vol. X, pp. 90–121). Beverley Hills: Sage Publications.

Elliott, D. S., Huizinga, D., & Menard, S. (1989). *Multiple problem youth: Delinquency, substance abuse, and mental health problems*. New York: Springer.

Elmhorn, D. (1965). Study in self-reported delinquency among school children in Stockholm. In K. O. Christiansen (Ed.), *Scandinavian studies in criminology* (Vol. 1). London: Tavistock.

Empey, L. T., & Lubec, S. G. (1971). *Explaining delinquency: Construction, test, and reformulation of a sociological theory*. Lexington, MA: Heath Lexington Books.

Enzman, D., Kivivuori, J., Marshall, I. H., Steketee, M., Hough, M., & Killias, M. (2018). *A global perspective on young people as offenders and victims*. New York: Springer.

Erickson, M., & Smith, W. B. (1974). On the relation between self-reported and actual deviance: An empirical test. *Humbolt Journal of Social Relations, 2*, 106–113.

Fabio, F., Loeber, R., Balmasubramani, G. K., Rorth, J., Fu, W., & Farrington, D. P. (2006). Why some generations are more violent than others: Assessment of age, period, and cohort effects. *American Journal of Epidemiology, 164*, 151–160.

Farmer, R. F., Seeley, J. R., Kosty, D. B., & Lewinsohn, P. M. (2009). Refinements in the hierarchical structure of externalizing psychiatric disorders: Patterns of lifetime liability from mid-adolescence through early adulthood. *Journal of Abnormal Psychology, 118*, 699–710.

Farrington, D. P. (1973). Self-reports of deviant behavior: Predictive and stable. *The Journal of Criminal Law and Criminology, 64*, 99–110.

Farrington, D. P. (1979). *Juvenile justice in England and Canada*. Ottawa: Solicitor General of Canada.

Farrington, D. P. (1986). Age and crime. *Crime and Delinquency, 7*, 189–250.

Farrington, D. P. (2019). The development of violence from age 8 to 61. *Aggressive Behavior, 45*, 365–376.

Farrington, D. P., Ohlin, L. E., & Wilson, J. Q. (1986). *Understanding and controlling crime: Toward a new strategy*. New York: Springer.

Farrington, D. P., Loeber, R., Stouthamer-Loeber, M., Van Kammen, W. B., & Schmidt, L. (1996). Self-reported delinquency and a combined delinquency seriousness scale based on boys, mothers, and teachers: Concurrent and predictive validity for African-Americans and Caucasians. *Criminology, 34*, 493–514.

Farrington, D. P., Auty, K. M., Coid, J. W., & Turner, R. E. (2013a). Self-reported and official offending from age 10 to age 56. *European Journal on Criminal Policy and Research, 19*, 135–151.

Farrington, D. P., Piquero, A. R., & Jennings, W. G. (2013b). *Offending from childhood to late middle age: Recent results from the Cambridge study in delinquent development*. New York: Springer.

Farrington, D. P., Ttofi, M. M., Crago, R. V., & Copid, J. M. (2014). Prevalence, frequency, onset, desistance and criminal career duration in self-reports compared with official records. *Criminal Behavior and Mental Health, 24*, 241–253.

Farrington, D. P., Lösel, F., Boruch, R. F., Gottfredson, D. C., Mazerolle, L., Sherman, L. W., & Weidsburd, D. (2018). Advancing knowledge about replication in criminology. *Journal of Experimental Criminology, 15*, 373. https://doi.org/10.1007/s11292-018-9337-3.

Farrington, D. P., Kazemian, L., & Piquero, A. R. (2019). *The Oxford handbook of developmental and life-course criminology*. New York: Oxford University Press.

Farrington, D. P., Barnett, A., & Blumstein, A. (2020). The meaning of intermittency in criminal careers. *Journal of Developmental and Life-Course Criminology, 6*, 524–528.

Forrest, W. E., & Vassallo, B. (2014). Individual differences in the concordance of self-reports and official records. *Criminal Behaviour and Mental Health, 24*, 305–315.

Fréchette, M., & Le Blanc, M. (1987). *Délinquances et délinquants*. Chicoutimi: Gaétan Morin.

Gagnon, F. (2004). *La gravité de la délinquance: Mesure, évolution, et prédiction*. Montréal: Mémoire de Maîtrise, École de criminologie, Université de Montréal.

Gibbs, J. (1972). *Sociological theory construction*. Hinsdale, IL: The Dryden Press.

Gibbs, J. (1985). The methodology of theory construction in criminology. In R. F. Meier (Ed.), *Theoretical models in criminology* (pp. 23–50). Beverly Hills, CA: Sage Publications.

Gillman, A. B., Kim, B. K. E., Newell, A., Hawins, J. D., & Farrington, D. P. (2014). Understanding the relationship between self-reported offending and official criminal charges across early adulthood. *Criminal Behaviour and Mental Health, 24*, 229–240.

Gleick, J. (1987). *Chaos: The making of a new science*. New York: Viking Penguin.

Glueck, S., & Glueck, E. (1930). *Five hundred criminal careers*. New York: Knopf.

Glueck, S., & Glueck, E. (1934). *Five hundred delinquent women*. New York: Knopf.

Glueck, S., & Glueck, E. (1937). *Later criminal careers*. New York: The Commonwealth Fund.

Glueck, S., & Glueck, E. (1943). *Criminal careers in retrospect*. New York: Commonwealth Fund.

Gold, M. (1966). Undetected delinquent behavior. *Journal of Research in Crime and Delinquency, 3*, 27–46.

Gold, M. (1970). *Delinquent behavior in an American city*. Belmont, CA: Brooks/Cole Publishing Company.

Gold, M & Reimer, D. J. (1975). Changing patterns of delinquent behavior among Americans 13 through 16 years old. *Crime and Delinquency Literature, 7*, 483–517.

Goldberg, L. R. (2006). Doing it all bass-ackwards: The development of a hierarchical factor structure from top down. *Journal of Research in Personality, 40*, 347–358.

Gomes, H. S., Maia, A., & Farrington, D. P. (2018). Measuring offending : self-reports, official records, sytematic observation and experimentation. *Crime psychology review, 4*, 26–44.

Gordon, A. D. (1999). *Classification*. New York, Chapman and Hall, CRC Press.

Gorman-Smith, D., & Loeber, R. (2005). Are developmental pathways in disruptive behaviors the same for boys and girls? *Journal of Child and Family Studies, 14*, 15–27.

Gorsuch, J. H. (1938). Scale of seriousness of crimes. *The Journal of Criminal Law and Criminology, 29*, 245–252.

Gottfredson, M. R., & Gottfredson, D. M. (1985). *Decision-making in criminal justice: Toward the rational exercise of discretion*. Cambridge, MA: Ballinger.

Gottfredson, M., & Hirschi, T. (1986). The true value of Lambda would appear to be zero: An essay on career criminals, criminal careers, selective incapacitation, cohort studies and related topics. *Criminology, 24*, 213–234.

Gottfredson, M., & Hirschi, T. (1987). The methodological adequacy of longitudinal research on crime. *Criminology, 25*, 581–614.

Gottfredson, M. R., & Hirschi, T. (1990). *A general theory of crime*. Stanford, CA: Stanford University Press.

Hardt, R. N., & Bodine, G. E. (1965). *Development of self-report instruments in delinquency research: A conference report*. Syracuse: Youth Development Center.

Hausmann, P., Beaufils, M., Boniver, M., & Kerger, A. (1982). *Le poids de l'inadaptation en milieu scolaire dans le processus delinquantiel*. Luxemburg: Luxemburg Center for Social and Pedagogical Research, Luxemburg University Foundation.

Hemphill, S. A., Herrenkohl, T. I., LaFazia, A. N., McMorris, B. J., Toumbourou, J. W., Arthur, M. W., Catalano, R. F., Hawkins, J. D., & Bond, L. (2007). *Crime and Delinquency, 53*, 303–321.

Hindelang, M. J., Hirschi, T., & Weis, J. G. (1981). *Measuring delinquency*. Beverly Hills: Sage.

Hirschi, T. (1969). *Causes of delinquency*. Berkeley, CA: University of California Press.

Hirschi, T., & Gottfredson, M. (1983). Age and the explanation of crime. *American Journal of Sociology, 89*, 552–584.

Huizinga, D., Esbensen, F.-A., & Weiher, A. W. (1991). Are there multiple paths to delinquency? *The Journal of Criminal Law and Criminology, 82*, 83–118.

Jason, C.-G. (1982). *Delinquency among Metropolitan boys: A longitudinal study of a Stockholm cohort*. Stockholm: Department of Sociology, University of Stockholm.

Jennings, W. G., & Hahn Fox, B. (2019). Acceleration, deceleration, escalation, and deescalation. In D. P. Farrington, L. Kazemian, & A. R. Piquero (Eds.), *The Oxford handbook of developmental and life-course criminology* (pp. 70–80). New York: Oxford University Press..

Jennings, W. G., & Reingle, J. (2012). On the number and shape of developmental/life-course violence, aggression, and delinquency trajectories: A state-of-the-art review. *Journal of Criminal Justice, 40*, 472–489.

Jennings, W. G., Loeber, R., Pardini, D. A., Piquero, A. R., & Farrington, D. P. (2016). *Offending from childhood to young adulthood.* New York: Springer.

Jessor, R., & Jesor, S. L. (1977). *Problem behavior and psychological development: A longitudinal study of youth.* New York: Academic Press.

Jolliffe, D., & Farrington, D. P. (2014). Self-reported offending: Reliability and validity. In G. J. N. Bruisma & D. L. Weisburd (Eds.), *Encyclopedia of criminology and criminal justice* (pp. 1054–1064). New York: Springer.

Junger-Tas, J., Terlouw, G.-J., & Klein, M. W. (1994). *Delinquent behavior among young people in the Western World.* New York: Kluger.

Junger-Tas, J., Marshall, I. H., & Ribeaud, D. (2003). *Delinquency in an international perspective: The International Self-Reported Delinquency Study.* The Hague: Kruger.

Junger-Tas, J., Marshall, I. H., Enzmann, D., Killias, M., Steketee, M., & Gruszczynska, B. (2010). *Juvenile delinquency in Europe and beyond: Results of the second international self-report delinquency study.* Berlin: Springer.

Junger-Tas, J., Marshall, I. H., Enzmann, D., Killias, M., Steketee, M., Gruszczynska, B., Lucia, S., & Jonkman, H. (2012). *The many faces of youth crime: Contrasting theoretical perspectives on juvenile delinquency across countries and cultures.* New York: Springer.

Kandel, D. (2002). *Stages and pathways of drug involvement.* New York: Cambridge University Press.

Kaplan, H. (1975). *Self-attitudes and deviant behavior.* Pacific Palisades, CA: Goodyear.

Kaplan, H. (1980). *Deviant behavior in defense of self.* New York: Academic Press.

Kaplan, H. (1984). *Patterns of juvenile delinquency.* Beverly Hills, CA: Sage.

Kaplan, H. (1986). *Social psychology of self-referent behavior.* New York: Plenum Press.

Kazemian, L., & Le Blanc, M. (2004). Exploring patterns of perpetration of crime across the life course: Offense and offender-based viewpoints. *Journal of Contemporary Criminal Justice, 20*, 393–415.

Kazemian, L., Le Blanc, M., & Farrington, D. P. (2008). Can we make long-term predictions about de-escalation in offending behavior? *Journal of Youth and Adolescence, 38*, 384–400.

Lanctôt, N. (2005). Que deviennent les adolescentes judiciarisées après la sortie du Centre Jeunesse? *Criminologie, 38*, 139–152.

Lanctôt, N. (2015). Development of antisocial behavior in adolescent girls. In J. Morizot & L. Kazemian (Eds.), *The development of criminal and antisocial behavior. Theory, research, practical applications* (pp. 399–412). New York: Springer.

Lanctôt, N., & Le Blanc, M. (2002). Explaining adolescent females' involvement in deviance. *Crime and Justice, 29*, 113–202.

Lanctôt, N., & Le Blanc, M. (2003). Deviance among females: Developmental pathways from adolescence to young adulthood. Life-course trajectories of deviant behavior in the Montreal longitudinal studies of adjudicated youths. American Society of Criminology, Annual Meeting, 13–16 November, Chicago.

Lanctôt, N., Émond, C., & Le Blanc, M. (2004). Adjudicated females' participation in violence from adolescence to adulthood: Results from a longitudinal study. In M. Moretti, C. Odgers, & M. Jackson (Eds.), *Girls and aggression: Contributing factors and intervention principles* (pp. 85–100). New York: Kluwer.

Langlois, S. (1999). *Tendances de la société québécoise (texte et tableaux).* Québec: Département de sociologie. Université Laval.

Langlois, S., Baillargeon, J.-P., Caldwell, G., Fréchet, G., Gauthier, M., & Simard, J.-P. (1991). *Recent social trends in Québec, 1960–1990.* Montréal: McGill-Queen's University Press.

Laub, J. H., & Samson, R. J. (2003). *Share beginnings, divergent lives, delinquent boys to age 70.* Cambridge, MA: Harvard University Press.

Le Blanc, M. (1969). *Inadaptation et classes sociales à Montréal*. Montréal: Département de criminologie, Université de Montréal.

Le Blanc, M. (1977). La délinquance à l'adolescence: de la délinquance cachée et de la délinquance apparente. *Annales de Vaucresson, 15*, 1–40.

Le Blanc, M. (1980). Le système de justice pour mineurs au Québec: quelques données statistiques. *Crime et Justice, 9*, 170–186.

Le Blanc, M. (1983). Vers une théorie intégrative de la régulation de la conduite délinquante. *Annales de Vaucresson, 20*, 1–34.

Le Blanc, M. (1983a). *Boscoville, la rééducation évaluée*. Montréal: HMH.

Le Blanc, M. (1983b). Delinquency as an epiphenomenon of adolescence. In R. Corrado, M. Le Blanc, & J. Trépanier (Eds.), *Current issues in juvenile justice* (pp. 41–48). Toronto: Butterworths.

Le Blanc, M. (1984a). L'opinion des juges, avocats de la défense et procureur de la couronne sur le système de justice pour mineurs et la loi sur les jeunes contrevenants. *Revue de Droit, 14*, 591–623.

Le Blanc, M. (1984b). La loi sur les jeunes contrevenants et les intervenants du système de justice pour mineurs au Québec. *Annales de Vaucresson, 21*, 67–92.

Le Blanc, M. (1984c). Les agents de relations humaines des centres de services sociaux, la loi sur les jeunes contrevenants et le système de justice pour mineurs. *Service Social, 33*, 324–356.

Le Blanc, M. (1984d). Les policiers, la loi sur les jeunes contrevenants et le système de justice pour mineurs. *Criminologie, 17*, 91–115.

Le Blanc, M. (1985). De l'efficacité d'internats québécois. *Revue Canadienne de Psychoéducation, 14*, 113–120.

Le Blanc, M. (1989). Designing a self-reported instrument for the study of the development of offending from childhood to adulthood: Issues and problems. In M. C. Klein (Ed.), *Cross-national research in self-reported crime and delinquency* (NATO ASI Series) (Vol. 50, pp. 371–398). Boston: Kluwer.

Le Blanc, M. (1995). Common, temporary, and chronic delinquencies: Prevention strategies during compulsory school. In P.-O. Wikström, J. McCord, & R. W. Clarke (Eds.), *Integrating crime prevention strategies: Motivation and opportunity* (pp. 169–205). Stockholm: The National Council for Crime Prevention.

Le Blanc, M. (1996). Changing patterns in the perpetration of offences over time: Trajectories from onset to the middle of the thirties. *Studies on Crime and Crime Prevention, 5*, 151–165.

Le Blanc, M. (1997). Socialization or propensity: A test of an integrative control theory with adjudicated boys. *Studies in Crime and Crime Prevention, 6*, 200–224.

Le Blanc, M. (1998). L'internat et la recherche évaluative. In G. Gendreau (Ed.), (pp. 265–290) *Bosco, la tendresse*. Montréal: Science et Culture.

Le Blanc, M. (1999). L'évolution de la violence chez les adolescents québécois, phénomène et prévention. *Criminologie, 32*, 161–194.

Le Blanc, M. (2002). The offending cycle, escalation and de-escalation in delinquent behavior, a challenge for criminology. *International Journal of Comparative and Applied Criminal Justice, 26*, 53–84.

Le Blanc, M. (2003). Évolution de la délinquance cachée et officielle chez les adolescents au Québec entre les années 1930 et 2000. In M. Le Blanc, M. Ouimet, & D. Szabo (Eds.), *Traité de criminologie empirique* (pp. 39–72). Montréal: Les Presses de l'Université de Montréal.

Le Blanc, M. (2006). Self-control and social control of deviant behavior in context: Development and interactions along the life course. In P.-O. Wikstrom & R. Sampson (Eds.), *The social contexts of pathways in crime: Development, context, and mechanisms* (pp. 95–242). Cambridge: Cambridge University Press.

Le Blanc, M. (2009). The development of deviant behavior, its self-regulation. *Monatsschrift für Kriminologie und Strafrechtsreform, 91*, 117–136.

Le Blanc, M. (2010a). *MASPAQ, Manuel sur des mesures de l'adaptation sociale et personnelle pour les adolescents québécois. (English, Spanish, Portuguese, and Arabic)*. Montréal:

Groupe de recherche sur l'inadaptation psychosociale à l'enfance, École de psychoéducation, Université de Montréal.

Le Blanc, M. (2010b). La délinquance officielle et rapportée chez les adolescents québécois de 1930 à 2007. In M. Le Blanc & M. Cusson (Eds.), *Traité de criminologie empirique. 4.* (pp. 49–74). Montréal: Les Presses de l'Université de Montréal.

Le Blanc, M. (2012). Twenty-five years of developmental criminology: What we know, what we need to know. In R. Loeber & B. C. Welsh (Eds.), *The future of criminology* (pp. 124–134). Oxford: Oxford University Press.

Le Blanc, M. (2015). Developmental criminology: Thoughts on the past and insights for the future. In J. Morizot & L. Kazemian (Eds.), *The development of criminal and antisocial behavior: Theory, research, and practical applications.* (pp. 507–538). New York: Springer.

Le Blanc, M. (2017). A criminological career within a new criminology. An amalgam of a multidisciplinary science and profession. In J. A. Winterdyk (Ed.), *Pioneers in Canadian criminology* (pp. 83–105). Ontario: Rock Mills Press.

Le Blanc, M. (2019). The interconnected development of personal controls and antisocial behavior. In D. P. Farrington, L. Kazemian, & A. R. Piquero (Eds.), *The Oxford handbook of developmental and life-course criminology* (pp. 193–223). New York: Oxford University Press.

Le Blanc, M., & Beaumont, H. (1992). The effectiveness of juvenile justice in Quebec: A natural experiment in implementing formal diversion and a justice model. In R. Corrado, N. Bala, R. Linden, & M. Le Blanc (Eds.), *Juvenile justice in Canada: A theoretical and analytical assessment* (pp. 283–312). Toronto: Butterworths.

Le Blanc, M., & Blumstein, A. (1972). Analyse du système de la justice criminelle. In D. Szabo (Ed.), *La crise de l'administration de la justice dans la zone métropolitaine* (pp. 245–280). Montréal: Centre international de criminologie comparée, Solliciteur Général du Canada.

Le Blanc, M., & Bouthillier, C. (2003). A developmental test of the general deviance syndrome with adjudicated girls and boys using hierarchical confirmatory factor analysis. *Criminal Behavior and Mental Health, 13,* 81–105.

Le Blanc, M., & Caplan, A. (1985). A cross-cultural verification of a social control theory. *International Journal of Comparative and Applied Criminal Justice, 9,* 123–138.

Le Blanc, M., & Caplan, M. (1993). Theoretical formalization, a necessity: The example of Hirschi's social control theory. *Advances in Criminological Theory, 4,* 329–431.

Le Blanc, M., & Fréchette, M. (1989). *Male criminal activity from childhood through youth: Multilevel and developmental perspectives.* New York: Springer.

Le Blanc, M., & Girard, S. (1997). The generality of deviance: Replication over several decades with a Canadian sample of adjudicated boys. *Canadian Journal of Criminology, 39,* 171–183.

Le Blanc, M., & Girard, S. (1998). Psychotropes et délinquance: Séquences développementales et enchâssement. *Psychotropes, 4,* 69–91.

Le Blanc, M., & Janosz, M. (1998). *The development of general deviance, course and processes: The contribution of the developmental and the chaos-order paradigms.* Washington, D.C.: Annual Meeting of the American Society of Criminology.

Le Blanc, M. & Kaspy, N. (1998). Trajectories of delinquency and problem behavior: Comparison of synchronous and nonsynchronous paths on social and personal control characteristics of adolescent. *Journal of Quantitative Criminology, 14,* 181–214.

Le Blanc, M., & Loeber, R. (1998). Developmental criminology updated. *Crime and Justice, 23,* 115–198.

Le Blanc, M., & McDuff, P. (1991). *Activités délictueuses, troubles de comportement et expérience familiale au cours de la latence.* Montréal: Groupe de recherche sur l'inadaptation psychosociale chez l'enfant, École de psychoéducation, Université de Montréal.

Le Blanc, M., & Morizot, J. (2003). Adjudicated males self-reported criminality trajectories from adolescence to midlife in the Montreal Longitudinal Studies of Adjudicated Youths. American Society of Criminology, Annual Meeting, 13–16 November, Chicago.

Le Blanc, M., & Tremblay, R. E. (1988). Homeostasis: Social changes plus modifications in the basic personality of adolescents equal stability of hidden delinquency. *International Journal of Adolescence and Youth, 1*, 269–291.

Le Blanc, M., Sarasin, M., & Caplan, A. (1977). *La construction des échelles de délinquance.* Montréal: Groupe de recherche sur l'inadaptation juvénile, École de criminologie, Université de Montréal.

Le Blanc, M., Ouimet, M., & Tremblay, R. E. (1988). An integrative control theory of delinquent behavior: A validation 1976–1985. *Psychiatry, 51*, 164–176.

Le Blanc, M., Morizot, J., & Lanctôt, N. (2003). Life-course trajectories of deviant behavior in the Montreal Longitudinal Studies of Adjudicated Youths. American Society of Criminology, Annual Meeting, 13–16 November, Chicago.

Le Blanc, M., Martin Lopez, T., Diego Espuny, F., Curto Fortuno, R., & Kazemian, L. (2004). Medidas de adaptacion social y personal para adolescentes espagnoles: Analisis de su coherencia interna, fiabilidad y validez. In F. Perez Alvarez (Ed.), *Serta in memorianm Alexandri Baratta* (pp. 236–267). Salamanca: Editiones Universidad.

Lerner, R. M. (1986). *Concepts and theories of human development.* New York: Random House.

Liberman, A. M. (2010). The long view of crime. In *A synthesis of longitudinal research.* New York: Springer.

Loeber, R. (1982). The stability of antisocial and delinquent child behavior: A review. *Child Development, 53*, 1431–1446.

Loeber, R. (1987). Natural histories of conduct problems, delinquency and associates substance use: Evidence for developmental progressions. In B. B. Lahey & E. Kazdin (Eds.), *Advances in Clinical Child Psychology* (Vol. 10, pp. 73–124). New York: Plenum.

Loeber, R. (2012). Does the study of the age-crime curve have a future? In R. Loeber & B. C. Welsh (Eds.), *The future of criminology* (pp. 1–19). New York: Oxford University Press.

Loeber, R. (2019). Developmental pathways to conduct problems and serious forms of delinquency. In D. P. Farrington, L. Kazemian, & A. R. Piquero (Eds.), *The Oxford handbook of developmental and life-course criminology* (pp. 159–172). New York: Oxford University Press.

Loeber, R., & Hay, D. (1997). Key issues in the development of aggression and violence from childhood to early adulthood. *Annual Review in Psychology, 48*, 371–410.

Loeber, R., & Le Blanc, M. (1990). Toward a developmental criminology. *Crime and Justice, 12*, 373–473.

Loeber, R., & Schmaling, K. (1985). Empirical evidence for overt and covert patterns of antisocial conduct problems: A metaanalysis. *Journal of Abnormal Child Psychology, 13*, 337–352.

Loeber, R., & Wilström, P.-O. (1993). Individual pathways in crime in different types of neighborhoods. In D. Farrington & R. J. Sampson (Eds.), (pp. 109–164). Stockholm: Swedish National Council for Crime Prevention.

Loeber, R., Stouthamer-Loeber, M., Van Kammen, W. B., & Farrington, D. P. (1989). Development of a new measure of self-reported antisocial behavior for young children: Prevalence and reliability. In M. Klein (Ed.), *Cross-national research in self-reported crime and delinquency* (pp. 203–225). Boston: Kluwer-Nijhoff.

Loeber, R., Stouthamer-Loeber, M., Van Kammen, W. V., & Farrington, D. (1991). Initiation, escalation, and desistance in juvenile offending and their correlates. *The Journal of Criminal Law and Criminology, 82*, 36–82.

Loeber, R., Green, S. M., Lahey, B. B., Christ, M. A. G., & Frick, P. J. (1992). Developmental sequences in the age of onset of disruptive child behaviors. *Journal of Child and Family Studies, 1*, 21–41.

Loeber, R., Wung, P., Keenan, K., Giroux, B., Stouthamer-Loeber, M., Van Kammen, W. B., & Maughan, B. (1993). Developmental pathways in disruptive child behavior. *Development and Psychopathology, 5*, 101–132.

Loeber, R., DeLamatre, M., Keenan, K., & Zhang, Q. (1998a). A prospective replication of developmental pathways in disruptive and delinquent behavior. In R. Cairns, L. Bergman, &

J. Kagan (Eds.), *Methods and models for studying the individual* (pp. 185–215). Thousand Oaks, CA: Sage.

Loeber, R., Farrington, D. P., Stouthamer-Loeber, M., & Van Kammen, W. B. (1998b). *Antisocial behavior and mental health problems: Risk factors in childhood and adolescence.* London: Cambridge University Press.

Loeber, R., Wei, E., Stouthamer-Loeber, M., Huizinga, D., & Thornberry, T. P. (1999). Behavioral antecedents to serious and violent offending: Joint analyses from the Denver Youth Survey, Pittsburgh Youth Study, and the Rochester Youth Development Study. *Studies on Crime and Crime Prevention, 8,* 245–263.

Loeber, R., Wim Slot, N., & Stouthamer-Loeber, M. (2006). A three-dimensional, cumulative developmental model of serious delinquency. In P.-O. H. Wikström & R. J. Sampson (Eds.), *The explanation of crime. Context, mechanisms, and development* (pp. 153–194). New York: University of Cambridge Press.

Loeber, R., Farrington, D. P., Stouthamer-Loeber, M., & White, H. R. (2008). *Violence and serious theft: Development and prediction from childhood to adulthood.* New York: Routledge.

Loeber, R., Jennings, W. G., Ahonen, L., Piquero, A. R., & Farrington, D. P. (2017). *Female delinquency from childhood to young adulthood: Recent results from the Pittsburgh Girls Study.* New York: Springer.

Lombroso. (1895). *L'homme criminel. Étude anthropologique et psychiatrique.* Paris: Alcan Éditeur.

Macleod, J. F., Grove, P. G., & Farrington, D. P. (2012). Explaining criminal careers. In *Implications for justice policy.* New York: Oxford University Press.

Magnusson, D., & Cairns, R. B. (1996). Developmental science: Toward a unified framework. In R. B. Cairns, G. H. Elder Jr., & E. J. Costello (Eds.), *Cambridge studies in social and emotional development. Developmental science* (pp. 7–30). London: Cambridge University Press.

Makel, M., Plucker, J. A., & Boyd, H. (2012). Replications in psychological research: How often do they really occur? *Perspectives on Psychological Science, 7,* 537–542.

Marceau, B., & Trépanier, J. (1985). La justice des mineurs. In D. Szabo & M. Le Blanc (Eds.), *Traité de criminologie empirique: Phénomène criminel et justice pénale* (pp. 238–270). Montréal: Les Presses de l'Université de Montréal.

Maxwell, S. R. (1999). Toward understanding antisocial behaviors and delinquency among Filipino youth. *International Journal of Comparative and Applied Criminal Justice, 23,* 257–266.

Mazerolle, P., & McPhedran, S. (2019). Specialization and versatility in offending. In D. P. Farrington, L. Kazemiam, & A. R. Jennings (Eds.), *The Oxford handbook of developmental and life-course criminology* (pp. 40–69). New York: Oxford University Press.

McGee, T. A., & Moffitt, T. E. (2019). The developmental taxonomy. In D. P. Farrington, L. Kazemian, & A. R. Piquero (Eds.), *The Oxford handbook of developmental and life-course criminology* (pp. 149–158). New York: The Oxford University Press.

McGee, T. R., Whitten, T., Williams, C., Jollife, D., & Farrington, D. P. (2020). Classification patterns of offending and life-course criminology, with special reference to persistence. *Aggression and Violent Behavior, 50,* 1–9.

McNeeley, S., & Warner, J. (2015). Replication in criminology: A necessary practice. *European Journal of Criminology, 12,* 581–597.

Menard, S., & Bowman-Bowen, L. C. (2015). Self-reported research. In D. Lewinson (Ed.), *The encyclopedia of crime and punishment* (pp. 1–5). New York: Wiley.

Messier, C. (1989). *Les troubles de comportement à l'adolescence et leur traitement en centre d'accueil de réadaptation à la suite d'une ordonnance de protection.* Québec: Commission de la protection des droits de la jeunesse. Ministère de la santé et des services sociaux du Québec.

Moffitt, T. E. (1993). Adolescence-limited and life-course-persistent antisocial behavior: A developmental taxonomy. *Psychological Review, 100,* 674–701.

Moffitt, T. E. (1994). Natural histories of delinquency. In E. G. M. Weitekamp & H.-J. Kerner (Eds.), *Cross-national longitudinal research on human development and criminal behavior* (pp. 3–61). Dordrecht: Kluwer.

Moffitt, T. E. (1997). Adolescent-limited and life-course persistent offending: A complementary pair of developmental theories. In T. P. Thornberry (Ed.), *Developmental theories of crime and delinquency* (pp. 11–54). New Brunswick, NJ: Transaction.

Moffitt, T. E. (2006). Life-course persistent versus adolescence-limited antisocial behavior. In D. Cicchetti & D. J. Cohen (Eds.), *Developmental psychopathology, vol. 3: Risk, disorder, and adaptation* (pp. 570–598). New York: Wiley.

Moffitt, T. E., Caspi, A., Rutter, M., & Silva, P. A. (2001). *Sex differences in antisocial behaviour: Conduct disorder, delinquency, and violence in the Dunedin Longitudinal Study*. London: Cambridge University Press.

Molinengo, G., & Testa, S. (2020). Analysis of psychometric properties of an assessment tool for deviant behavior in adolescence. *European Journal of Psychological Assessment, 26*, 108–115.

Morange, E. R. (1979). *La criminalité réelle à Aix-en-Provence*. Aix-en-Provence: Université de droit, d'économie et des sciences d'Aix-Marseille.

Morizot, J. (2019). Trajectories of criminal behavior across the life course. In D. P. Farrington, L. Kazemian, & A. R. Piquero (Eds.), *The Oxford handbook of developmental and life-course criminology* (pp. 97–125). New York: Oxford University Press.

Morizot, J., & Kazemian, L. (2015). *The development of criminal and antisocial behavior. Theory, research, practical applications*. New York: Springer.

White, R. H. (2019). Developmental influences of substance use on criminal offending. In D.P. Farrington, L. Kazemian & A. H. Piquero. (2019). *The handbook of developmental criminology and life-course criminology*. (pp.454-474). New York: Oxford University Press.

Morizot, J., & Le Blanc, M. (2003). Using cluster analysis for the identification of multivariate trajectories. American Society of Criminology 2003 Annual Meeting, 13–16 November, Chicago.

Morizot, J., & Le Blanc, M. (2003a). Continuity and change in personality from mid-adolescence to mid-life: A 25-year longitudinal study comparing conventional and adjudicated men. *Journal of Personality, 71*, 705–755.

Morizot, J., & Le Blanc, M. (2003b). Searching for a developmental typology of personality in an adjudicated men's sample and its relations to antisocial behaviors from adolescence to midlife: A 25-year longitudinal study. *Criminal Behavior and Mental Health, 13*, 241–277.

Morizot, J., & Le Blanc, M. (2005). Searching for developmental types of personality and their relation to antisocial behaviors: A 25-year longitudinal study comparing conventional and adjudicated men from adolescence to midlife. *Journal of Personality, 73*, 139–182.

Morris, A., & Giller, H. (1987). *Understanding juvenile justice*. London: Croom Helm.

Murphy, F. J. (1946). The incidence of hidden delinquency. *American Journal of Orthopsychiatry, 26*, 686–696.

Muthén, L. K., & Muthén, B. O. (2007). *Mplus: Statistical analysis with latent variables: User's guide (Version 8)*. Los Angeles, CA: Authors.

Nagin, D. S., & Tremblay, R. E. (2005). Developmental trajectory groups: Fact or useful statistical fiction? *Criminology, 43*, 873–918.

Naylor, R. T. (2003). Toward a general theory of profit-driven crimes. *British Journal of Criminology, 43*, 81–100.

Nettler, G. (1974). *Explaining crime*. Toronto: McGraw-Hill.

Nunnaly, J. C. (1967). *Psychometric theory*. New York: McGraw-Hill.

Nye, J. C. (1957). *Family relationships and delinquent behavior*. Westport, CO: Greenwood Press.

Nye, F. I., & Short, J. F. (1957). Scaling delinquent behavior. *American Sociological Review, 22*, 326–331.

Nye, F. I., Short, J. F., & Olson, V. J. (1958). Socioeconomic status and delinquent behavior. *American Journal of Sociology, 63*, 381–389.

Nylund-Gibson, K., Asparouhov, T., & Muthén, B. O. (2007). Deciding on the number of classes in latent class analysis and growth mixture modeling: A Monte Carlo simulation study. *Structural Equation Modeling: A Multidisciplinary Journal, 14*, 535–569.

Osgood, D. W., Johnston, L. D., O'Malley, P. M., & Bachman, J. G. (1988). The generality of deviance in late adolescence and early adulthood. *American Sociological Review, 53*, 81–93.

Ouimet, M. (2005). *La criminalité au Québec durant le vingtième siècle*. Québec: Les Presses de l'Université Laval.

Ouimet, M. (2010). Analyse de l'évolution des données de la criminalité, des tribunaux criminels et des services correctionnels. In M. Le Blanc & M. Cusson (Eds.), *Traité de criminologie empirique* (pp. 21–48). Montréal: Les Presses de l'Université de Montréal.

Parker, P. N., & McDowall, D. (1986). Constructing an index of officially recorded crimes: The use of conformatory factor analysis. *Journal of Quantitative Criminology, 2*, 237–250.

Patterson, G. R., & Yoerger, K. (1993). Developmental models for delinquent behavior. In S. Hodgins (Ed.), *Mental disorder and crime* (pp. 140–172). Newbury Park, CA: Sage.

Patterson, G. R., & Yoerger, K. (1997). A developmental model for late-onset delinquency. In D. W. Osgood (Ed.), *Nebraska Symposium on Motivation, Vol. 44. Motivation and delinquency* (pp. 119–177). Lincoln: University of Nebraska Press.

Patterson, G. R., & Yoerger, K. (2002). A developmental model for early- and late-onset antisocial behavior. In J. B. Reid, G. R. Patterson, & J. Snuder (Eds.), *Antisocial behavior in children and adolescents: A developmental analysis and model for intervention* (pp. 147–172). Washington, DC: American Psychological Association.

Patterson, G. R., Reid, J. B., & Dishion, T. J. (1992). *Antisocial boys*. Eugene, OR: Castalia Press.

Peak, D., & Frame, M. (1994). *Chaos under control*. New York: Freeman.

Piquero, A. R. (2010). Taking stock of developmental trajectories of criminal activity over the life-course. In A. M. Liberman (Ed.), *A long view of crime; a synthesis of longitudinal research* (pp. 23–78). New York: Springer.

Piquero, A. R., Blumstein, A., Brame, R., Haapanen, R., Mulvey, E. P., & Nagin, D. S. (2001). Assessing the impact of exposure time and incapacitation on longitudinal trajectories of criminal offending. *Journal of Adolescent Research, 16*, 54–74.

Piquero, A. R., Farrington, D. P., & Blumstein, A. (2003). The criminal career paradigm. *Crime and Justice, 30*, 359–506.

Piquero, A. R., Farrington, D. P., & Blumstein, A. (2007). *Key issues in criminal career research: New analyses of the Cambridge study in delinquent development*. Cambridge: Cambridge University Press.

Piquero, A. R., Hawkins, J. D., & Kazemian, L. (2012). Criminal career patterns. In R. Loeber & D. P. Farrington (Eds.), *From juvenile delinquency to adult crime: Criminal careers, justice policy and prevention* (pp. 14–46). New York: Oxford University Press.

Piquero, A. R., Reingle Gonzales, J., & Jennings, W. G. (2015). Developmental trajectories and antisocial behavior over the life-course. In J. Morizot & L. Kazemian (Eds.), *The development of criminal and antisocial behavior. Theory, research, practical applications* (pp. 75–88). New York: Springer.

Platt, A. M. (1969). *The child savers: The invention of delinquency*. Chicago: University of Chicago Press.

Podgorecki, A. (1976). *Problèmes de psychologie sociale*. Varsovie: Panatwowe Wydawnictwo Naukowe.

Popper, K. R. (1992). *The logic of scientific discovery*. New York: Routledge.

Porterfield, A. (1946). *Youth in trouble*. Fort Worth: Leo Potishman Foundation.

Pridemore, W. A., Makel, M. C., & Plucker, J. A. (2018). Replication in criminology and the social sciences. *Annual Review of Criminology, 1*, 19–38.

Québec. (1979). *Youth Protection Act*. Québec: Gouvernement du Québec.

Quételet, A. (1831). *Recherches sur le penchant au crime aux différents âges*. Brussels: M. Hayez, Imprimeur de l'Académie Royale.

Quetelet, A. (1835). *Sur l'homme et le développement de ses facultés, ou essai de physique sociale*. Paris: Bachelier.

Quételet, A. (1869). *Physique sociale, essai sur le développement des facultés de l'homme*. Brussels: C. Muquard.

Reiss, A. J. (1975). Inappropriate theories and inadequate methods as policy plagues: Self-reported delinquency and the law. In N. J. Demerath, III, O. Larson, & K. Schuessler Social policy and sociology, (pp. 211–222). Academic Press, New York.

Remschmidt, H. (1978). Recent results of juvenile delinquency research – West Germany. *Praxis der Kinderpsychologie und Kinderpsychiatrie, 27*, 29–40.

Rocque, M., Posick, C., & Hoyle, J. (2015). Age and crime. Encyclopedia of crime and punishment. In W. G. Jennings, G. E. Higgins, M. M. Maldonado-Molina, & D. N. Khey (Eds.), (pp. 1–8). Hoboken, NJ: Wiley. https://doi.org/10.1002/9781118519639.wbecpx27.

Salmi, V. (2009). *Self-reported juvenile delinquency in Finland 1995–2008*. Helsinki: National Research Institute of Legal Policy.

Sampson, R. J., & Laub, J. H. (1993). *Crime in the making, pathways and turning points through life*. Cambridge, MA: Harvard University Press.

Schmidt, S. (2009). Shall we really do it again? The powerful concept of replication is neglected in the social sciences. *Review of General Psychology, 13*, 90–100.

Sellin, T. (1938). *Culture conflict and crime*. New York: Social Science Research Council.

Sellin, T., & Wolfgang, M. E. (1964). *The measurement of delinquency*. New York: Wiley.

Selvin, H. C. (1965). Durkheim's suicide: Further thoughts on a methodological classic. In R. A. Nisbet (Ed.), *Émile Durkheim* (pp. 113–136). Englewood Cliffs, NJ: Prentice-Hall.

Shaw, C. R. (1930). *The Jack-Roller, a delinquent boy's own story*. Chicago: University of Chicago Press.

Siennick, S. E., & Osgood, D. W. (2008). A review of research on the impact on crime of transitions to adult roles. In A. M. Liberman (Ed.), *The long view of crime: A synthesis of longitudinal research* (pp. 161–187). New York: Springer.

Skardhamar, T. (2009). Reconsidering the theory of adolescent-limited and life-course persistent antisocial behavior. *British Journal of Criminology, 49*, 863–878.

Slobodian, P. J., & Browne, K. D. (1997). Car crime as a developmental career: An analysis of young offenders in Coventry. Psychology. *Crime & Law, 3*, 275–286.

Snow, J. (1855). *On the mode of communication of cholera* (2nd ed.). London: Churchill.

Stouthamer-Loeber, M. (2012). The next generation of longitudinal studies. In R. Loeber & B. C. Welsh (Eds.), *The future of criminology* (pp. 94–102). New York: Oxford University Press.

Stouthamer-Loeber, M., & van Kammen, W. B. (1995). *Data collection and management: a practical guide*. Newbury Park, CA: Sage.

Sutherland, E. H. (1947). *Principles of criminology*. Philadelphia: Lippincott.

Sylvester, S. F. (1984). *Research on the propensity for crime at different age: Introduction and translation of Quételet (1931)*. Cincinnati: Anderson.

Theobald, D., Farrington, D. P., Loeber, R., Pardine, D. A., & Piquero, A. R. (2014). Scaling up from convictions of self-reported offending. *Criminal Behavior and Mental Health, 24*, 265–276.

Thornberry, T. P. (1987). Toward an interactional theory of delinquency. *Criminology, 25*, 963–892.

Thornberry, T. P., & Krohn, M. D. (2000). The self-reported method for measuring delinquency and crime. *Criminal Justice, 4*, 1–83.

Thornberry, T. P., & Krohn, M. D. (2003). Taking stock of delinquency. In *An overview of findings from contemporary longitudinal studies*. New York: Kluwer.

Tolan, H., Gorman-Smith, D., & Loeber, R. (2000). Developmental timing of onsets of disruptive behaviors and later delinquency of inner-city youth. *Journal of Child and Family Studies, 9*, 203–220.

Tracy, P. E., & Kempf-Leonard, K. (1996). *Continuity and discontinuity in criminal careers*. New York: Plenum Press.

Tracy, P. E., Wolfgang, M. E., & Figlio, R. M. (1990). *Delinquency careers in two birth cohorts*. New York: Plenum Press.

Tremblay, R. E., Le Blanc, M., & Schwartzman, A. (1986). *La conduite délinquante des adolescents à Montréal (1974–1985)*. Montréal: École de psychoéducation et École de criminologie, Université de Montréal.

Trépanier, J. (2003). La justice des mineurs. In D. Szabo, M. Le Blanc, & M. Ouimet (Eds.), *Traité de criminologie empirique* (pp. 585–647). Montréal: Les Presses de l'Université de Montréal.

Tzoumakis, S., Lussier, P., Le Blanc, M., & Davies, G. (2012). Onset, offending trajectories, and specialization in violence. *Youth Violence and Juvenile Justice, 2*, 1–22.

Van Der Westhuizen, J. (1981). *Measurement of crime – quantification.* Pretoria: University of South Africa.

Van Dulmen, M. H. M., Goncy, E. A., Vest, A., & Flannery, D. J. (2009). Group-based trajectory modeling of externalizing behavior problems from childhood through adulthood: Exploring discrepancies in the empirical findings. In J. Savage (Ed.), *The development of persistent criminality* (pp. 288–314). New York: Oxford University Press.

Van Nieuwenhuizen, M., Junger, M., Velderman, M. K., Wirfferink, H., Paulussen, T., Hox, J., & Reijneveld, S. A. (2009). Clustering of health-compromising behavior and delinquency in adolescents and adults in the Dutch population. *Preventive Medicine, 48*, 572–578.

Wadsworth, M. (1979). *Roots of delinquency, infancy, adolescence, and crime.* Oxford: Robertson.

Wallace, M., Turner, J., Matarazzo, A., & Babyak, C. (2009). *Measuring crime in Canada: Introducing the crime severity index and improvements to the uniform crime reporting survey.* Ottawa: Statistics Canada. Ministry of Industries.

Wallerstein, J. S., & Wyle, D. J. (1947). Our law-abiding law-breakers. *PRO, 25*, 107–112.

Weis, J. G. (1986). Issues in the measurement of criminal careers. In A. Blustein, J. Cohen, J. A. Roth, & C. A. Visher (Eds.), *Criminal careers and "career criminals"* (Vol. 2, pp. 1–51). Washington: National Academy Press.

Werner, H. (1957). The concept of development from a comparative and organismic point of view. In D. B. Harris (Ed.), *The concept of development.* Minneapolis: University of Minnesota Press.

West, D. J. (1969). *Present conduct and future delinquency.* New York: International Universities Press.

West, D. J., & Farrington, D. P. (1973). *The delinquent way of life.* London: Heinemann.

White, H. (2015). A developmental approach to understanding the substance use-crime connection. In J. Morizot & L. Kazemian (Eds.), *The development of criminal and antisocial behavior. Theory, research, practical applications* (pp. 379–308). New York: Springer.

Whitehead, P. C., & Smart, R. G. (1974). Validity and reliability of self-reported drug use. In C. L. Boydell (Ed.), *Deviant behavior and reaction* (pp. 25–42). Toronto: Holt, Rinehart, Winston.

Williams, J. R., & Gold, M. (1972). From delinquent behavior to official delinquency. *Social Problems, 20*, 209–229.

Wohlwill, J. F. (1973). *The study of behavioral development.* New York: Academic Press.

Wolfgang, M. E., Figlio, R. M., & Sellin, T. (1972). *Delinquency in a birth cohort.* Chicago, IL: University of Chicago Press.

Wolfgang, M. E., Figlio, R. M., Tracy, P. E., & Singer, S. I. (1985). *The national survey of crimes severity.* Washington: U.S. Department of Justice, Bureau of Statistics.

Wolfgang, M. E., Thornberry, T. P., & Figlio, R. M. (1987). *From boy to man, delinquency and crime.* Chicago: University of Chicago Press.

Zamboanga, B., Carlo, G., & Raffaelli, M. (2004). Problem behavior theory: An examination of the behavior structure system in Latino and non-Latino college students. *Interamerican Journal of Psychology, 38*, 253–262.

Index

© Springer Nature Switzerland AG 2021
M. Le Blanc, *The Development of Antisocial Behavior and Crime*,
https://doi.org/10.1007/978-3-030-68429-7

CPSIA information can be obtained
at www.ICGtesting.com
Printed in the USA
LVHW082048230922
729069LV00008B/204